always n

practicing faith
in a new media landscape

ANGELA WILLIAMS GORRELL

Baker Academic
a division of Baker Publishing Group
Grand Rapids, Michigan

Published by Baker Academic
a division of Baker Publishing Group
PO Box 6287, Grand Rapids, MI 49516-6287
www.bakeracademic.com

Printed in the United States of America

Library of Congress Cataloging-in-Publication Data
Names: Gorrell, Angela, 1982– author.
Title: Always on : practicing faith in a new media landscape / Angela Gorrell.
Description: Grand Rapids : Baker Publishing Group, 2019. | Series: Theology for the life of the world | Includes bibliographical references and index.
Identifiers: LCCN 2018038579 | ISBN 9781540960092 (pbk. : alk. paper)
Subjects: LCSH: Social media—Religious aspects—Christianity.
Classification: LCC BV652.95 .G635 2019 | DDC 261.5/2—dc23
LC record available at https://lccn.loc.gov/2018038579

ISBN: 978-1-5409-6204-1 (casebound)

Portions of this book appeared in an earlier form in Angela Gorrell, "Spiritual Care in a Social Media Landscape," *Journal of Pastoral Care & Counseling* 72, no. 3 (September 2018): 221–23, https://doi.org/10.1177/1542305018801477.

19   20   21   22   23   24   25   7   6   5   4   3   2   1

In keeping with biblical principles of creation stewardship, Baker Publishing Group advocates the responsible use of our natural resources. As a member of the Green Press Initiative, our company uses recycled paper when possible. The text paper of this book is composed in part of post-consumer waste.

For my mom,
Virginia (Jenny) Grace Douglas

In third grade, I told you I would write a book someday.
And you believed me.

contents

gratitudes

Mom, this book is in honor of your love for your children and your own passion for writing. From the moment I began writing (at a very early age), you have supported me. You have always shown extraordinary enthusiasm for my work and for me. And you have taught me to believe that anything is possible with God. You modeled and nurtured the work ethic necessary for writing this manuscript. I cannot say enough about what an awesome mom you are, so I'll just say this: Thank you for *everything*. I am especially grateful for your and Don Douglas's faith in Jesus and your encouragement of your children. Special thanks to Don for sending me comic strips to keep me laughing through this process. I love you both.

Paul Gorrell, my amazing husband and best friend, thank you for listening to my musings on new media for the past six years! Thank you for letting me read this book aloud to you and for verbally processing ideas with me. Thanks also for the book's chapter titles and your poetry and ideas that went into this manuscript. And thank you for your willingness to move to Connecticut with me so I could work at the Yale Center for Faith and Culture. It is impossible to recount the numerous ways you helped me during the writing process. Do you remember when you brought dinner to my office (multiple times) so I could keep typing? Wow. I am so grateful to you for the many delicious, creative meals you made and the extra house duties and responsibilities you took on during especially difficult months. There were many, many days that I did not believe that finishing this book was possible. But you prayed for me and loved me well, and you believed this book was meaningful. I love you to the moon and back.

Jenna and Rob Olney, your love, stories, and humor sustain my life in ways that are difficult to articulate well. I love you both. Stefanie Poulin and Allison

Williams, I love you too. I am especially glad us sisters have been able to help each other through the last year and a half. Who would have thought that our texting sister group would bring such comfort and hope? To the rest of my awesome family, thank you for your encouragement.

Writing this book was an emotional and difficult process. Things like care packages, cards, and texts from my amazing family and friends inspired me to finish this manuscript. Molly Galbraith, thank you for the extraordinary number of gifts you sent in the mail to lift my spirits and for your visits. I have been counting on you since ninth grade. Macy Workman, I am grateful for every phone call and prayer and each card and gift you sent to reassure me. Since college, you have been a source of strength. To my LA besties (though some are in other cities now)—Audra Luzell, Beth Chiaravalle McQuitty, Chloe James, Christine Allen, Katie Eischen Nickols, Liz McQuitty, Lyndsey Deane Ratchford, Michaela O'Donnell Long, and Molly Stuckey—seriously, what would I do without you? Thank you for cheering me on and being wonderful friends.

During the spring of 2012, I was the director of children, youth, and family ministry at Pasadena Mennonite Church (PMC) and in my first year of PhD work at Fuller Theological Seminary. I must extend my gratitude to those who nurtured my passion for understanding the relationship between social media and Christianity. Thank you to the youth and youth leaders of PMC. Our conversations in that church basement mean the world to me. You helped me to see God's presence and love, even in the most difficult moments. Our discussions around the dinner table and on couches are among the most formative of my life. You are fantastic human beings.

From the moment I told Mark Lau Branson, my incredible PhD mentor, that I wanted to write my dissertation on social media, he was supportive. We had numerous conversations where he listened to me verbally process my ideas. It was Mark who, after reading my dissertation, said I should write a book on media literacy. I don't use this phrase much in this book because it's esoteric (Mark would probably agree), but this book was written in light of Mark's inspiration and my desire to help Christian communities develop competencies related to theological new media literacy. Thank you, Mark, for your mentorship, and especially for teaching me to always look for what God is up to and to listen to the Spirit.

Mark introduced me to Fuller professor Ryan Bolger. I emailed Ryan out of the blue one day asking to meet and talk about social media. Our conversation at the former Coffee by the Books near Fuller's Pasadena campus was pivotal for my media studies. Ryan, thanks for sharing your passion for new media with me, for your innovation at Fuller in this area, and for your guidance.

I have the privilege of serving at Yale Divinity School (YDS) as a research faculty member. Specifically, I am an associate research scholar at the Yale Center for Faith and Culture (YCFC). I am grateful for the space, time, and encouragement to do meaningful research. Thanks especially to Dean Greg Sterling. I am currently working on the Theology of Joy and the Good Life Project, a grant generously funded by the John Templeton Foundation (JTF).[1] This book was made possible through the support of JTF.

Thank you, fellow associate research scholars—Sarah Farmer, Matt Croasmun, and Drew Collins—for your remarkable friendship, love for Jesus, and feedback on my writing and ideas. Your pep talks made a huge difference. And Ryan McAnnally-Linz, what would I do without your editing skills and passion for theology? Thank you so much for editing nearly every chapter of this book. You have a remarkable mind and heart. Thanks for your leadership of YCFC and for believing in this book. Ryan, Sarah, Matt, and Drew, dialoguing about theology and pedagogy with you over the past two years has changed my life.

I am also grateful to Miroslav Volf, the founding director of YCFC. Thank you for your feedback on this book, for your compelling questions, and for urging me not just to invite conversation but to provide a glimpse into a Christian vision for true life in a new media landscape. You elevated my work.

I want to also express my gratitude to other staff at YCFC. Thanks to YDS's lifelong learning director, Debora Jackson, and to Team Ops—Phil Love, Leon Powell, Susan dos Santos, Karin Fransen, Skip Masback, and Shivhan Allen—for all you do at YCFC, for the ways you have supported this book, and for being wonderful colleagues. Thank you to Brendan Kolb for organizing the research seminar where great ideas were shared with me. And thank you to Tori McGraw-Rowe for being an awesome, dedicated research assistant. Thanks for your hard work and for the many conversations we had about this manuscript. I am also very grateful to David Dalwood. Thanks for your careful attention to this manuscript. It is a far better book because of your editing and feedback.

During this process, I was able to present my research ideas to several groups of people. I especially want to thank the Association of Youth Ministry Educators (AYME). In the fall of 2015, I had the privilege of speaking at AYME and it was then that I met Robert Hosack, acquisitions editor at Baker Publishing. Bob, thank you for your enduring enthusiasm for my work and for your belief in me throughout the years. Thanks for the many times you have

1. The opinions expressed in this publication are mine and do not necessarily reflect the views of JTF. For more information on the project, see YCFC's website (http://faith.yale.edu).

come to hear me speak and met with me. I am very grateful that you advocated for this book to be published. Thanks also to the many hardworking, helpful teams at Baker Academic for their guidance and support. I am very grateful to Melisa Blok. Thank you for your attention to detail, creativity, kindness, and writing and decision-making skills.

Lynne Baab (http://www.lynnebaab.com) reviewed the first draft of this manuscript. Thank you, Lynne, for your helpful feedback and for your encouragement! Also, Andy Root, thanks for reading chapter 3 and for the uplifting conversation we had while walking through Yale's campus. Deborah Kapp, thank you for our dinners and for bringing me to Chicago many times over to share my research. And Willie Jennings, I am grateful for our inspiring conversation at the YDS faculty Christmas party. Your words helped me to shape chapters 4–6.

Several groups of students have allowed me to stumble my way through deeper understanding of the new media landscape. Special thanks to Art, Cieara, Chosen, Damon, Daneen, Daren, David, Dickson, Eric, Georgia, Janet, Joyce, Kevin, Lily, Leah, Marietta, Nannette, Richard, Ryan B., Ryan H., and Will, former students at McCormick Theological Seminary, and Ben, Calvon, Jordan, Joseph, Kyle, and Pearl, former YDS students. Thank you for your feedback, for your presentations, and for reading parts of this manuscript in its earliest stages. Also, I must express my gratitude to the Yale College Life Worth Living students whom I have been privileged to teach. Your cards, questions, and support during this process sustained my enthusiasm for writing this book. Thank you, Alice, Annie, Caitlin, Cam, Carman, Charlotte, Carter, Ethan, Grace, Henry, Hope, Ian, Jack, Kate, Katherine, Leigh, Lina, Luke, Mahrukh, Marwan, Matthew, Sadé, Salaar, SGH, Shivam, Thanh, Tony, and Trina!

Even with so much dedicated support, this book is not perfect—not even close. Any of the book's weaknesses are entirely due to personal limitations and failings.

During the process of writing this book, several people I care about and admire passed away. I am so thankful for the well-lived lives of my coworker in Christ Dr. Scott Cameron, my high school friend Aaron Jackson, my brother-in-law Paul Jenkins, my nephew Mason Rice, and my pastor Rev. Debra Williams. Also, my dad, David Lee Williams, passed away. Dad, I miss you. Thanks for your enduring love and the many phone calls we had about my PhD research while I was walking around Victory Park. Thanks for the ways you called me "my Angel" and "my Angela" throughout my life. I can still hear you saying these words in my mind. You always told me you were proud of me, and you always ended your time with me in prayer. Thanks especially for your silly faces and big hugs.

My dear mamaw, Delores Christine Applegate Spencer, passed away just a few weeks ago. She told me recently that she was looking forward to reading this book. The night before her funeral, some family members were gathered at mamaw and papaw's house. When everyone lined up for dinner, I walked outside to get something from the car. I took a moment to look around and take everything in—the acres of green grass, the barn I played in as a kid, the house I have been visiting for over thirty years. As I was walking back inside, I heard boisterous laughter and conversation flowing out from the windows; it was exactly how mamaw liked her home—full of people she loves, eating and talking together. My heart was overflowing with gratitude (as it is today) for my entire family and all the years we have gathered in those rooms to share life, and for her love that has been a uniting force.

introduction

"Alexa, turn up the lights." The lights change from a dim glow to a bright light that illuminates the entire room. "Alexa, turn on Frank Sinatra." Sinatra's voice is suddenly booming throughout the house. "Alexa, turn the music down a little." The song is quieted. I suddenly realize that my friend Chloe and I have barely entered the front door and without moving or touching anything or exerting much effort, the ambiance of the house has been changed.

My husband, Paul, and I are using streaming software to watch a film on our smart TV. I check my mobile phone and notice a text from my mom. She wants to know if I have received her card, the one with the comic strip from my stepdad, Don, that mentions Yale (where I am a researcher and lecturer). I text back that the comic strip was funny and is now on my refrigerator, and then I go back to watching the film. A few minutes later, I remember that I need to update my phone, which requires deleting as many photos and videos as possible. I keep getting the maddening message that my storage is full. I plug my phone into my laptop to import the photos and videos that I want to keep. This process involves reviewing highlights of my experiences over the past year and a half: highs, lows, and everything in between. I spend most of the movie clicking through photos and reflecting on the joys and sorrows of recent months, while still being somewhat attuned to the film's plot. I've seen it before anyway.

"When we go out to eat, we put all of our phones in the middle of the table. The first person to pick up their phone has to pay the bill," Joe explained. I had read about this practice, but it was even more interesting to hear a senior in college tell me about it in person. I was eating dinner with Joe's family. He

1

went on to say, "It works! No one picks up their phone because no one wants to pay the bill."

These three vignettes demonstrate a few of the massive shifts that have taken place recently, and they invite multiple questions: Is Alexa a good technology? What makes technology *good*? Does daily access to multiple modes of communication shape and change human beings, and if so, how? Have mobile phones become so intrusive that we need mindful practices that help us be more attentive to our friends? And what do these vignettes have to do with Christian faith? Does God care about the sorts of technology we develop and engage with? Simply by reflecting on these illustrations, we can come up with many more questions.

There are several reasons I think we need to spend time reflecting on our current "new media landscape" (this term is examined at length in chap. 2). First, it is likely that you engage with new media more than you realize because "new media" encompasses many forms and devices, including blogs, the internet, podcasts, social networks, streaming services, e-books, computers, cell phones, e-readers, and so on.[1] The term "old media" includes print newspapers, television, radio, and traditional books. You use new media if you email or text; if you use a Kindle to read books, Google maps to navigate, a digital device for listening to music (e.g., mobile phone, iPod, etc.), or a service for watching television or movies (e.g., Netflix); or if you buy things online. New media is a large category that includes current forms of social media. So what qualifies as social media?

The term "social media" is commonly used to describe a variety of online sites, technologies, and activities. There are four main categories for social media platforms.[2]

1. Social networking sites (e.g., Facebook, Twitter, LinkedIn) are online platforms primarily designed for connecting with other people.
2. User-generated content sites (e.g., YouTube, Flickr, Wikipedia) are online platforms where people can upload content (e.g., videos, photos) they have created, curated, or remixed and share it with other people.
3. Trading and marketing sites (e.g., Amazon, Groupon, Craigslist) are online platforms where people buy, sell, and/or trade material goods.

1. For more on the term "new media" and a description of its main characteristics (e.g., numerical representation, modularity, automation), see Campbell and Garner, *Networked Theology*, 40–48.
2. Van Dijck, *Culture of Connectivity*, 8.

4. Play and game sites (e.g., Angry Birds, Farmville, The Sims Social) are online platforms for playing internet games with other people.

However, social networking sites are rarely clearly defined by these platform categories. This is because each platform is in unending competition with others of its type and is constantly reaching into the niche industry of others. The market more or less guarantees that this will always be the case.[3] For example, Facebook connects people, allows people to upload created content and invite others to play games, and has created ways for people to buy, sell, and trade items through the site.

Even if most of what I described does not apply to your daily life, it most likely applies to the lives of many of the people in your community. This is the second reason I hope you will read this book and spend time reflecting on our current new media landscape. If you want to be attentive to what is impacting people's lives, critical and theological reflection on new media development and engagement is essential. Donna Freitas surveyed and interviewed college students at thirteen campuses about their concerns regarding new media. In her fascinating book *The Happiness Effect*, she writes, "Students want to know what their peers think about social media and whether they experience the same struggles. They want, in other words, information about how their generation is handling one of the most significant and dramatic cultural shifts of our time. Most of all, they want to know that they are not alone in feeling the way they do."[4] Young people want space to discuss their new media experiences and their struggles with it, and they desire guidance.[5] From leading seminars and courses on new media, I have discovered that older generations deeply appreciate the opportunity to discern the implications of new media development and engagement for their lives and their Christian faith. When I lead conversations about new media, people often tell me they are relieved to have an opportunity to discuss their experiences. I have found that conversation and reflection on new media development and engagement create opportunities to explore some of the most beautiful and painful realities in people's lives.

Third, new media extends suffering that occurs in physical spaces into digital spaces, and issues of suffering are increasingly integrated across people's online and in-person lives. If you care about issues like poverty, sexism, depression, anxiety, and racism, you may want to know more about how

3. Van Dijck, *Culture of Connectivity*, 8.
4. Freitas, *Happiness Effect*, 10.
5. Freitas, *Happiness Effect*, 245–46.

new media is being developed and how people are engaging with it. Finally, artificial intelligence (AI; e.g., Alexa) and robotics (e.g., Sophia[6]) already exist, but new technologies are continuously being developed using AI; and robotics will have significant implications for work, health care, travel, and many other categories of human existence. New media is always changing, and Christian communities need lasting Christian visions of true life that will guide them well into the future.

What This Book Is About

This book begins by proposing that new media has both glorious possibilities and profound brokenness.[7] Glorious possibilities arise when new media is designed and used in view of Christian visions of the flourishing life.[8] New media spaces and devices *can* be sites and instruments of God's unconditional love. However, in view of malformed visions of what the good life is, new media is developed and used for damaging purposes, which only deepens the conditions of the false life: malign circumstances, harmful practices, and destructive feelings. This is why new media is often a source of profound brokenness.

New media *can* be a site and instrument of the home of God if Christian communities discern, articulate, and live Christian visions of the good life for this new landscape. Therefore, articulating such visions must be the central focus of conversation about new media in Christian communities. Regrettably, communities mainly engage in fruitless conversation about new media. In chapter 1, I support this point by outlining the content of four common types of fruitless conversation about new media, encouraging readers to assess their own communities. The chapter ends by offering a way forward: interested conversation.

6. Sophia is a robot. The website Hanson Robotics explains:
Designed to look like Audrey Hepburn, Sophia embodies Hepburn's classic beauty: porcelain skin, a slender nose, high cheekbones, an intriguing smile, and deeply expressive eyes that seem to change color with the light. . . . Her creator is Dr. David Hanson, founder of Hanson Robotics and a modern-day renaissance man who has built a worldwide reputation for creating robots that look and act amazingly human. After working at Disney as one of its "Imagineers," Dr. Hanson aspired to create genius machines that are smarter than humans and can learn creativity, empathy, and compassion—three distinctly human traits Hanson believes must be developed alongside and integrated with artificial intelligence for robots to solve world problems too complex for humans to solve themselves. ("Sophia," Hanson Robotics Ltd., http://www.hansonrobotics.com/robot/sophia/)
7. I was inspired by Graham Ward's use of "glorious possibility" in his book *Cultural Transformation and Religious Practice*, 57.
8. Throughout the book I will use the terms "flourishing life," "true life," and "the good life" interchangeably.

Interested conversation is meaningful, imaginative, critically and theologically reflective, Spirit-guided, and fruitful dialogue. This is conversation that is *interested* in what God is up to in this new media landscape and *interested* in reasons why new media has glorious possibilities and profound brokenness. Interested conversation is also invested in discerning and articulating visions that Christian communities can live toward in a new media–saturated culture. Christian visions of true, flourishing life that guide new media design and use aim, by God's grace, to nurture a healing Christian community in a new media landscape. Interested conversation is not just dialogue; rather, it inspires action. Genuine Christian visions transform the trajectory and content of people's beliefs, desires, and practices. By doing so, as in the case of new media, such visions nurture hybrid faithful living. "Hybrid" is a term I use throughout the book to describe the integrated nature of both physical and digital spaces and in-person and mediated practices; I discuss the idea of "hybridity" in chapter 2. Hybrid faithful living encompasses the true life of righteousness, peace, and joy—online and in person—even while living under the conditions of the false life, until the new world is established.

Chapter 2 explores the new media terrain and provides insight into why new media is connected to Christian faith and is meaningful to people and Christian communities. Chapter 3 describes cultural narratives that shape the social contexts that designers and developers of new media live within. By describing these narratives, we begin to get a sense of the conditions of the false life we are all living within. I argue that the communication techniques and priorities of these social contexts form the structure—the practices and values—of new media. Additionally, I propose that new media not only deepens these narratives but also contributes to them.

Chapter 4 takes a turn toward imagining Jesus's life and ministry as a methodology for articulating Christian visions of the true life. This chapter discusses Luke 4 and 7 to help us imagine how a person formed in the image of God, which is Jesus Christ, would act and feel when using new media, and what kinds of new media circumstances Jesus would seek to create. In chapters 5 and 6, I discuss the nature of hybrid faithful living. Since various visions converge in a new media landscape, living a life of righteousness, peace, and joy—a Christian vision of true life—can be difficult. I argue that hybrid faithful living requires a commitment to regularly practicing discernment and nurturing a hybrid, healing community. Chapter 5 offers methods for practicing discernment about new media. And chapter 6 describes ways to develop hybrid Christian practices and design a rule for life in a new media landscape.

Whom This Book Is For

If you are interested in new media, this book is for you. If you want to learn more about new media and its glorious possibilities and profound brokenness and more about discerning, articulating, and living the true life in a new media landscape, this book was written with you in mind.

That being said, this book was specifically written for Christian communities—with implications for leaders of those communities, for the communities as a whole (i.e., organizations, institutions), and for individual community members. I use the term "Christian community" in this book as a way of talking about groups (e.g., congregations, parishes, classrooms, small groups, youth groups, parachurch groups, Christian nonprofit organizations) that are committed to following Jesus and doing life together by teaching, practicing, and reflecting on Christian faith. I wrote this book to prepare pastors, lay leaders, and other types of Christian religious educators (in the academy, parachurch organizations, Christian secondary schools, etc.) to facilitate interested conversation about new media and therefore to guide Christian communities in articulating, discerning, and living Christian visions of the good life while traversing the new media terrain.

How to Use This Book

I hope you will read this book with other people. This book provides discussion questions, frameworks, and other pedagogical aids along the way that will help your Christian community reflect on contextual faith for a way of life in our new media landscape. Once your community has talked about a chapter's themes, the discussion questions can be used to practice interested conversation.

In chapter 1, the questions will help your community begin to reflect on new media's glorious possibilities and profound brokenness, as well as the community's feelings and typical conversation regarding technology. Chapter 2's questions will nurture dialogue about the new media terrain. And the questions at the end of chapter 3 will help your community critically reflect on cultural stories. Chapter 4 is an invitation for your community to imagine Jesus's life and ministry, in order to articulate how a representative of Christ's kingdom would act and feel online and what sorts of conditions they would seek. The chapter itself is an example of this sort of imagining. At the end of chapter 4, there are two exercises that your community can use to reflect on Jesus's life and ministry and articulate a Christian vision of true life. Chapter 5 describes several processes of discernment and provides three sets of discussion questions. Finally, chapter 6 offers numerous ways to develop hybrid Christian practices and has an outline for designing a rule for life in a new media landscape. At the end of chapter 6, you will find an example of a method of prayer called the Examen (or the Daily Examen), a spiritual discipline that is helpful for assessing hybrid living. I hope your community will use these resources to practice interested conversation.

New Media Is Daunting, but You Are Better Than Google

When I recall the first time I preached or led a seminar or walked into a classroom to teach, I remember one primary feeling: vulnerability. I preached my first sermon in seventh grade. The sermon was for my youth group and was called, "The Masks We Wear." What I didn't know then was that the vulnerable feeling would stick around and reappear many times when I have felt inadequate, like an imposter with weaknesses that disqualify me as an educator. I was sure that when I opened my mouth to give my first lecture, people would wonder why I had been chosen to speak. Perhaps they might even believe that their time would have been better spent elsewhere. I am naturally very much myself when I preach, speak, and teach, which I hope people find distinctive and humanizing, but I often worry that it makes me appear naive, less "academic," or worse: incompetent. That seventh-grade feeling followed me around and was there the first time I walked into a seminary classroom as an "instructor-in-training"—a title that assures students will not respect you. I was terrified. Every time I went to the whiteboard, I was afraid students would discover how much I need spell-check.

I felt exposed and vulnerable when I started leading, preaching, speaking, and teaching. I bet most of you did too. Now, with the internet, and with new online platforms and phone apps (it's alright if you need to google "app" right now) and websites appearing daily, many of you may be feeling vulnerable. Some of you may be counting the days until you can retire so you do not have to use social media in ministry, or teach online, or even get a social media account. New media is a daunting topic for everyone, especially for people who feel responsible for helping other people reflect on new media. If you are feeling unnecessary or inadequate in this digital age, I have some good news: *you are better than Google.*

While new media has some incredible benefits, you are better. For example, Google is primarily invested in making money. Google treats people like objects of strategy, rather than human beings made in the image of God. But you are better. When engaging with them, you take into consideration who your community members are, where they have been, and who they are becoming. The lives of the people in your Christian community matter deeply. Google doesn't realize this, but you do.

If you were to ask Google, "What do you think of me?" it would not be much help. I know, because I googled this question. It will give you articles and books related to reputation management. Obviously, Google cannot actually tell anyone what it thinks about them. But you can. You can provide meaningful feedback. You can watch your community members act and think in various contexts, across time, and tell them what you see. You can affirm them and help them in ways that Google cannot.

Have you ever used Google to figure out how to do something? Sometimes it works; other times, not so much. For example, I googled the question, "How do I do a back handspring?" and discovered that WikiHow provides eleven steps with pictures. Unfortunately, for most of us, these steps are not enough to help us actually perform a back handspring. But you are better than Google. You do not assume that the people in your Christian community will learn something on their own and do it correctly the first time or that people will practice alone. You curate educational settings (whether in person or online) where community members can practice, experiment, and fail, and where you will be there to mentor them.

Also, Google does not even know if the information it provides is what people need. The information it offers can be inaccurate and meaningless. This is why *you* are needed more than ever. You can teach critical reflection. You can help members of your Christian community understand that they use the internet *and* that the internet uses them. And even better, you have the Holy Spirit as your companion and guide as you are a companion to others in your Christian community.

Finally, Google automatically produces an answer to every question. But you are different. You understand that the point of being a pastor or Christian leader is *not* having all the answers. Richard Rohr in *Things Hidden* writes, "What I've learned is that not-knowing and often not even needing to know is a deeper way of knowing and a deeper form of compassion."[9] This type of educating nurtures people who will do the same things within the groups they lead. Sure, Google can provide an "answer" to almost every question. And yes, it usually finds the right TED talk or a great YouTube video. But Google cannot do what the best leaders do. And that is why *you are better*.

9. Rohr, *Things Hidden*, 39.

About the Author

My Twitter account (@AngelaGorrell) describes me this way: "research. teach. write. repeat. fascinations: people, asking why, examining life, media, practical theology, education and formation, contemporary culture."

My Instagram page provides this summary: "Wife. Sister. Daughter. Aunt. Friend. Professor. Researcher. Writer. Lover of God and people."

My Facebook profile describes my work, education, places I have lived, my birthday, relationship status, and even several life events. By reading it, you would learn that I work at the Yale Center for Faith and Culture and teach at Yale University. You would also discover that I obtained a degree from Azusa Pacific University and two degrees from Fuller Theological Seminary. You would see that I have lived in Kentucky, California, and Connecticut. You would also find out that I am married to Paul Gorrell. You would even learn from my timeline of life events (curated for me by Facebook) when I met Paul Gorrell and when we were married.

My LinkedIn profile says, "Associate Research Scholar and Lecturer at Yale." The summary below this title says,

> I am passionate about investing in people's lives, building and nurturing teams, and cultivating learning communities where people are invited to hunt their assumptions and think critically while feeling connected to others, heard, free to be creative, and safe to ask questions and tell their stories. I especially enjoy teaching; mentoring and coaching; learning, distilling, and examining ideas; asking compelling, capacious questions; problem-solving; activating; innovating; and leading (and helping groups to navigate) change. One of my greatest research interests is discerning ways new media can be designed, developed, and engaged to nurture relationships, explore the world and the fundamental questions of human existence, extend education, and contribute to the common good.

My website (https://www.angelagorrell.com) provides a way to contact me for speaking, teaching, consulting, and research. It shows photos of the people I have partnered with and learned from.

You would learn quite a bit about me by reviewing my social media profiles and website. However, I would like you to know a few other things about me. I pursued ordination in the Mennonite Church USA because of my Christian commitments to peacemaking, preventing violence, seeking justice, and engaging in radical hospitality. I felt called to youth ministry in seventh grade, and I have dedicated the majority of my work life to church and parachurch ministry. I began teaching in the academy in 2014. I teach courses related to theology, ecclesiology, philosophy, contemporary culture, and education and formation. I am energized by teaching and care deeply about investing in the lives of students. As a wife, family and community member, friend, pastor, and professor, I try to continually choose true life by listening to God's voice, holding fast to God, and recognizing that the Lord is my life (Deut. 30:19–20).

one

interested conversation

Occupants of the unsaid sides of silence move
single-file by force through paths of grief and grace,
variegated planks for feet rough cut and worn
smooth with the friction-chatter of naked toes and heels.

Words worth saying often go unsaid—
worthwhile,
quieted,
words.

> *If you bring forth what is within you what you bring*
> *forth will save you.*
> *If you do not bring forth what is within you what you*
> *do not bring forth will destroy you.*

Paul Gorrell,[1] "Words Worth Saying"

This past year, a high school friend of mine, Aaron Jackson, was dying. Hundreds of people used social media to stay updated on his cancer treatment, hoping that he would be healed. Each week his Facebook page was flooded with encouragement. People reminded Aaron often that they

1. Paul Gorrell is a poet and the founder and director of Peace Right Here, which "works to recover and reshape imaginations to embrace, practice, and champion alternatives to violence." See "About," Peace Right Here. Paul is also my husband and partner in life. This poem is from an unpublished collection of his poetry.

loved him and were praying for him. He spent the last months of his life sharing his cancer journey with us: the joyful, the ugly, and the mundane. In the midst of it all he continued to use the phrases, "God is in control," "Stay strong," and "Never give up." In November, he posted his last two Facebook status updates: one, an enthusiastic post dedicated to his favorite basketball team, and the other, a sobering post promising to watch over everyone and asking friends to let him know who to say "hey" to on the other side. Like so many others, I will be forever grateful for Aaron's online vulnerability and positivity, and his insights into the experiences of those trying to survive cancer. For most of the last months of his life, Aaron was unable to leave his hospital room and could only have a few visitors because his medical team was trying to get him into remission. Social media was his connection to his friends and to the world.

Glorious Possibilities

God is online. God is active in every place and at every point of our lives. God's investment in creation extends to the various developments of human culture, including internet spaces like social media sites.[2] The Holy Spirit can be our companion in online spaces, as in all other aspects of life—teaching us; reminding us; empowering us; encouraging us; revealing truth to us; bringing us grace, joy, hope, and peace; praying on our behalf; telling us what to say; setting us free; making us holy; and, thus, inviting human beings to be receptive to and share in God's loving, reconciling ministry in our hearts and in the world (Luke 2:26; 10:21; 12:12; John 14:26; Acts 1:8; 9:31; 13:9; Rom. 8; 14:17; 15:13; 2 Cor. 5:14–21; 1 Pet. 1:2). God is with us during our engagement with new media just as God is with us when we engage in physical spaces and activities and use other tools. Given God's dynamic participation in people's lives and the entire world, new media has glorious possibilities. In other words, incredible, meaningful things can happen as people use new media—because of God's guidance, love, and active presence in our new media landscape.

Reflecting on Aaron's story, I can see that he demonstrated God's love, strength, and hope toward his family, girlfriend, coworkers, and friends online, and an extraordinary number of people mirrored that love, strength, and hope back to him through social media. Each week I witnessed people

---

2. God is missional in the sense that God is actively engaged in the world and the Spirit is consistently inviting human beings to participate in God's activities. Consequently, "God is at work in the world beyond the church." Van Gelder, *Ministry of the Missional Church*, 59. See also Gorrell, "Social Media, Churches," 11, 215.

online rejoicing with Aaron when he rejoiced. When he posted about being able to spend time with people he loved in person, when he shared videos and photos of himself walking the halls of the treatment center (his will to survive and remain hopeful never wavered), and when the treatment he received was working and helping him feel more like himself, people wrote joyful, compassionate replies.

I also observed people mourning when Aaron mourned. They expressed sadness when he displayed a photo of the effects of chemotherapy on his mouth and explained that he was unable to eat even though he was starving; they communicated grief when he shared his sadness about missing events that were important to him; and they conveyed pain when he posted that doctors were struggling to find other remedies for curing him.

When Aaron posted his last status updates, the rejoicing and mourning were intermingled, as often joy and sorrow are. People wrote things like, "You have brought laughter and humor to such a heartbreaking time. You have had every right to complain and instead, you chose love." And, "With tear-filled eyes all I can do is look at the sun rising over the clouds and imagine the beauty you are entering. Well done my friend, what a wonderful life you have led here. You are so loved." And, "Your strength, faith in God, and determination have changed so many lives."

Social media was used to keep people updated about Aaron's treatment plans, support him with practical resources, shower him with love, and invite people to pray for his healing. For example, a sock campaign was started in his honor. He loved to wear crazy, colorful, decorative knee-high socks. Everyone who knew him, knew he loved wild socks, a beautiful idiosyncrasy that people used to share his story and let him know that he was seen and heard. His family, friends, and coworkers wore crazy socks and posted photos on social media of them wearing the socks with special hashtags dedicated to him and with loving words of support. One friend made an image in his honor of a cancer awareness ribbon in blue and white (the colors of his favorite Kentucky basketball team: University of Kentucky), and many of his Facebook friends replaced their profile picture with it.

People held events on his behalf—a softball tournament and social events at a local restaurant—to raise money for whatever he needed, and they posted about the events on social media to acquire additional funds. Then, three months before he passed away, friends used technology (in fewer than forty-eight hours) to gather a large group of over one hundred people outside the cancer center where Aaron was being treated. He had been at the center for ninety-two days and was about to be moved from Kentucky to a new cancer center in Texas. The purpose of gathering people was twofold: (1) to encourage him to stay strong by bringing him to the balcony of the cancer center to look down on the crowd and see how loved he was and (2) to raise more money for the new type of treatment he was about to receive. To raise the money, someone filmed the gathering and posted it on Facebook so people could find the website to donate money for the treatment that everyone was hoping would save his life. In the video, you can see the crowd cheering and holding up handmade signs with loving words like "Stay Strong," "You are our Superhero," and "We love you."

Connection

The major possibility that new media use affords is *connection.* In the early days of AOL, message boards allowed people to discuss, among other things, their hobbies. My aunt Teri told me that one day she was messaging a group that discussed favorite childhood books. She mentioned that hers was a book about a girl visiting the circus and seeing female riders and horses with plumes on their heads, but she could not remember the name of the book. Instantly a man in the group recognized the book and provided the title; he even asked for an address where he could mail her a vintage copy for free. Teri said this was when she was first awakened to new media's possibilities and reawakened to the kindness of strangers.

Most online activity comes from a desire to connect. In *It's Complicated,* danah boyd explores the important reasons young people stay online, arguing that "most teens are not compelled by gadgetry as such—they are compelled by friendship. The gadgets are interesting to them primarily as a means to a social end."[3] Basically, if young people can find a way to hang out with their friends, they will. Youth have a way of "socializing" technology—that is, always finding a way of using technology to nurture relationships with their friends.[4] When cars became popular, youth went cruising with their friends and drove to parking lots to sit around and talk to each other. For teens today, having a cell phone means having access to friends. And teens love to talk to their friends.

3. Danah boyd, *It's Complicated,* 18. As a Microsoft researcher, danah boyd talked with teens in eighteen states from a wide array of socioeconomic and ethnic communities between 2006 and 2010, conducted 166 formal, semistructured interviews with teens, and observed teens online and offline (see boyd, *It's Complicated,* 27, 215–20). Sometimes media scholars, such as boyd, and media platforms do not capitalize words that are normally capitalized and, likewise, may use capitalization when convention would suggest otherwise. I will follow norms concerning trademarks and allow authors' preferred nonstandard usage in book titles, chapter titles, names, and digital vocabulary (e.g., website names and internet terminology).

4. Zirschky, "Technology, Education." In his book *Beyond the Screen,* Zirschky explores why young people frequently use technology and provides guidance for people who care about and work with young people.

New media is not just being used to connect with friends though; it is also being used to help young people have healthier experiences with their peers and to feel empowered. "Connected Camps" offers a weeklong program that allows kids to have a camp experience by playing games and engaging in various activities online. There are even counselors who monitor and lead the experiences. Paul Darvasi tells the story of Karen Gilbo's daughter. She is twelve years old, loves LEGO and playing Minecraft and also happens to have a form of autism (Asperger's syndrome), which causes her to struggle to read social cues in person.[5] In the past, Gilbo sent her daughter to in-person camps (the type most people are familiar with), but her daughter needed an aide with her at all times, and this made her feel different. However, at online camp, she did not see herself as different, and she had positive social interactions with other campers while enjoying some of her favorite activities.

There are also adults who find that the internet helps them relate to others and embrace and participate in God's love when it would otherwise be difficult or even impossible. Numerous online support groups have been created for people who are facing similar things in life: the challenges of parenting, specific diseases like migraines, various addictions, and so on. Social media use can be deeply encouraging to people who feel alone or marginalized in the community they live in or in the organizations they are a part of.

Internet spaces can also be inspiring and motivating, spaces that nurture learning. Tori McGraw-Rowe, a friend and research assistant for this book, described the importance in her life of the Vineyard Women website, a hub for women's pastoral voices in the Association of Vineyard Churches.[6] It aggregates sermons preached by women in Vineyard churches in North America. For Tori, a young seminarian, recently ordained in the Vineyard church, the sermons have been encouraging and empowering examples of preaching. She is also part of a monthly coaching group, composed of women Vineyard pastors in Pennsylvania, Colorado, and Tennessee. Without the social media site that hosts their monthly meeting, the women would probably not know each other, and each would likely be on her own.

The internet has also become an important space for people to relate with those they would otherwise not know. I met Jedidiah Haas while working at an in-person summer camp in high school, approximately eighteen years ago. I have kept up with him somewhat through social media. Jed has cystic fibrosis, and during the last few years this has made working as an in-person pastor unmanageable. His doctors did not want him to interact with many

---

5. Darvasi, "Online Communities Lower Social Barriers."
6. "Homepage," Vineyard Women.

Jedidiah Haas
May 5, 2017

A quick update for my friends—I spend a lot of time on Facebook these days (it is easy to scroll and see people I love). I am either in the hospital in an isolation room or home bound these days. My health takes up about 90% of my focus (lots of time for Kendra and other family too) so I can stay healthy enough for a potential double lung transplant. I have about 10% to spend on my other priorities. As you can see my time is limited and visitors are super limited. I am a people guy so naturally this drives me crazy, yet, I am cherishing the time I have in person with my family and extended family (in other words my "oikos," which includes family and some friends). Texting is my new way of life because I don't have to use breath. I am moving to primarily virtual communication, and I am super thankful to be part of the ministry of virtualdisciplemaker.com. I want to thank everyone for your continued prayer and support. We feel at peace and loved big time. I weep at times thinking of the amazing relationships I have been blessed with, and I continue to see love in action through each one of you. My heart is for as many people as possible to know the love of Jesus. Keep spreading the joy! Keep focusing your eyes on Jesus.

 Like   Comment   ⤷ Share

people in person for fear of them making him sicker. In 2017, I watched Jed use the power of the internet to disciple other people while awaiting a lung transplant.[7] Jed explains in a Facebook post (above).

Jed mentors and coaches other people by using an online platform called Zoom. His website and Zoom help him continue to invest in people's lives, despite being in a hospital room.[8]

One of my best friends, Lyndsey Deane Ratchford, has dedicated her life to helping people have access to clean water. She uses social media to post status updates and live videos that encourage responsiveness to the needs of some of the world's most vulnerable communities. Her posts urge viewers to understand the far-reaching implications of this issue (e.g., education, health) and to learn the stories of people whose lives have been saved by clean water

7. Jed received new lungs in late 2017 and is doing really well!
8. virtual DISCIPLEMAKER, http://www.virtualdisciplemaker.com/about.html.

as well as those working to solve this problem.[9] She uses both her in-person ministry (preaching and speaking) and social media to invite members of Christian communities to partner with her and World Vision by running half and full marathons, donating money, and sponsoring children. Her goal is to help provide clean water to every person on the planet during her lifetime; social media has assisted her in making headway toward this goal.

Online platforms can provide nonthreatening space for people's imagination and feelings to be engaged so that they can participate in God's work and be transformed. Social media use can even cause people to feel empathy and compassion for people they have never met.[10] One of the most powerful displays of internet-nurtured compassion occurred in 2015 when an online photo of three-year-old Syrian refugee Alan Kurdi lying dead on a beach instantly went viral. Bryan Walsh writes in a *Time* article about the photo, "A few minutes into the journey to Greece, the dinghy capsized. Alan, his older brother Ghalib and his mother Rihanna all drowned, joining the more than 3,600 other refugees who died in the eastern Mediterranean. . . . In death, Alan became a symbol of all the children who lost their lives trying to reach safety in Europe and the West."[11] A digital photo shared on multiple online platforms awakened the world to what was happening in Syria. The photo of Alan humanized the horrifying war zone in Syria and caused many people across the globe to give money toward aiding refugees.[12] (The refugee crisis remains, and we need to keep responding.)[13] These are a few examples of possibilities related to connection that new media use affords.

New media spaces and devices *can* be sites and instruments of God's home among mortals (Rev. 21:3) where new media development and engagement is determined by Christian visions of the good life.[14] You *can* live a true life of

---

9. "Clean Water." See also World Vision International at https://www.wvi.org.

10. Mary Hess, in her article "Mirror Neurons," explores the effectiveness of digital storytelling for faith formation due to possible connections between digital storytelling and the development of empathy.

11. B. Walsh, "Alan Kurdi's Story."

12. Deutsche Welle, "Refugee Donations Surge."

13. For information on the refugee crisis, including ways to help, see "Refugee Crisis."

14. Miroslav Volf and Matthew Croasmun refer to the kingdom of God as "God's home among mortals" in their book *For the Life of the World*. As they explain, this home of God that "Jesus proclaimed and enacted is a particular kind of *dynamic relation* between God and the world: it is 'the world-with-God' and 'God-with-the world'" (68). They quote Revelation 21:3, which says, "I heard a loud voice from the throne say, 'Look! God's dwelling is here with humankind. He will dwell with them, and they will be his peoples. God himself will be with them as their God.'" Volf and Croasmun invite serious discussion "about how doing theology fits into the grand goal of God: fashioning each human and the entire world into God's home and our true home as well" (8).

righteousness, peace, and joy in the Holy Spirit (Rom. 14:17) and practice faith in this new media landscape, although it will be lived under the conditions of the false life, until the new world is established (Rev. 21:1–22:5).[15] God has not yet fully made this new media landscape God's home; rather, it is still on its way to becoming God's home. Online and in person, we experience glimpses of God's activity and loving embrace, but we experience these glimpses in the midst of a world that is broken—marred by sin and its consequence: suffering.

Profound Brokenness

While the stories I have shared display some of the most glorious things that can happen through social media, embedded in other stories are the ways social media use contributes to malign circumstances, harmful practices, and destructive feelings. I am not quite a digital immigrant, nor am I a digital native.[16] One might call me a first-generation internet citizen.[17] I did not have a mobile phone until college, and I have never taken a keyboarding class. However, my mother bought a desktop computer for my bedroom when I was sixteen years old. Looking back, I realize this was a significant privilege. After receiving this computer and learning how to connect to AOL through a dial-up connection, I often visited various chat rooms first thing after arriving home from school. If you were around at the beginning of AOL and had access to a desktop computer, you probably recall both the familiar noise the modem made when it was connecting to the internet and your own excitement about talking to your friends through a computer. It was incredible.

I was an early adopter of MySpace, the first social media site that helped me create a social network online. However, MySpace was also how I found out that my college boyfriend of two-and-a-half years was simultaneously

15. There are two forms of flourishing life: ultimate and secondary. Volf and Croasmun explain, "Then and there, in the new world that comes from God, all God's creatures will flourish in God's presence; the flourishing of each will aid the flourishing of all and the flourishing of all will in fact be an aspect of the flourishing of each. This is the flourishing life in its ultimate form. . . . Flourishing life in the secondary and penultimate sense is *the mode of the true life under the conditions of the false life*." *Life of the World*, 76, 79.

16. "A digital immigrant is an individual who was born before the widespread adoption of digital technology. The term digital immigrant may also apply to individuals who were born after the spread of digital technology and who were not exposed to it at an early age. Digital immigrants are the opposite of digital natives, who have been interacting with technology from childhood." "Digital Immigrant."

17. "Born between 1977 and 1997, Net-generation [is] the first generation to grow up surrounded by home computers, video games, and the Internet." Leung, "Net-Generation Attributes," 333.

in a relationship with someone else. Obviously, this was painful. While new media has expanded my understanding of the world in meaningful ways, kept me connected with friends and family, and provided rich resources for teaching (among many other things I could name), it has also been a source of pain, anxiety, frustration, and sadness on many occasions. I know what it feels like to post something and then regularly check to see if people have responded or liked what I have said. And more than this, I know what it feels like to have a post "fall flat," the kind of post that so few people respond to that you want to delete it. I *have* deleted those kinds of posts.

I understand how social media can contribute to jealousy. I have several friends who seemingly, no matter what they post, get hundreds of likes each time. I look at their posts and sometimes compare myself to them and feel "less than"—less smart, less funny, less beautiful, less successful. And I understand why social media can extend worry. After posting something potentially controversial, I know what it feels like to try to work (or do school assignments) only to find myself wondering, "What are people thinking about what I just shared? If I glance at my page, will I find hateful remarks?" And then there was 2016, the year that I came to understand, like so many of you, how hurtful social media rants and posts about politics and religion can be. I began to recognize how angry I can get when using social media. I started to notice that when I read certain posts, tweets, or news stories, my stomach would tighten, and I would feel like my blood was boiling. Long after leaving my newsfeed, I obsessed over what I could say or do in response.

Too many days this year, I have read things online and thought, "I cannot believe this is the world we live in. I cannot believe people really think this way." You may resonate with these sentiments. My friends have reminded me that, unfortunately, the world *has* been this way (divided in many respects, violent, racist, misogynistic, etc.), and social media's exposure of recent events (and people's ability to constantly share their thoughts on the events) has simply surfaced these longtime realities in new ways that are forcing *everyone* to feel them and confront them.

Beyond all of this, there are the devastating stories—genocide, modern slavery, mass shootings, white supremacy demonstrations, starvation. Even though I realize that too much of history is filled with these kinds of violence, I also recognize that social media has given me access to this information in new ways. I often read, in rapid succession, stories of violence, sometimes even as they are occurring, from the very people who are living them. It is one thing to hear about violence and another thing to watch it in real time. During these online moments, I see the depth of need in the world and how far it reaches. I see the heartbreaking reality of too many people's lives; and like so many of you, on too many days I am overwhelmed by what I encounter online. On top of this, I often realize (again) that these needs and these heartbreaks have something to do with how I live my life—what I buy, how I take care of the environment, who I vote for, how I spend my time, what I do with the information I encounter online. In the midst of this kind of new media engagement, I often find myself unsure of what to pray for and crushed by my seeming inability to do anything about, well, anything.

Diminished Humanness

The new media landscape definitely presents new challenges, chief among which is the risk for *diminished humanness*. Online, some dimensions of humanity become more prominent, like our sense of sight and hearing. However, some dimensions of humanity remain opaque, like smell and touch (other than touching keys on a keyboard or touching a mobile phone). And even though sight and hearing are engaged when using new media, we usually use them to see words and images and to hear music, podcasts, notifications, and videos, rather than seeing and hearing *the people* we are engaging with (with the exception of new media like video calling). Given that most forms of mediated communication do not engage all our senses or require that we actually see or hear the people we are interacting with, these forms of communication tend to make it easier to minimize the humanness of yourself and other people.

Diminished humanness is the result of not seeing *yourself* or *other people* as full beings with minds, hearts, emotions, hopes, friends, families, reputations, struggles. With respect to yourself, you can believe that what you do and say online or through a device is not the "real" you. New media "freezes" what you do in time so that, normally, you can go back to things you have said or done and review them. Perhaps this fact creates an actual separation between the person and their words and actions, which gives them the sense that their words and actions can be distanced from who they understand their "self" to be. In general, humans have a hard time believing that certain things they have said or done represent aspects of their personality or character. Nietzsche explains it best: "'I did that' says my memory. 'I couldn't have done that'—says my pride, and stands its ground. Finally, memory gives in."[18] Social media only exacerbates this issue.

Social media sites can also give you the impression that what you are doing and saying online is a performance, and so you are not really being you; rather,

---

18. Nietzsche, *Beyond Good and Evil*, §68, p. 59.

you are merely acting for an imagined audience. Game sites, for example, encourage people to try on different personas by creating an online identity. In this way, you might believe that there is both a gamer version of you and an "actual" you. You might think of new media as enhancing or exaggerating aspects of who you are or allowing you to exhibit characteristics or personality traits that you wish you had, and so you might consider the online version of you as either amplified (for better or for worse) or fake. All of this could be true. However, the real (pun intended) issue at hand is that these lines of thinking can change what you believe is humane and permissible online, make you ignorant of the fact that new media engagement both reveals and shapes aspects of who you are, and cause you to believe that what you do and say online is somehow detached from who you are connected to and responsible to and who you are called to be.

Minimizing the humanity of *other people* online contributes (at the very least) to saying and doing hurtful things online that are normally more private—that is, things that are said or done between friends and family or acted out when alone (whether in your thoughts or through actions). For example, diminished humanness causes people to be less careful with their words when sending an email or posting online, which can be damaging to relationships. A Facebook friend recently shared the post you see below.

> **Anonymous**
> October 13, 2017
>
> Ninety percent of the time I can handle angry emails, name-calling, critiques of my leadership, etc. Ninety percent of the time I can look for a constructive nugget in it and try to figure out how to work with someone. But sometimes words just hurt. A lot. The people you're yelling at through your screen are real people, y'all.
>
> 👍 Like   💬 Comment   ↪ Share

As this friend suggests, not only does minimizing humanness online damage relationships; it extends destructive ideologies, like racism, from physical spaces to digital spaces. At its very worst, it destroys people's lives.

Christian Rudder, in *Dataclysm*, describes a colleague's awful, racist tweet. Before boarding a plane for Cape Town, Justine Sacco tweeted, "Going to Africa. Hope I don't get AIDS. Just kidding. I'm white!" She then turned off her phone for the eleven-hour flight.[19] In a single tweet, she dismissed the humanness of African people, of people living with HIV and AIDS, and of people of color. Her violent words were met by millions of people responding on Twitter with hate-filled words back to her. Social media users were morally outraged, and they wanted Sacco to be punished.

The hashtag #HasJustineLandedYet was seen by 62 million people in its first day.[20] People tweeted about anxiously awaiting her demise. Pictures of her family were circulated online; her nephew received numerous threatening phone calls; and BuzzFeed featured her face on its homepage with a large "LOL" scrawled across it.[21] Once she landed and discovered the firestorm, Sacco tweeted that she was having panic attacks because she worried that her family would be harmed. Both Sacco's racism and the crowd's shaming manifested themselves in horrific ways because it was difficult to associate tweets with actual human beings.

Like racism, moral outrage online can be easier and less costly than moral outrage in person. A person can express their outrage in a few clicks and then be anonymous in an angry crowd.[22] Normally, the "cost of outrage expression is empathic distress" because "punishing and shaming involves inflicting harm on other human beings, which for most of us is naturally unpleasant." However, "online settings reduce empathic distress by representing other people as two-dimensional icons whose suffering is not readily visible. It's a lot easier to shame an avatar than someone whose face you can see."[23] Diminishing and dismissing the humanity of yourself and other people online is what makes multiple forms of violence possible: vicious thoughts, cruel words, brutal actions.

It is one thing for social media users to label what Sacco did as racist, thoughtless, and wrong. What she did *was* wrong. However, it is quite another thing to shame her, to threaten and bully her and her family, and to express joy (*schadenfreude*[24]) over destroying her life. These sorts of responses to racism only mirror the sort of hatred that fuels racism in the first place. Martin Luther King Jr. explains:

> If I respond to hate with a reciprocal hate I do nothing but intensify the cleavage in broken community. I can only close the gap in broken community by

19. Rudder, *Dataclysm*, 141.
20. Rudder, *Dataclysm*, 143.
21. Rudder, *Dataclysm*, 142–43. LOL is an acronym for "laugh out loud."
22. Crockett, "Moral Outrage."
23. Crockett, "Moral Outrage," 770.
24. *Schadenfreude*, which literally means "harm-joy," is a German word for when people experience joy over another person's misfortune.

meeting hate with love. If I meet hate with hate, I become depersonalized, because creation is so designed that my personality can only be fulfilled in the context of community. Booker T. Washington was right: "Let no man pull you so low as to make you hate him." When he pulls you that low he brings you to the point of working against community; he drags you to the point of defying creation, and thereby becoming depersonalized.[25]

Shaming, threatening, and bullying exacerbate destructive ideologies, like racism, and destroy community rather than provide responses that nurture justice and healing.

Exploitation in the physical world is also present in the digital realm. Sometimes exploiting others online is done maliciously, other times out of ignorance. For example, when people visit low-wealth communities during mission trips, social media users like to post photos of the trip, which often include photos of people they meet. However, taking photos of kids and adults who have illnesses or are malnourished and living in dire conditions can be dehumanizing and objectifying. Photos of people in low-wealth communities that are particularly problematic are those taken without consent (especially photos of children) or those showing people who appear helpless or sick rather than capable and dignified. Also problematic are photos that contribute to stereotyping. For example, photos of healthy, privileged Americans posing with or offering handouts to underprivileged people can suggest that people who lack access to adequate resources are incapable of acting for their own benefit; these photos can perpetuate the idea that wealthy people save people in low-wealth communities.[26]

Another form of online exploitation is human trafficking. It is modern slavery. Children and adults are being sold, confined, oppressed, and abused. Polaris has identified twenty-five job fields that involve human trafficking, including carnivals, hotels and hospitality, and agriculture. Their report explains that "each [field] has its own business model, trafficker profiles, recruitment strategies, victim profiles, and methods of control that facilitate human trafficking."[27] It is estimated that over twenty million people are enslaved today; the internet makes this possible, as it offers anonymity and efficient, discreet communication between traffickers.[28] Dehumanization not only contributes to horrific forms of abuse in person; it contributes to destructive abuse online.

25. King, *Stride toward Freedom*, 94. Both Washington and King use gendered language. It would have been good for both of them to use inclusive language instead, as their words apply to all human beings.

26. "Ethics and Photography"; Gharib, "Volunteering Abroad?"

27. "Typology of Modern Slavery."

28. "Human Trafficking."

If Christian communities care about new media use contributing to damaged relationships, destructive ideologies, and significant problems like modern slavery, they need to have constructive conversations about the new media landscape. Unfortunately, these important matters—the kinds of glorious possibilities and profound brokenness described thus far—are usually not the focus of conversations about new media in most Christian communities. There are significant reasons why.

Essential Questions

The emerging and rapidly changing new media landscape provokes *fear* of one kind or another in Christians who respond to it. And fear often leads Christian communities to neglect essential questions that motivate faithful living in a new media landscape.

- What is the new media landscape like and what does it have to do with Christian faith?
- Why is new media design and use profoundly broken?
- How would Jesus Christ—a person formed in the image of God—act and feel when using new media, and what kinds of new media circumstances would Jesus seek to create?
- What would it take and how would it look to live a life of righteousness, peace, and joy in the Holy Spirit in a new media landscape?

Neglecting critical questions like these, combined with inadequate resources for leading communities in critical and theological reflection on the new media landscape and limited time for Christian education about new media, means that those of us who lead churches, nonprofit ministries, classrooms, and other types of Christian learning communities often "major on the minors." For example, a community might focus on debating whether its members are texting too much rather than focusing on trying to understand the experiences and feelings of those doing the texting and discerning whether texting might have something to do with living a righteous and joyful life in a new media landscape. Additionally, the glorious possibilities and profound brokenness of new media are not merely linked to new media tools (e.g., social media sites). Rather, multiple factors matter—the people using new media, its context and aims, the developers of new media, and its embedded values—and thus new media and people's engagement with it must include attention to multiple factors.[29]

---

29. These convictions are connected to the perspective on technology, "media as social institutions," which takes seriously the people (individuals and groups) that are both designing

Healing profound brokenness related to new media development and engagement cannot be reduced to choosing the right social media site to use. Given the complexity of issues named, Christian learning communities default to allowing perceptions of new media and the feelings it engenders to guide their responses to it, and regrettably, the responses of too many organizations and institutions are *fruitless*.

Fruitless "Conversations"

There are four types of fruitless "conversations" about new media that are worth highlighting. Each is related to one of four core feelings: nostalgia, enthusiasm, anxiety, and apathy.[30] These feelings correspond to four characteristic unreflective movements: looking backward, leaping forward, sitting stagnant, and wandering aimlessly. And these movements develop into a variety of habits, which I will highlight in each section below. I will also discuss an underlying malformed conviction that usually informs each type of conversation. Each type thus has a dominant feeling, a characteristic habit, and a malformed conviction that are *interconnected*. This is because human beings' desires (guided by our feelings), practices, and beliefs are interrelated. Additionally, each conversation has negative consequences, which are often unintended but ultimately thwart the practice of faith in a new media landscape. While each of these conversations is inadequate, each is driven by something *true*, what I call "accurate intuitions": (1) our relationship to new media *is* often broken; (2) new media *does* offer exciting new possibilities; (3) new media *does* present new challenges; and (4) leaders of learning communities need to feel equipped to guide conversation about new media.

---

and using the technology and acknowledges that social values must be taken into account when considering new media. Ferré, "Media of Popular Piety," 88–90. See also Campbell and Garner's read of Ferré in *Networked Theology*, 98–100. Designers and developers are embedded in social contexts that shape the media they create. The communication techniques and priorities of these social contexts form the structure of the media. When users adopt particular forms of media, social, economic, governmental, and cultural factors influence how they use the media and for what purposes. See Baym, *Personal Connections*, 40.

30. I have noticed these types of unconstructive conversations during teaching and speaking experiences, which include teaching courses that consider the relationship between theology, philosophy, and culture at Fuller Theological Seminary, McCormick Theological Seminary, Yale College, and Yale Divinity School, as well as leading seminars on new media in multiple contexts and conducting a national survey on social media, churches, and Christian formation for my dissertation. However, the four types of conversation I describe in this chapter are not the only types of conversations about new media, and their diagrams are not meant to be exhaustive; rather, they are meant to be talking points for dialogue about the relationship between feelings, habits, and convictions regarding new media.

Table 1.1 Four Types of Fruitless Conversation about New Media

Conversation Type and Unreflective Movement	Core Feeling	Habit	Malformed Conviction	Negative Consequences	Accurate Intuition
Homesick Monologue *looking backward*	nostalgia	critique new media while reminiscing about the way things used to be	new media engagement cannot deepen or extend genuine human seeing and relating	neglect the experiences of media users and God's agency in this new media landscape	our relationship to new media *is* often broken
Misplaced Hope *leaping forward*	enthusiasm	highlight new media's usefulness	new media is a neutral tool, and if it is used with good intentions, it contributes to God's purposes	neglect new media's embedded values and practices and become shaped by, and thus practiced at embodying, narratives other than the gospel (e.g., marketplace narratives)	new media *does* offer exciting new possibilities
Anxious Inaction *sitting stagnant*	anxiety	regularly use new media and discuss new media's challenges but never adequately address them	believe there is no guide for new media and thus disregard that the Spirit is speaking and leading in this new media landscape	neglect critical and theological reflection	new media *does* present new challenges
Oblivious Silence *wandering aimlessly*	apathy	ignore the implications of new media development and engagement on individuals, communities, and the practice of faith	assume someone else will lead learning communities in discerning, articulating, and embodying Christian visions of true life in a new media landscape	neglect the social milieu that new media is developed and engaged within, as well as connections between faith and media	leaders of learning communities need to feel equipped to guide conversation about new media

When reflecting on these conversations, you may immediately connect your community to one of the four types of conversations. As you read, you may personally connect with a particular type too. Or you may find that you or your community is experiencing some combination of the feelings, convictions, and intuitions of several of these conversation types or that your community is having a different type of conversation altogether. The important thing, as you read, is to engage in critical reflection about how your community is talking about new media and people's engagement with it. Likewise, reflect on the ways your community's feelings and beliefs about new media have guided your communal and personal responses to it, and consider the possible consequences of these responses.

HOMESICK MONOLOGUE—LOOKING BACKWARD

Homesick monologues are characterized by fondness for older forms of media. Discussion about new media stirs affectionate reference to older forms of communication. These conversations idealize the past, and nostalgia generally manifests itself in the habit of critiquing new media use and only discussing its brokenness (e.g., saying things like "new media is distracting us from what is important and making us addicted to devices at the expense of relationships"). Embedded in a homesick monologue is a prevailing malformed conviction: new media engagement cannot deepen or extend genuine human seeing and relating.[31]

These types of conversations have unhelpful consequences in Christian communities. They neglect God's agency. "The earth is the LORD's and everything in it" (Ps. 24:1), even the internet. If indeed the Triune God is active, prompting truth, goodness, beauty, and redemption and countering sin, brokenness, and other human practices of destructiveness in the world, then the Spirit of God is active during communication in person *and* online. Social media is a space, like all other spaces in people's lives, where people can be invited to be open to God's initiatives by being receptive to the Spirit's voice. Additionally, homesick monologues too often neglect theological and critical reflection involving adequate theology and research studies about how and why people are using new media.[32] The implication of this neglect

---

31. There are a number of books that are shaped by these types of convictions: e.g., Kallenberg, *God and Gadgets*; Turkle, *Alone Together*; Turkle, *Reclaiming Conversation*.

32. Danah boyd invites readers to not overlook the fundamental desire for social connection that motivates social media use (*It's Complicated*, 17). For example, when she observed teens at a football game, she noted that most were using their phones to take photos or find their friends at the game rather than using their phones to ignore the people around them (3). In fact, her research has led her to believe that "most of those who are 'addicted' to their phones

is attachment to more familiar forms of media. Likewise, the unfamiliarity of newer forms presses me into ignoring the actual value of newer forms for ends that I actually approve of. This initiates a one-sided conversation, a monologue rather than a dialogue.

In Christian communities where most community members are nostalgic and do not use social media, users of new media are silenced and discussion of new media is unwelcome because it is labeled "deficient" by those who prefer older forms of communication (e.g., phone calls and bulletins). Communities who primarily engage in homesick monologues disregard the lived experiences of members of the community who engage with new media. Additionally, nostalgic communities neglect any positive benefits new media engagement affords in people's lives, especially nurturing significant relationships (i.e., the very sense of healing that nostalgic institutions desire to nurture but label as "not genuine" when formed using new media).

The major point here is that assuming new media engagement is always deficient forecloses more fruitful and life-giving *conversations* about how new media *is* reshaping human modes of embodiment. It is important to note, however, that homesick monologues accurately intuit that our relationship to new media *is* often broken. Mindless engagement with new media contributes to malformed desires, wasted time, unhealthy habits, and destructive feelings.

Misplaced Hope—Leaping Forward

On the other end of the spectrum, conversations based on *misplaced hope* are fueled by unreflective enthusiasm about new media. These conversations focus on describing the incredible potential of new media and highlighting its contribution to progress and to the improvement of people's lives. Members of Christian communities who exhibit unreflective enthusiasm regarding new media habitually describe it in terms of its utility. The hope I am highlighting here is utilitarian rather than Christian. The basic idea in utilitarian conversations is that if the institution can become more skilled (or find the right staff) or spend more money on better forms of new media, it can use new media to do God's work in the world.[33] People who are excited by technology often neglect to critically assess the malformed visions it is shaped by and its damaging values and practices. The malformed conviction that informs this

---

or computers are actually *focused on staying connected to friends* in a culture where getting together in person is highly constrained" (18, emphasis added).

33. A number of books are shaped by these types of convictions. They tend to focus on social media strategies rather than addressing new media's adaptive challenges, especially its embedded values. See, e.g., Drescher and Anderson, *Click 2 Save*; Gould, *Social Media Gospel*; Lazarus, *Connected Church*; Southerland, *Digital Witness*; Wise, *Social Church*.

type of conversation is that new media is just a tool, and if used with good intentions, it contributes to God's purposes. This is too simplistic.[34] The Christian church has a long history of viewing communication technologies as neutral, believing we can use new tools to share Christian content without critically and theologically reflecting on the ways new tools contribute to what is being communicated. This neglects the fact that various media forms are created in light of particular values and therefore have and nurture those values.[35] And some of the values, as well as practices embedded in media, are contrary to the values of Christianity.

Often, the motivating principle in dialogue centered on misplaced hope is that using new media will fix the church's and the academy's contemporary problems (e.g., declining church participation or declining enrollment). New media is posited as the essential remedy, which disregards that many contemporary issues in Christian institutions are adaptive (rather than technical) challenges and require new vision, not just new skills.[36] Along with this goes the misguided belief that churches and academic institutions can use technology to strategize their way into a sustainable future. Instead, Christian communities need to develop capacities for discerning God's initiatives and shaping interpretive communities who participate in God's work in a new media landscape. Sustaining Christian learning communities requires discerning, articulating, and embodying Christian visions of the true life, not just technical tweaks. This calls for accepting God's grace, abiding in Jesus's love, and being receptive to the Spirit's leading, which is more complex than simply finding useful tools and using them with good intentions.

The effects of misplaced hope can be detrimental to institutions and humans. Constantly trying to keep up with new forms of media overwhelms

34. This type of conversation about new media is connected to the perspective on technology known as "instrumentalism" or "media as a conduit." From this perspective, people use tools to share their messages, and media is itself neutral. See Ferré, "Media of Popular Piety," 86.

35. This is connected to the perspective on technology known as "determinism" or what Ferré calls "media as a mode of knowing." Media as a mode of knowing views technology as having embedded messages that change and impact the content that is being delivered. Ferré, "Media of Popular Piety," 86. See also McLuhan, *Understanding Media*, 9, who explains that "the medium is the message." For McLuhan, technologies have characteristics that are transferred to users.

36. Heifetz and Linsky, *Leadership on the Line*, 13–20. As the authors explain, technical challenges are those that individuals and institutions have the know-how to face. The problem and the solution are relatively clear. Adaptive challenges require a response that is outside of the current repertoire. There isn't an expert who can fix the problem, and the current know-how isn't sufficient. Adaptive challenges "require experiments, new discoveries, and adjustments from numerous places in the organization or community" (13). For Heifetz and Linsky, the single biggest cause of leadership failure "is that people, especially those in positions of authority, treat adaptive challenges like technical problems" (14).

(sometimes even devastates) staff and members of the community, and unreflective use of new media is a waste of resources. Most importantly, the church
and the academy can become shaped by, and thus practiced at embodying, narratives other than the gospel (e.g., marketplace narratives), which extend and
contribute to malformed desires, unhealthy practices, and destructive feelings.
The fundamental critique of misplaced hope is that enthusiasm for new media
without theological and critical reflection can be destructive to institutions
and can be dehumanizing. However, there are embedded accurate intuitions in
these types of conversations: new media *does* offer exciting new possibilities.
Christian communities certainly need to be open to reflecting on new media
in terms of its opportunities, recognizing that new media can provide space
for expression and learning (self-understanding), for nurturing relationships,
and for contributing to the common good, among many other possibilities.[37]

Anxious Inaction—Sitting Stagnant

During conversation marked by *anxious inaction*, communities who use
new media portray it as overwhelming. Participants in these types of conversations use new media daily while simultaneously critiquing its pace and
negative impact on their lives. The core sentiment of this conversation is
anxiety. However, these types of conversations often result in inaction regarding anxiety and other named challenges because users are apprehensive about
unplugging. Institutions and individuals are afraid of getting behind on news
or work, missing out, feeling unseen, being forgotten, and neglecting important work or social communication. Fear is one source of anxiety. Another
source is the constant demand for new skills.[38] Often these communities and
their members become anxious about new forms of technology because there
is always something new to learn, and users can feel overwhelmed about their
inability to use new media in a functional or intentional way.

Individuals in these conversations continue to use multiple forms of new
media on a daily basis, and institutions do what they think is necessary to
stay relevant (e.g., set up a website, create a Facebook page), but they never
take time with their community to discuss how to adequately address new
media's challenges. Likewise, communities stuck in anxious inaction do not

37. There are a number of books that thoughtfully describe such opportunities. See, e.g.,
Castells, *Networks of Outrage and Hope*; Davidson, *Now You See It*; Jenkins, Ford, and Green,
Spreadable Media; Shirky, *Cognitive Surplus*.

38. Everyone will have a certain level of anxiety when it comes to engaging with new media.
It is new, after all. But the sort of anxiety I am referring to is the kind that is felt and then not
examined. People engaged in anxious inaction are not actively seeking to learn about new media
or reflect on their use of it.

focus on learning how to engage with new media in healthy ways or on discussing which media to use and when (which could empower media users). Additionally, these types of communities do not dedicate time to articulating any sort of Christian vision for new media use.

The malformed conviction in conversations related to anxious inaction is that institutions and individuals believe there is no guide for the current new media landscape and therefore neglect the role of the Spirit in this new environment. Additionally, members of these communities often believe (wrongly) that they do not have time to reflect on their media use. Members may simply feel too busy, or they may feel that they have too little knowledge of media, that there is no place in the community's programming to reflect on new media, or that other issues are more important. The consequences of these kinds of conversations are neglect of both human agency and the agency of the Triune God, which results in stagnation and feelings of powerlessness. Likewise, new media users do not consider ways to practice faith online or take time to mitigate the destructive effects of new media use. To flourish in a media-saturated culture, it is essential to be receptive to the Spirit's voice and take time with one's community to articulate a Christian vision for new media engagement, including making decisions about limits for engagement and times of disengagement. However, anxious inaction conversations *do* accurately intuit that new media presents new challenges. The challenges are real and their effects are widespread, and these challenges must be addressed.

Oblivious Silence—Wandering Aimlessly

Many Christian communities never address new media, and thus there is no conversation at all. *Oblivious silence* ignores the reality of new media and its effect on people's lives of faith. Generally, organizations and institutions apathetic to new media give the impression (by their neglect) that it is unimportant to create space to discuss the implications of new media. In oblivious communities, discussing new media is separate from reflecting on faith for a way of life.[39] For example, a member might talk to a friend about whether a political Facebook post offended someone in their office but never connect this to their practice of faith since their community has never spent time discerning possible connections between practicing faith and writing status updates.

There are many reasons for apathy. Apathetic communities may believe that new media is something for communication specialists to reflect on, but

---

39. I borrow the phrase "for a way of life" from Volf, "Theology for a Way of Life."

not for them. They may believe that reflection on new media is unsuitable for a "serious" pastor, professor, or theologian, or that people will naturally discern faithful living in a new media landscape on their own. There is also the issue of *time*. Many leaders of Christian communities are swamped as it is. The prevailing malformed belief shaping oblivious silence is that someone else will do the difficult work of helping people traverse the new media terrain and discern, articulate, and embody Christian visions of true life in a new media landscape.

There are several consequences of oblivious silence. One is that communities entirely disregard the social milieu within which people are practicing their faith. Additionally, people in these Christian communities feel like it is up to them to figure out how to navigate the new media landscape on their own (or within their immediate family) or believe their faith has nothing to do with new media. However, there is an accurate intuition behind these conversations (or lack of conversations)—there is wisdom in being silent on a topic that you are not equipped to discuss in a helpful way. More and more pastors and Christian religious educators are sensing the importance of reflecting on new media use in their learning communities, but they do not feel equipped to do so.

A Way Forward

Besides being largely fruitless, these four kinds of conversation have something else in common. They neglect to engage the looming, dominant emotion that lurks in the shadows of thoughts about new technology: fear. It is the driving force behind each of the previously described conversation types. There is the fear of change (homesick monologue), the fear of an unsustainable future (misplaced hope), the fear of not being relevant (anxious inaction), and the fear of not being adequately equipped to discuss new media with community members (oblivious silence).

We need a way forward that helps Christian communities attend to fears while also addressing the most important matters of the new media landscape: its glorious possibilities and profound brokenness. Donna Freitas provides insight into this way forward in her fascinating book *The Happiness Effect*. Freitas surveyed and interviewed college students at thirteen campuses about their concerns regarding new media. Freitas explains that attentiveness to faith and critical reflection helped students she interviewed have a healthier and more empowered relationship to social media. She interviewed students at faith-based institutions who connected their faith and religious practices to their social media engagement and seemed to benefit significantly. Freitas explains,

What is unusual about them is that they are, more so than their peers, empowered in their use of social media. Those students who allow the devotion to their faith to permeate their online worlds use their religious traditions as a framework for navigating their behavior and posts—one they find far more meaningful and sturdier than warnings about future employers and prescriptions for curating one's online image. They are learning the dos and don'ts of social media from a higher power, and this makes an enormous difference. . . . And while these students are just as image-conscious and as aware as everyone else that they have an audience, having God and their faith tradition filtering their online decision-making seems to help them stay grounded.[40]

Freitas also interviewed college students at a prestigious institution that was not faith based. The students here were also able to easily engage in critical reflection on their social media engagement. Regardless of the kind of school students attended, they all benefited from being able to critically reflect on social media use. She writes, "Knowledge—in the form of critical analysis—quite literally seems to translate into power. Being able to think clearly about social media, believing that they have the intellectual skills to best Mark Zuckerberg at his own game and understand some of the more manipulative ways that social media infiltrates our lives and relationships, gives them a healthier, more empowered relationship to it."[41]

Considering new media in view of Christian visions of the true life by nurturing critical and theological reflection on the new media landscape—its connections to Christian faith, devices, spaces, developers, and new media users—is empowering. And more than this, it is essential for flourishing in a new media landscape. It is time to *change the conversation*.[42]

Interested Conversation

Throughout this book, I advocate for a particular type of meaningful, imaginative, critically and theologically reflective, Spirit-guided, and fruitful conversation about new media: *interested conversation*.[43] Interested conversation

---

40. Freitas, *Happiness Effect*, 110.

41. Freitas, *Happiness Effect*, 60.

42. I borrow the italicized phrase from Robinson and Roxburgh, "Changing the Conversation," who use this phrase to discuss needed changes in conversation about missiology.

43. For me, interest involves sincere desire to learn and be attentive, for the sake of the kingdom of God. Aspects of interested conversation were inspired by Mark Lau Branson's practical theology method (Branson and Martínez, *Churches, Cultures, and Leadership*, 42–45). In *Networked Theology*, Campbell and Garner describe religious-social shaping of technology as a four-stage process (103–14). Throughout this book, movements of interested conversation

signals just that—*interest* in the Spirit's leading in this new media landscape—not negativity, not unreflective enthusiasm, not assumptions. Christian communities who participate in interested conversation are initially *interested* in new media's glorious possibilities and profound brokenness. Therefore, they are *interested* in asking and answering the essential questions that motivate faithful living in a new media landscape.

The important questions outlined earlier in this chapter are guiding concerns that make up the mosaic of movements embedded in interested conversation. I am inviting Christian communities to be *interested* in assessing what type of conversation their community is having about new media (this chapter), *interested* in exploring the new media landscape (chap. 2), *interested* in critically reflecting on cultural narratives that guide new media development and consequently people's use of new media (chap. 3), *interested* in articulating a Christian vision of flourishing life regarding new media (chap. 4), and *interested* in hybrid faithful living (chaps. 5 and 6).[44]

Interested conversation is meant to cultivate dialogue, curiosity, storytelling, understanding, and hope. Interested conversation is also meant to be a process that happens over time. Each movement of interested conversation involves prayer. I invite your community to pray together about God revealing new media's possibilities and brokenness. Similarly, pray that God will teach your community what God is up to in this landscape. With each movement of interested conversation, invite the Spirit to lead and teach your community and to help you listen to and care for one another as you discern what it means to be a Christian community traversing the new media terrain. I hope Christian communities will continue to engage the movements of interested conversation as new forms of media are developed in the future.

Interested conversation does not require a conversation guide who understands (or even frequently uses) media. Interested conversations can be facilitated by people who have a great deal of experience or very little experience

---

will integrate aspects of their four-stage process. For example, by considering what kind of conversation your Christian community is having and why, your community will be reflecting on part of its technological history (an aspect of stage 1 of Campbell and Garner's process). When your community imagines Jesus's ministry and articulates a Christian vision of flourishing life, you will be unearthing core beliefs of the Christian faith that should relate to new media decisions and use (an aspect of stage 2). In chap. 5, your community will be encouraged to make decisions about which media to use by assessing its values (an aspect of stage 3). Finally, designing a new media rule for life, described in chap. 6, is a particular way of developing a formal statement about technology (a key aspect of stage 4).

44. A number of books are shaped by similar convictions regarding new media. See, e.g., Baab, *Reaching Out in a Networked World*; Crouch, *Tech-Wise Family*; Schnekloth, *Mediating Faith*; Zsupan-Jerome, *Connected toward Communion*.

using forms of new media. Interested conversation needs only initiators who are open to practicing discernment. The outcomes of interested conversation in your community will be particular, contextual, and culturally responsive.

In order to critically and theologically reflect on new media, we need to have a basic understanding of the new media landscape. We need to know what sort of ground we are standing on. What is new media's connection to Christian faith? What activities are taking place in this new environment? What questions and theological issues arise from such activities? In short, what is this new media landscape like—what are its elements and dimensions? And how are Christian communities traversing this new media terrain? In the next chapter, we take on these questions and begin to explore this (relatively) recently discovered new media terrain.

interested conversation in practice

Discussion Questions

1. What are the possibilities and challenges of new media, and what do they have to do with Christian faith?
2. What feelings, thoughts, and questions surface as you reflect on the four types of unconstructive conversation?
3. What is the core feeling about new media in our community (e.g., family, church, organization, institution)? Are we nostalgic, enthusiastic, anxious, apathetic, or something else regarding the use of new media?
4. When we discuss new media in our community, do we tend to focus on reminiscing about old media, cultivating skills for using new media well, describing its challenges, keeping it separate from faith for a way of life, or something else?
5. What might our community learn about itself by considering our conversations about new media?

two

traversing the new media terrain

Jonathan Timothy Stoner
April 19

Delonte Gholston is my favorite Facebook pastor. Don't know what I would do without his daily exhortations & encouragements. Can I get an "Amen!" or a "Hallelujah!" from other members of this social media church?

 Like   Comment   Share

Delonte Gholston
Man, yall are too much. Yall bout to make this Bapticostal preacher take up a love offering, a pastor's anniversary, and a seed offering lol. Seriously tho yall, I really have been sitting in gratitude when I realize that, "wow, it is my job to listen to the Spirit, to meditate on Scripture, and to sit with people through every stage of their life and walk with the Lord? Wow, that's my job?! Incredible. What a joy it is to serve."

The Facebook post above received many replies—a beautiful mix of "amens," clapping emojis, compliments, and an amazing GIF of a woman dancing in the aisles of a church. In Reverend Delonte Gholston's reply he articulates how grateful he feels for his job as a pastor. He asks, "Wow, it is my job to listen to the Spirit, to meditate on Scripture, and to sit with people through every stage of their life and walk with the Lord?" He articulates the sense of joy he has at the opportunity to serve. Reverend Delonte is the senior pastor of a Christian community in Washington, DC, which means he has a group of people he regularly leads, worships with, and cares for. However, Reverend Delonte does not just minister to people he sees in person each week or to those who are members of his Christian community. As evident in Jonathan Stoner's post, Reverend Delonte is a social media pastor too. Reverend Delonte's Facebook friends (like me) look forward to his posts because they embody God's grace and love, invite us to reflect critically and theologically on our lives, and challenge us to use our voice and our actions to practice Christian faith.

Discerning what God is doing in our current new media landscape requires asking important questions about our current context and inviting the Spirit to help us see our environment anew. Discerning, articulating, and living Christian visions of the flourishing life regarding new media design and use necessitates initial *interest in exploring this new media landscape—its connection to Christian faith and its activities, language, and distinctions.*[1] To that end, this chapter provides a basic understanding of the current new media terrain. Keep in mind, this terrain is vast and largely uncharted. Consider this a map from my perspective.[2] My map is likely to turn out more like one of those misshapen sixteenth-century maps of the Americas than today's GPS-supported, down-to-the-centimeter-precise online maps. Hopefully, despite its limitations, this map will begin to help you think about what it looks like to traverse this terrain wisely.

1. "Web 2.0 [early 2000s] is the name used to describe the second generation of the world wide web, where it moved static HTML pages to a more interactive and dynamic web experience. Web 2.0 is focused on the ability for people to collaborate and share information online via social media, blogging and Web-based communities. Web 2.0 signaled a change in which the world wide web became an interactive experience between users and Web publishers, rather than the one-way conversation that had previously existed. It also represents a more populist version of the Web, where new tools made it possible for nearly anyone to contribute, regardless of their technical knowledge." "Web 2.0."

2. My perspective on the new media landscape is deeply shaped by my experiences and personal characteristics. I grew up and currently live in the United States. I use social media on a daily basis. I am an older millennial. Additionally, I'm female, have an advanced degree, and am able to use and afford access to new media (and have since high school). And I'm a member of a privileged ethnic-racial group (to most people I appear "white," although white is a social construct, and my ethnic heritage includes Indigenous peoples). All these give particular shape to my assessment of contemporary culture and my perspective on the new media landscape.

Connecting Faith and Media

For some Christian communities, connections between faith and media are not immediately obvious. It is helpful to reflect on historic connections between faith and media in order to reason why it is important to consider the practice of faith in light of contemporary media. Scripture is itself a medium for God's revelations to humankind and for communicating the gospel. Scripture is made up of several genres, such as narrative, poetry, wisdom, and epistles. Each biblical genre is a mediator of what is being discussed. In other words, the type of a particular biblical book matters when interpreting what the book is communicating. For example, the book of Psalms is an entire book of hymns and song lyrics and should be understood differently than should a medium for communicating directions for a particular community, like the letters to the Corinthians. Each biblical genre helps Christian communities deepen their understanding of God, human beings, and the world (Acts 8:26–39; Rom. 15:4; 1 Cor. 10:6–11).

The Bible includes multiple instances of all sorts of media being used for communication between humans and God. The Triune God spoke and led through multiple mediums—a whirlwind, a cloud, fire, sheer silence, and angels (Exod. 13:21; 1 Kings 19:11–18; Job 38–39).[3] In Exodus 12, blood on the doorposts communicated that God should not execute judgment on that house. In Luke 1–2, a young, lowly girl delivered *the message*, Christ, and with Mary as the medium, God announced what type of king Jesus would be (very different than people were imagining). Second Corinthians 3:18 provides the image of Jesus as God's principal medium. The first chapter of John describes Jesus as the word that became flesh and lived among people in order to show us God (John 1:1–5, 10, 14).

The Bible also includes instances of media being used for communication between people, often to share God's messages with one another. Exodus and Deuteronomy describe two stone tablets that conveyed the covenant that the Lord made with the Israelites. In Joshua 2 and 6, a crimson cord in the window communicated that Rahab's household should be protected from invasion. Nehemiah 6:1–9 discusses a series of important messages sent back and forth using messengers between Nehemiah and Sanballat and Geshem. Messengers between Esther and Mordecai gave Esther the courage to approach the king on behalf of the Jews (Esther 4). In Luke 10, Jesus sent out a large group of disciples in pairs, directing them to share peace in various communities, participate in village life, and contribute to the households they

---

3. Angels (literally "messengers") show up over three hundred times in Scripture.

stayed within. This was a form of mass communication of the gospel in an oral culture.[4] From Jesus's perspective, the gospel was communicated by the way it was practiced and embodied by these disciples.

In his comprehensive survey of media, *From Jesus to the Internet*, Peter Horsfield describes early Christian communities as "multimedia communities" because of their multisensory engagement.[5] Horsfield supports this claim by describing how their gatherings included written, oral, and physical communication through reading and singing Jewish Scriptures, shared meals, prayers (kneeling, lying prostrate, etc.), and greeting one another with a holy kiss.[6] Whenever Christians eat the bread during the Lord's Supper (i.e., Eucharist, communion), depending on our denomination, we remember Jesus or believe it is Jesus's body (Luke 22:19–20). The bread and the wine are mediums, and the act of eating the bread and drinking the wine communicates a message, "broadcast[ing] the death of the Lord until he comes" (1 Cor. 11:26).

If media is defined as tools of communication, then we can see that Christianity has been communicated through a variety of media ever since the days of its earliest adherents. Therefore, the question of how Christianity relates to media, even to forms of social media, is nearly as old as the faith itself. Tools like letters and the printing press had and continue to have implications for the practice and communication of faith. The New Testament letters were created and shared to encourage faithful living among churches, provide guidance, and nurture relationships. Interestingly, Paul's Second Letter to the Corinthians describes the difference between him being in person versus writing a letter to the community (2 Cor. 10:1). Paul admits that he appears bolder in letters than in person. In fact, he feels the need to say that he is not trying to intimidate people with his letters (v. 9). Even in the New Testament, we see that media (in the form of letter writing) created tension between people. Paul wants his readers to know that his in-person actions will parallel his written words (v. 11). Paul wanted to be the same in person as he was in his letters.

The printing press, invented in 1450, is partly responsible for one of the major shifts in Christianity: the Reformation.[7] The printing press made it possible to quickly and cheaply produce copies of illustrations and words. Ideas could suddenly be widely distributed for little money and in a relatively short amount of time. The printing press quickly spread the ideas of the Reformation, which gave voice to the laments of laity and raised questions about clerical abuses and

4. Thiessen, *New Testament*, 20.
5. Horsfield, *From Jesus to the Internet*, 43.
6. Horsfield, *From Jesus to the Internet*, 44.
7. Edwards, *Printing, Propaganda and Martin Luther*, 15.

the price of salvation, as well as the intercessory role of the papacy and clergy.[8] Additionally, pamphlets contained messages or illustrations that encouraged the reader to share the pamphlet and read it aloud.[9] Social relationships thus played a part in spreading new ideas, especially ideas related to the Reformation. In this light, pamphlets and illustrations could be categorized as social media.

There are countless historical connections between faith and media. When nostalgic, enthusiastic, anxious, and apathetic individuals and communities consider historic connections between faith and media, the decision to be interested in the relationship between contemporary forms of media and Christianity becomes simultaneously glaringly obvious and somewhat less intimidating, since we can trust that the God who has been historically present and faithful continues to be actively present and faithful in this new media terrain. Beginning to uncover God's agency regarding new media by attending to historic connections between media and Christianity is a vital and helpful starting point. It is important that Christian communities own this history between media and Christianity and teach it.

Seeing Online Actions as Meaning-Filled

Dismissing new media and people's engagement with it as something unnecessary for Christian education and formation appears justifiable to some Christian communities. A major reason social media use is not considered an important issue is that the activities people engage in online appear either empty and shallow or too mundane to be of much spiritual interest. After all, social media use involves selfies and celebrity gossip, and it seemingly wastes so much of people's time. Christian leaders might wonder why they should spend time creating space for members in their community to reflect on their online posts and their Instagram and Snapchat stories when there are more pressing issues Christian communities should be discussing.

However, every time someone gets online, their choices about what to view, share, post, or express emotion about—what to "like" or get angry at or share tears about—*matter*. Social media engagement requires people to constantly (and often unconsciously) answer difficult questions such as:

- Whom should I interact with?
- When should I speak and when should I be silent?
- What should I click?

8. Eire, *Reformations*, 150–51.
9. Scribner, "Oral Culture," 87.

These activities reveal a person's beliefs, values, desires, and judgments. Actions online, like the actions we engage in during in-person conversation, both expose and form our attachments, allegiances, and assumptions, as well as demonstrate how much or how little we engage in critical and theological reflection about these choices.

In fact, a person's feelings, habits, disciplines, and activities, online and in other forms of communication, both *reveal* and *continually shape* a person's theology. This is because theology (whether malformed and deficient or healthy and sound) is embodied, exercised, and practiced. Theology is performative. Theology is not merely a set of beliefs, convictions, or ideas about the nature of God; theology is lived. As human beings perform theology in their actions and habits, they learn to reflect on it, describe it, shape it, and reform it. Let's consider how online engagement is embodied theology by reflecting on normative new media behaviors, considered in order from extremely passive to exceptionally participatory actions. It may seem strange to talk about these seemingly simple actions in such detail, but doing so will help your community uncover just how *meaning-filled* these mundane activities are.[10]

Streaming and Scanning

On the passive side of the spectrum is *streaming*, which includes watching TV shows, films, and other kinds of video online. Close to streaming in its passivity is *scanning*. The majority of online engagement involves viewing others' posts on social media sites. It is not unusual for people to get online multiple times per day just to read or view content that other people have posted. Decisions, whether thoughtfully made or not, go into streaming and scanning.

For example, I scan my Facebook newsfeed while drinking my morning cup of coffee. In a matter of minutes, I see several posts: a funny animal meme created by a church friend, a post by a friend I have not seen in years asking for prayer, an interesting article on managing stress, a vulnerable post related to a trending hashtag about sexual harassment and assault (#metoo), a set of

10. Your objection may not be that these are ordinary activities but instead that these activities concern trivial things and waste time that is better used for more important things. I would not disagree that at points new media engagement wastes time. However, my concern here is that billions of people get online every day and engage in these types of actions thinking they are mundane, when instead they are meaning-filled (even if not engaged in a way that reaches this potential), and therefore Christian communities need to consider why these activities matter. On practices as meaning-full, see Bass, "What Is a Christian Practice?" The Valparaiso Project launched PracticingOurFaith.org as a way of extending the invitation offered in Bass, *Practicing Our Faith.*

photos from a close friend's trip to Greece, a post asking for financial support of refugees, and a long post written by a seminary friend about reducing gun violence after another national tragedy.

I have approximately five minutes to reply to one or more of these posts before needing to get ready for work. What should I view? What should I read carefully? Whose posts should I dismiss along the way? Again, these seemingly ordinary actions are infused with choices informed by what people value and believe. Intentionality also matters. Thoughtful streaming and scanning is distinct from thoughtless streaming and scanning. Scanning a newsfeed or streaming a video because of boredom versus doing so for the purpose of learning (e.g., wanting to know what people think about a particular current event or trying to find a video for making a point in a sermon) are quite different.

Friending and Following

Other types of actions, such as *friending* and *following* (and allowing following on platforms like Instagram), are significantly more dynamic. When people join a social media site, they have to make choices about "the who" as it relates to friending and following. Who will I accept, and who will I reject, and what are the terms? Who matters to me and why? Who do I want to see my posts? Whose posts do I want to view? Will I friend everyone? How many friends and followers do I hope to have?

Responding

Even more participatory is *responding*, which can take several forms, including emotional expressions, written and visual replies, and private dialogue. Responding to a post implies value. It is interesting to consider why some posts feel worthy of a response and others do not. How should we decide? Several social media sites have a single form of expressing emotion when responding to posts: "liking" the post (by clicking a heart, for example). However, on the most widely used social media site, Facebook, a person can choose from several options: like, love, laugh, surprise/awe, sadness, or anger. It is interesting to consider the various kinds of posts a person might encounter when scanning a newsfeed. In a short amount of time, a person might view something political, religious, tragic, hilarious, mundane, or extraordinary. It is easy to quickly go from "laughing" (clicking the "haha" emoji) at a meme, to "awe" (clicking the "wow" emoji) at someone's new job offer, to "sorrow" (clicking the "sad" emoji) because a friend's grandmother just passed away—in three clicks and often in under ten seconds. One has to wonder about the implications of feeling all of these emotions in such quick succession or, indeed, whether we're truly feeling any of them. But when people express emotions toward our posts, it can feel really good. It is comforting to write something sad and have multiple people express sadness back to us. It gives us a sense of solidarity.

Replies can also involve words or photos or background images. Replying to a post by writing something or sharing a link or even an image (e.g., a photo or meme) in one's response versus just liking it generally means the post or the person who wrote the post is even more valuable to the responder. These sorts of replies require more time and, in theory, thought. There are also replies that become an ongoing dialogue where users go back and forth talking to (or past) one another several times under a particular post. An even more engaged form of replying happens privately (e.g., messaging someone directly).

Posting

Another online activity is *posting* (e.g., a status update, image, story, tweet). Posting, like responding, can take several forms: sharing, updating, tagging, and producing. Sharing has taken on new meaning in the realm of social media, where it refers to passing on content (originally posted by someone else) and inviting others to read or view, to absorb, and possibly to respond to information that one believes is worthy of attention. This content can include videos, tweets, diagrams, art, articles, photos, memes, and so on. People might also add their own comments, and thus appraisal, to the content they share. For example, sometimes the user will pick a quote from an article and post it above the link to the article. By doing so, the user is pointing out what is particularly meaningful, engaging, frustrating, or confusing in the article. A user might also share content and comment on its value, suggesting to others that they should watch or read or pay attention to the content for a specific reason. The person sharing may desire the audience to gain specific knowledge, laugh, cry, stand up for something, or be inspired, among other actions and emotions.

Passing on content does not necessarily mean the sharer agrees with it. Sometimes content is shared because of adamant disagreement. The person who is sharing the content might be frustrated or appalled by it. Likewise, the sharer may want others' opinions on the matter, so they may post or tweet an article and ask their audience, "What do you think?" Participants on social media have the ability, through sharing, to dissect ideas or movements, join in global conversations, spread important data, and evaluate and critique information. The circulation and recirculation of ideas has led to the migration of information and stories across the globe. The more content is shared, the more "spreadable" it is. Perhaps unsurprisingly, the types of content that are most spreadable are "shared fantasies, humor, parody and references, unfinished content, mystery, timely controversy, rumors."[11] A user considers several questions before sharing content: Should I share this? Why? Is this interesting? Should I add my own comments when sharing this? And perhaps a user asks: Will it get the sort of response I am hoping for from my followers or friends?

A post can also have original content. Generally, this is an update of sorts about the person's recent thoughts and experiences. This content can vary from being extremely personal ("I am feeling depressed. Need prayers.") to being less personal, like an evaluation of a TV show ("I can't believe it ended that way!"), or even to a "story" on Instagram of the user at a concert or a party. Users make a number of decisions when they post online. How personal do I want to be? Do I want people to know I am at this event? Should I say something about that tragedy? Posting can include the entire spectrum of the human experience (depending on how much one wants to share): location, feelings, attendance (e.g., at a concert), achievement, belief, evaluation, illuminations, hope, grief.

Embedded in the activity of posting online is the ability to "tag" an idea (#joy), event (#birthday), place (#nature), social issue (#GivingTuesday), or another person (@POTUS). Users do this with the pound sign or "hashtag" (#), the @ symbol, and by clicking people's faces in a photo. Tagging creates an association between someone's post and something or someone else. This association can mean a number of positive things: friendship, affiliation, connection, and solidarity. Tagging can invite dialogue or grow a movement or include people. Conversely, it can be shaming ("@soandso, why did you say that?") or opposing and can therefore cause frustration, obstruct conversation, and demonstrate how small (if its hashtag has limited use) or hated an idea or event is. Tagging can then also exclude people.

The most active form of posting is producing content (e.g., blog, video, presentation, website) that is then distributed. There are a number of decisions you have to make when creating content. What do I want to say and how should I say it? What is the best medium for explaining my ideas? Who do I hope to share my ideas with? Should I draw attention to other people or include other people's thoughts when sharing my ideas, and if so, who?

11. Jenkins, Ford, and Green, *Spreadable Media*, 202.

How long should my post or video be? What do I hope the outcome(s) of producing this content will be?

Seeing and Relating

The actions discussed above—streaming, scanning, friending, following, responding, and posting—are involved in various kinds of online activities: playing games, networking and dating, as well as trading, selling, and buying material goods. Recognizing these routine actions as meaning-filled could be viewed as overwhelming. Or it could be seen as an incredible gift. As we discover the meaningfulness of ordinary actions, we also find the meaningfulness imbued in our lives, every day. People often look up to find God, as if God is above us, in the clouds somewhere. Yet Christian faith teaches that the Spirit is our constant companion who lives with us and will be with us (John 14:17). Christianity, like Jesus's parables, invites faith that is postured toward being receptive to the Spirit who dwells within us and thus toward embracing and participating in God's unconditional love in the ordinary activities of our everyday lives.[12]

Critical reflection reveals that all these actions are integrated into the larger themes of seeing and relating. And these themes present their own sets of questions about online actions. Regarding seeing, we might examine our online actions and consider questions like, Whom and what do I see? Whom and what do I pay attention to? Whom and what do I respond to? Whom do I ignore? And these ideas, people, and experiences I am seeing—am I seeing them rightly? Truthfully? All of these questions raise a pressing theological question: What does it mean to see rightly and truthfully?

Similarly, many of these online actions produce questions about relating. What does it mean to relate well with someone else? Toward what end is my relating aimed? What conversations do I join? What or whom do I stand for or against? To whom am I responsible? These questions point toward a larger theological question as well: What does it mean to relate rightly and truthfully?

Each day, we live answers to these questions. Again, theology is performative. In the midst of this living, as in all the activities of our lives, the Spirit is inviting us to share in how God's unconditional love sees and relates. It

---

12. Jesus's parables teach us to find God's work in the ordinary—in lamps, wine, soil, work, mustard seeds, yeast, sheep, coins. See Matt. 5:14–15; 9:17; 13:3–23; 20:1–16; Mark 4:30–32; Luke 13:20–21; 15:3–10. Bass and Dykstra, "Times of Yearning, Practices of Faith," 8, discuss how when we see ordinary practices as Christian, we come to perceive how they are related to God's work in the world.

is not a matter of whether the Spirit is leading us, only a matter of whether we are receptive to the Spirit's prompting and open to participating in God's unconditional love. Once we recognize that we are being led by the Spirit while engaging in these ordinary online actions and see the possibility that God's love can be embraced and shared through our online seeing and relating, it makes sense that what we might have once thought to be virtual (i.e., artificial) is actually quite real.

Acknowledging Hybrid Living

Recognizing online actions as meaning-filled helps Christian communities to consider our current online and in-person reality in terms of its hybridity, rather than in terms of digital dualism (thinking of online as virtual and in person as real). "Hybridity" describes "the coming together of online and offline, media and matter, or, more dynamically, . . . the interplay between the online and offline dimension."[13] Most Americans live hybrid lives because our online and offline lives have become integrated.[14] Interactions online shape offline experiences, and offline communication and practices shape people's online engagement.[15]

It could be argued that human beings lived hybrid lives before new media since people have used tools to mediate their communication and spread information for a long time (as we examined earlier in this chapter). But there are significant differences in the current landscape. The main differences between old media hybrid living and new media hybrid living are related to how often most people use new media (daily), the quantity of modes of media people engage with (many more), and how quickly new media spreads information (much faster).

The conversations I have with some of my distant friends are a good example of the nature of living in a hybrid reality. I have a fantastic group of LA friends who keep me grounded, honest, engaged, and hopeful. We consistently stay in touch with one another, even though I live in Connecticut

13. Lindgren, Dahlberg-Grundberg, and Johansson, "Hybrid Media Culture," 2. Other terms that are used to describe the merging of the digital and physical are "mixed reality" and "hybrid reality." See, e.g., Milgram and Kishino, "Taxonomy"; and de Souza e Silva and Sutko, *Digital Cityscapes*.

14. "The vast majority of Americans—95%—now own a cellphone of some kind. The share of Americans that own smartphones is now 77%, up from just 35% in Pew Research Center's first survey of smartphone ownership conducted in 2011." "Mobile Fact Sheet."

15. Lindgren, Dahlberg-Grundberg, and Johansson, "Hybrid Media Culture," 6. See also Campbell and Garner, *Networked Theology*. The authors discuss connectedness between the physical and the digital throughout their book. They write, "This [love of God and neighbor] has obvious implications for life in a hybrid of physical and digital worlds" (91).

Dualism vs. Hybridity

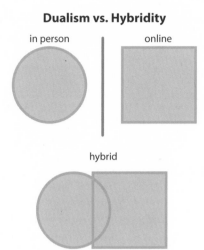

and the members of the group travel frequently. Our friendships are made up of hybrid interactions. We especially enjoy dialoguing about work, family, politics, and religion. These conversations occur during in-person gatherings (at each other's houses and at restaurants), through group text messaging (our group is labeled "The Girls" in our phones), while engaging in one-on-one phone calls or FaceTiming one another (video conferencing through mobile phones), and by responding to each other's social media posts. It is becoming increasingly difficult to discern the starting point of any conversation. For example, if I were to try to describe what we said to each other recently about our reflections on women in leadership (we are all in positions of leadership within various organizations), I would draw on several conversations that occurred across time and numerous mediated forms. It was a hybrid dialogue.

Living hybrid lives has become normal for many people because the internet functions like a place.[16] The internet has essential aspects of other sorts of spaces (e.g., schools, churches, cafés, living rooms, dinner tables) for meaningful human interaction in that it allows for dialoguing, connecting, learning, sharing, planning, and dreaming. Author and minister Lynne Baab explains, "Engaging with the internet as a place where people spend time with their friends and look for information enables the internet to be considered as one of the many places on earth where humans engage with each other, where we sin in multiple ways like we do anywhere else, and where God works."[17]

16. "The internet is a place where, for many people, identity is formed, memory is structured and attitudes are determined." Baab, "Theology of the Internet," 280.

17. Baab, "Theology of the Internet," 288.

Likewise, people engage in practices online that are similar to practices they engage in in other spaces and activities—such as concerts, sports events, rallies, and vigils—that nurture human connection through celebration, truth-telling, lament, and so on.[18] Online groups have qualities found in many definitions of community: "sense of space, shared practice, shared resources and support, shared identities, and interpersonal relationships."[19] These characteristics— that it functions as a place for meaningful human interaction and common practices and qualities of community—contribute to the significance of social media in people's lives and reveal the importance of interested conversation in a new media landscape that demonstrates awareness of the integrated nature of our in-person and online lives.

One last thought on hybrid living comes from Nathan Jurgenson, who proposes that digital and physical spaces mix together to form an "augmented reality,"[20] where online and in-person experiences are considered "mutually constitutive."[21] This perspective recognizes a relationship between online and in-person actions, interactions, and feelings. For instance, if I see someone post online about getting a new job and then I run into them at the grocery store, I might talk in person with them about what I saw online. Likewise, if I check my Twitter feed and see negative reactions to something terrible that is happening in the world and it makes me worried, I am likely to go offline and continue worrying. Worry will not immediately go away the moment I get off my mobile phone.

The augmented perspective argues that rather than labeling in-person interactions as "real" and digital communication as "virtual," we should understand both to be real and mutually constitutive but with recognizable differences. From this view, online and in-person interactions are along a

18. Michel Foucault calls places that juxtapose several spaces into one single real space and render time relative "heterotopias" (e.g., cemeteries, theaters, boats, sacred places). I would argue that the internet fits his description. Heterotopias "have a function in relation to all the space that remains. This function unfolds between two extreme poles. Either their role is to create a space of illusion that exposes every real space, all the sites inside of which human life is partitioned, as still more illusory (perhaps that is the role that was played by those famous brothels of which we are now deprived). Or else, on the contrary, their role is to create a space that is other, another real space, as perfect, as meticulous, as well arranged as ours is messy, ill constructed, and jumbled. This latter type would be the heterotopia, not of illusion, but of compensation." Foucault, "Of Other Spaces, Heterotopias, 8."

19. Baym, *Personal Connections*, 75.

20. Jurgenson, "Digital Dualism versus Augmented Reality." "Augmented reality" is also a term used by tech companies to describe how their products enhance the physical world and how digital information can be made more interactive in physical realms—for example, visualizing how a piece of furniture will look in your apartment or navigating an airport on a smartphone. See "Augmented Reality" on Apple's website.

21. Jurgenson, "Defending and Clarifying."

continuum where various kinds of engagement can be categorized differently.[22] For example, human interactions can be described in terms of depth of relationship (anonymous versus established) or in terms of time (asynchronous versus synchronous; long versus short duration) rather than real or virtual.[23] These sorts of realizations—online experiences being real and having the possibility of being meaning-filled and the mutually constitutive nature of online and in-person engagement—invite Christian communities to accept and continually acknowledge that both in person and online interactions can be authentic and beneficial, as well as deficient and harmful.

Hybrid Christian Communities

Christian communities are a medium for God's love. Paul's missionary strategy was to form small Christian communities that, as Richard Rohr explains, "would make the message believable: Jesus is Lord (rather than Caesar is Lord); sharing abundance and living in simplicity (rather than hoarding wealth); nonviolence and suffering (rather than aligning with power)."[24] Christian communities live this message by engaging in practices that reflect these values in both private and public settings. Hybrid Christian communities embody God's love and "make the message believable" through meaningful conversations and faithful habits that are both in person and mediated, that take place at various times, and that happen in both physical and digital spaces.

I do not think it is too daunting for Christian communities to think about their community as being hybrid, given Paul's letters and specifically his use of the metaphor of "the body of Christ." Paul's letters are a clear example of hybrid Christian community, since his letters were extensions of his in-person ministry within particular communities and also provided mediated guidance for those communities. Paul's metaphor of the body of Christ describes how Christians are united members of one body despite being in different places and existing in different times (1 Cor. 12:27). Peter Simonson explains Paul's metaphor: "First Corinthians envisions the Body of Christ as a medium that traverses space and time and binds the faithful together as an intercommunicating community. . . . As they ate from the loaf, the Corinthians consumed

22. Lindgren, "Towards a Heterotopology," 141.
23. Asynchronous communication happens when people communicate with one another at different times. For example, if I email someone at 5 p.m. on a Saturday and they email me back at 7 p.m. on Monday, we are communicating asynchronously.
24. Rohr, "Church."

the Body of Christ and drew themselves together as the multi-membered *ekklesia* of God."[25] By eating the bread and drinking the cup, members of Christian communities are not just joined to one another locally but also incorporated into the global Christian community across time and space. Likewise, mediated and online practices can nurture connections with the larger Christian community.

It is possible to nurture a hybrid Christian community. Many Christian communities *are* hybrid Christian communities (though they would probably not yet use this terminology) because they are nurturing relationships, growing spiritually, and engaging in ministry both in-person and online. Through social media, members are cultivating connections online that are not that different from the relationships that prevailed before the internet and mobile phones.

Social media is being used to nurture relationships in between in-person gatherings. For example, my former youth group had a Facebook messaging thread that usually started after a youth group meeting and kept going until the next time we gathered. We shared jokes, told stories, and discussed what we were doing each day. The digital era has provided Christian communities that regularly meet in person with tools and techniques for planning together asynchronously, raising money for community members affected by illness or needing other kinds of assistance, supporting members through encouragement, and praying for one another. For example, some Christian communities have a special hashtag for prayer requests or a phone number people can text to share prayer requests during the week. Additionally, some Christian communities are using websites and apps to set up meetings (https://doodle.com), plan worship services (https://worshipplanning.com), and organize bringing meals to community members (https://www.mealtrain.com).

Social media is also helping community members participate in mediated conversations (e.g., about theological matters) when they cannot be physically present at a meeting. By allowing leaders to arrange discussions between remote interlocutors, social media is particularly beneficial for parents with young children, those who lack access to transportation, and those who live with disabilities or a long-term illness. Some Christian communities have members who meet in online groups to study the Bible and other books. Communities are also using sites like Zoom (the same site my friend Jed uses) for mentorship and spiritual direction meetings, as well as pastoral care visitations. One of my former students told me he usually meets once a month with seniors in his church who are homebound. However, during class he was inspired to begin using Zoom to increase visits to once a week.

25. Simonson, *Refiguring Mass Communication*, 50–51.

New media is also being used by members of Christian communities to gather meaningful information, obtain access to theological resources, and nurture faith. An abundance of online resources—sermons, resources for programming (e.g., children's ministry materials), TED talks, YouTube videos, reviews of books related to Christianity, and blogs—integrate theological reflection on real-life issues. Facebook and Instagram posts and stories, Twitter tweets, and blogs are positively impacting people's faith formation. And some Christian communities are using YouTube to learn songs for worship services.

Christian communities are increasing their missional capacities by inviting new or different perspectives into ministry activities since social media posts and stories, videos, articles, and art that is shared online are all valuable materials for sharing diverse viewpoints. New media is also used to create resources—videos, Bible studies, devotions, prayer guides, multimedia presentations.

Additionally, Christian communities are encouraging members to use new media to create presentations, videos, or art, and to share such creations with the entire community. For example, in the youth group I led, youth were invited to send me videos they had made and photos they had taken related to the topics we were going to explore during youth group. I shared these creations to begin conversations and provoke imaginations.

I have been moved by visiting and worshiping with Christian communities that are using new media to participate in the kingdom of God. It is becoming increasingly apparent that all Christian communities need to think about what it means to be a hybrid Christian community. Likewise, members of Christian communities need to be taught to view their social media practices as both meaning-filled and real. It is important for every Christian community to spend time discerning and articulating God's invitations to their community regarding ministering online and using technology.

While new media can be used to practice faith (evident in all the examples I just provided), it is too often built with embedded aims and values that change what users think is meaningful as well as what users believe about and desire for themselves, other human beings, and the global common good. So using new media is not merely a matter of using it well but also of choosing well (what forms of technology and social media to use) and training people to be cognizant of new media's aims and values that often negatively impact people. In the next chapter, I will examine a destructive, dominant cultural narrative that shapes many of the social contexts new media is designed and developed within.

interested conversation in practice

Discussion Questions

1. What are some examples of media and mediated communication in Scripture?

2. What surprises you about the new media landscape?

3. Why are online actions meaning-filled, and what are possible connections between online actions and practicing faith? If you maintain that online actions are trivial and have nothing to do with practicing faith, why?

4. When considering online actions (such as streaming and posting) in light of larger themes (such as seeing and relating), what are some possible theological implications?

5. What is meant by the term "hybridity"? How does it impact your view of technology's role in contemporary culture and the practice of Christian faith?

6. Is our community a hybrid Christian community? If so, how? If not, why not?

three

shaping stories

Part of our contemporary crisis is created by a lack of meaningful access to truth. That is to say, individuals are not just presented untruths, but are told them in a manner that enables most effective communication. When this collective cultural consumption of and attachment to misinformation is coupled with the layers of lying individuals do in their personal lives, our capacity to face reality is severely diminished as is our will to intervene and change unjust circumstances.

bell hooks, *Teaching to Transgress*

The college students sat quietly as they watched me write personal branding expert Dan Schawbel's words on the board: "You are a brand and the success of your personal brand lies in your hands."[1] I read the words aloud and asked the students to come to the board to write responses to Schawbel's statement.[2] On the board, students could pose questions, write sentences of support or disagreement, and/or make connections (by drawing lines) between various replies. Their reflections, both on the board and in the discussion afterward, were fascinating. The students shared thoughtful criticisms of the statement, but no one actually disagreed with it. Eventually I said, "You know you're not actually a brand, right? You are a human being."

1. Schawbel, *Me 2.0*, 1. This is a paraphrase of Schawbel's words.
2. This is a pedagogical tool that I learned from Stephen Brookfield in *Teaching for Critical Thinking*, 186–87. Brookfield learned this from a student, Steven Rippe, who learned this from Hilton Smith of the Foxfire Fund.

The setting (or milieu) in which people live, including the social aspects of their lives, is significant for how they organize their lives and relate to themselves, others, society, and God. Your milieu is shaped by cultural stories that present guiding convictions about how you should act and feel and what sorts of conditions you should seek to create for yourself, your community, and the world. Cultural narratives influence the way you relate to other people, and they shape your perceptions, affecting what you think is worth doing, desiring, and feeling. They help you to determine what is meaningful.

Like you, the designers of new media are embedded in social contexts that have been influenced by cultural narratives. The communication techniques and priorities of these social contexts, shaped by cultural stories, form the structure—the practices and values—of the new media they create.[3] Therefore, another step in interested conversation is *interest in critically reflecting on cultural narratives that guide new media design and people's use of new media.* Knowing the language and agenda of cultural narratives, and thus developing sensitivities for recognizing how their themes shape new media development and engagement, is vital for discerning and articulating Christian visions of flourishing life in a new media milieu.

This chapter describes a dominant cultural narrative (and its subplot) and how this narrative shapes the American cultural milieu, thus defining some of the convictions, values, and practices of the social contexts new media is being designed within. The description of this narrative will give you a sense of the convictions, values, and practices that are shaping contemporary conditions of the false life. This dominant cultural narrative and its subplot resist Christian visions of flourishing life. Rather than presenting a Christian vision of true life, this story provides *malformed* convictions about what a good life is. It is important to recognize that the dominant cultural narrative being described affects all aspects of Americans' lives—home, work, educational systems, government, religious institutions. I will focus on its impact on new media design, especially social media sites, although it affects more than technology use. In view of malformed visions of human flourishing, new media is developed and engaged in for economic gain, with little consideration for its implications on people's lives. This only intensifies the false life, which is characterized by harmful conditions, wounding practices, and destructive feelings.

The good news is that Jesus's alternative vision of flourishing life is simultaneously breaking in. I will discuss Jesus's vision in the next chapter and its impact on our hybrid new media landscape throughout the rest of the book,

---

3. Baym, *Personal Connections*, 40.

but it is also important to understand elements of malformed contemporary visions of the good life that compete with Christian visions of true life.

The Main Story

New media—its development and people's use of it—is shaped by a dominant cultural narrative that motivates many aspects of American culture. This story informs the convictions and thus the goals, beliefs, desires, and practices of institutions, organizations, businesses, families, and individuals. It is not discussed widely enough as a leading story that drives contemporary American culture; yet it is widely *lived*.

The story goes something like this: Be true to yourself.[4] You do you.[5] Do what you want, whatever feels right to you.[6] Be happy.[7]

The story's predominant message is that your life's meaning and self-fulfillment are discovered through, and therefore dependent on, your ability to authentically express yourself—that is, to find your unique way of being human that does not imitate anyone else. If you are unable to do this, you

4. I want to express my gratitude to Ryan McAnnally-Linz for his insights regarding modes of expressive individualism and for connections he helped me to make between being true to yourself and desire. This chapter was inspired by his dissertation (see later footnotes), ongoing research, lectures I have heard him give, and many conversations we have had. Ryan is the managing director of YCFC as well as my friend and trusted colleague. The notion of "being true to yourself" is connected to "expressive individualism," the idea that your identity and meaning comes from expressing yourself in your own authentic way. Charles Taylor discusses authenticity at length in *A Secular Age*, 473–504. Robert Bellah's *Habits of the Heart* provides a rich exploration of the roots and development of expressive individualism. According to Bellah, "Expressive individualism holds that each person has a unique core of feeling and intuition that should unfold or be expressed if individuality is to be realized" (333–34). Further, on Bellah's account, expressive individualism asserts that human beings are self-made and thus self-reliant (55).

5. "You do you" is the current mantra for being true to yourself. See Taylor, *Ethics of Authenticity*, 4, 14–23. "You do you" treats normative commitments as strategies for self-fulfillment. Bellah, *Habits of the Heart*, 48.

6. From the perspective of expressive individualism, "Acts, then, are not right or wrong in themselves, but only because of the results they produce, the good feelings they engender or express." Bellah, *Habits of the Heart*, 78.

7. Adam Potkay traces the roots of happiness in his book *The Story of Joy*. Potkay explains, "The noun 'happiness' is a surprisingly recent coinage in English. Although it can be found sparingly in Spenser, Shakespeare, and Milton, it does not take wing until the eighteenth century, as a rendition of the Greek *eudaimonia* either directly or through the Latin *beata vita*" (21). Potkay explains that eighteenth-century writers described public happiness in terms of "civic, social and material conditions for widespread individual flourishing" (22). Therefore, public happiness could be determined by "a calculus of material conditions" (23). Combine the beliefs of expressive individualism with these terms of happiness and it is no wonder the United States has lots of individuals relying on themselves to procure social and material conditions for happy feelings.

will miss the point of your life.[8] From this story's perspective, authentic self-expression involves being who you are and defining yourself without regard for moral demands or demands stemming from your connections to others.[9] In this story no one else should tell you what to choose or do; so a truly good society will not propose that there are right and wrong ways to lead your life, or right and wrong circumstances to seek, or right and wrong feelings.[10] The right way to live is up to you. In fact, there is no wrong way to "do you." Your guide in your pursuit of this vision of human flourishing is personal preference based on desire.[11] Being true to who you are means being true to your desires, so decision-making is centered on your feelings, whatever you *feel* compelled by, usually whatever you think will make you feel happy.[12] Truth, like decision-making in this story, is subjective. Being true to yourself involves believing what feels true to your experience over and against objective facts.[13] Both morality and epistemology, then, are also personal.[14]

This story, like most stories, has heroes and sheroes. In the United States, the heroes and sheroes of this story are what we call "celebrities." American culture rewards people who appear to live this sort of life well (by being true to themselves, "doing them") by making them famous (e.g., reality TV stars), or by making them even more famous (music icons or movie stars). Think about it for a moment. Many of the most well-known, rich, and admired celebrities are those who exemplify what it looks like to be led by desire. And they appear extremely happy, as if their life is full of things and people that exist solely for their self-fulfillment. Watch one of the top music videos, review the top tweets, or scan the most viral Instagram photos of the past year, and you will notice that the United States worships people who appear to be enjoying life free of moral demands—ultimately, those who give the impression they are being true (only) to themselves.

8. Taylor, *Ethics of Authenticity*, 28–29.

9. This is one mode of expressive individualism. Taylor's critiques of this mode invite a higher standard—self-fulfillment that regards ties to others and the demands emanating from something more than human desires or aspirations; see Taylor, *Ethics of Authenticity*, 35, 73.

10. Taylor, *Ethics of Authenticity*, 14, 17–18.

11. The freedom to choose what you feel drawn to because you desire it is a natural next step.

12. Expressive individualists imagine the self as the intuitive center and the evaluator of good and bad feelings. Bellah, *Habits of the Heart*, 78.

13. The Oxford Dictionary's word of the year in 2016 was "post-truth." This is an adjective. Post-truth is defined as "relating to or denoting circumstances in which objective facts are less influential in shaping public opinion than appeals to emotion and personal belief." See "Word of the Year 2016 Is . . ."

14. Taylor, *Ethics of Authenticity*, 18.

The Subplot

There is a subplot too—if you will, a story within the story. Daily, you are being told that the proof of whether you are living this dominant cultural story well lies in your ability to make money and to consume.[15] The celebrities American culture celebrates are rich (or give the appearance of being so). They generate consumption, defined in part by what they wear on the red carpet (or out on their morning jog). And more often than not, they are purveyors of consumer goods: Matthew McConaughey sells cars, Beyoncé sells clothes, and Jennifer Aniston sells skin-care products. In this story's subplot, your truest sources of identity, meaningfulness, and self-fulfillment—and thus what you should especially feel drawn to choose, regardless of moral demands or demands stemming from your connections to others—are money and what having it enables: namely, consumption.[16] Sociologist and philosopher Zygmunt Bauman explains the nature of this subplot well:

> To sum up, the culture of liquid modernity has no "populous" to enlighten and ennoble; it does, however, have clients to seduce. Seduction, by contrast with enlightenment and ennoblement, is not a one-off, once and for all task, but an open-ended activity. The function of culture is not to satisfy existing needs, but to create new ones—while simultaneously maintaining needs already entrenched or permanently unfulfilled. Its chief concern is to prevent a feeling of satisfaction in its former subjects and charges, now turned into clients, and in particular to counteract their perfect, complete and definitive gratification, which would leave no room for further, new and as yet unfulfilled needs and whims.[17]

This subplot suggests that what will give you significance and thus what you *really* should desire and what will *really* make you happy is making money and consuming—that is, buying or obtaining access to as many contemporary goods (e.g., gadgets, news, fashion, beauty products, celebrity gossip, television shows, sports, food, alcohol, exercise programs, conferences, vacation packages) as possible.[18] There is an increasing emphasis not just on

15. Andrew Root examines the duty to consume in *Faith Formation*, 21–27.

16. Helga Dittmar describes this as "materialistic value orientation," in which the self is constructed through material goods. See her paper for a YCFC consultation, "Materialistic Value Orientation," as part of the Theology of Joy and the Good Life Project.

17. Bauman, *Culture in a Liquid Modern World*, 16–17.

18. A growing body of theorists think the dominant economic structures and ideology today are no longer built around *consumer* capitalism but around *finance* capitalism, which is important for theologians to examine. However, finance (or debt) capitalism depends on the continued power of consumer ideology. Additionally, the concern of this book is media, and its connections to the accumulation of material and cultural goods that depend on nurturing

buying material objects and cultural goods but also on buying remarkable experiences. It is even becoming more common to view people who spend their money on remarkable experiences as better than people who spend their money on material goods, as if they are more moral and making wiser choices. Yet remarkable, short-lived experiences are often just another part of consumerism, another thing offering a "hit" of happiness that people mistake for the supreme good in a good life. When remarkable experiences become the ultimate marker of the good life, ordinary life easily seems depressing, unimportant, and void of the goodness of God.

Implicitly and explicitly, you are being reminded daily by advertisements, businesses, and even your friends and family that no matter what you do for a living, your *real job* is to make money. And so goes the cycle: Earn money (or borrow it). Consume.[19] Repeat. And if you won't do this job for yourself, at least do it for your kids: Make money. Create opportunities for your kids to consume. Repeat.

Visions of the Good Life

Every vision of a good life presents convictions related to the sorts of circumstances—social, material, political, economic—you should pursue, how you should act, and how you should desire to feel.[20] Incongruously, the dominant cultural narrative and its subplot (the one that says "you do you" by making money and buying things) provide a set of convictions about the type of life you ought to live. It is a vision of the right sort of life to live. In sum, this vision (integrating the main plot and subplot) tells you to lead your life well by *authentically expressing yourself*, which looks like *pursuing your desires ("doing you"), making money*, and *consuming as much as possible*.[21] Accordingly, access to cultural and material goods, money, and an ever-increasing amount of personal preference–based choices centered on your happiness are the measures of a life that is going well. If you lead your life well and pursue the right circumstances as prescribed, you will be fulfilled, which means you will feel happy; and of course, being happy is the way life *should* feel—or so the story goes.

desire and connecting happiness to material objects, two keys of consumer capitalism that I want to critique.

19. Cavanaugh discusses the formative power of consumer culture in *Being Consumed*, 47–52.

20. Volf and Croasmun discuss visions of the good life in terms of how a vision articulates life being led well, going well, and feeling as it should in *Life of the World*, 16–17; see also Volf and McAnnally-Linz, *Public Faith in Action*, 13–15.

21. Root, *Faith Formation*, 59.

How Can This Be True?

Not many people want to admit that these are some (or all) of the convictions guiding their lives or the lives of those in their families and communities. The convictions of this main story and its subplot are often masked in our hopes for our children. I regularly hear parents say that what they want most for their children is for them to be happy and successful. Embedded in the American dream is the desire for wealth. And some of American culture's famous slogans celebrate living for desire and doing whatever you want, like "What happens here, stays here." Implicitly, values related to this story—its main plot and subplot—are also exhibited in social media hashtags. For example, among the top ten most used hashtags on Instagram are #happy, #fun, #fashion, and #me.[22]

It is also important to note that this story's convictions are usually integrated into the convictions of other stories that shape you, like the Christian narrative. This is why it can be difficult to delineate differences between American visions of flourishing and Christian visions of flourishing. Often, they are intermingled.[23] For example, God is who you pray to in order to have your desires met and to feel good about yourself, and the acquisition of happiness, wealth, or success is seen as a sign of God's blessing (#blessed).[24] Too often, elements of malformed visions merge with elements of Christian visions of flourishing life, and we mistake values shaped by expressive individualism and capitalism, for example, for Christian values.

How exactly did this story's main plot and subplot become so alluring? In short, its allure is that it taps into human desires. Humans need to develop an identity, a sense of who they are—their personality, gifts, passions. Healthy humans feel seen, known, and loved for who they are. Money is not inherently

22. Anić, "'Hashtag a Day.'"
23. Vincent Miller explores how religious belief and practice are transformed by the structures and practices of consumer culture in *Consuming Religion*. Root discusses how Jesus has emerged as a product or an idea that you could commit to (or not) in *Faith Formation*, 83.
24. C. Smith and Denton studied the religious and spiritual lives of American teenagers from 2001 to 2005 and identified what they term "therapeutic individualism," which sees the "individual self as the source and standard of authentic moral knowledge and authority, and individual self-fulfillment as the preoccupying purpose of life" (*Soul Searching*, 173). On this view, religious and spiritual practices are about satisfying wants (175); hence, "religion becomes one more product among many others existing to satisfy people's subjectively defined needs, tastes, and wants" (176). Kenda Creasy Dean explains the effects of "Moralistic Therapeutic Deism" in *Almost Christian*, 29–37; she writes that "Moralistic Therapeutic Deism has little to do with God or a sense of divine mission in the world. It offers comfort, bolsters self-esteem, helps solve problems, and lubricates interpersonal relationships by encouraging people to do good, feel good, and keep God at arm's length" (29). Kate Bowler explores the prosperity gospel movement and how wealth, success, and capitalism became associated with the gospel in her book *Blessed*.

bad. It allows people to buy material goods that sustain their lives. Additionally, humans appreciate choices; those who lack them usually live in oppressive conditions. And it is natural to prefer and desire happiness. I am not suggesting that any of these normative human needs and desires are inherently bad. In fact, these are legitimate and good things; identity, resources, choice, and happiness are gifts. What I am suggesting is that this story deforms the shape and aims of these natural needs, and of our desires for them, in ways that nurture harmful living conditions, damaging practices, and destructive feelings.

Malformed Vision

This story—the dominant cultural narrative—has several issues that make it a malformed vision of the good life and mean that its prevalence deepens the conditions, practices, and destructive feelings of the false life. First, it shames imitation, emphasizing self-creation and self-reliance, suggesting that you do not need a relationship with God or community to know who you are or to have meaning in your life. There are several problems with this line of thinking. Human beings are imitative creatures. Our relationships with God and others are formative. We have connections to God and others whether we recognize it or not. We *need* God and other people, and we need their recognition, which allows us to know ourselves and develop an identity. As relational creatures, we need our self-expression to be seen and affirmed by other people.

This alerts us to a second issue. Embedded in this story are conflicting desires. On the one hand, as relational beings we long for other people to validate our authenticity, so we find ourselves trying to be interesting and likeable; on the other hand, we strive to be as self-reliant and distinctive as possible. Bauman describes the paradox this way:

> The contradictory yearnings and desires spoken of here are a longing for a sense of belonging within a group or an agglomeration, and a desire to be distinct from the masses, to acquire a sense of individuality and originality; a dream of belonging and a dream of independence; the need for social support, and the demand for autonomy; a wish to be like everyone else, and a pursuit of uniqueness. . . . Or, if we look at this conflict from another perspective: the fear of being different, and the fear of losing individuality.[25]

This conflict of desires is extremely difficult to navigate and perhaps contributes to the perpetual anxiety of people (especially young people) in the United States (more on anxiety in chap. 5).

25. Bauman, *Culture in a Liquid Modern World*, 20.

A third issue that the dominant cultural narrative suffers from is its idealization of personal preference based on desire (alone). The story neglects that there is something better than merely the ability to do whatever you want—namely, the ability to choose something meaningful. Having choices only matters if some choices are more significant than others.[26] For example, if you walk into my office and I show you a table with a bunch of bananas on it, but all the bananas are exactly the same, my saying "Choose any banana you like" would be puzzling to you. Yes, you could pick any banana, but you would also recognize that the decision actually does not matter. Having the personal choice to select a banana would be insignificant. Similarly, if life's meaning and self-fulfillment are found through a series of choices between tons of the same thing, life seems pointless. Fortunately, life is made up of all types of choices, and some of those choices are *more significant* than others. Our horizons of significance are always *social*. Consequently, we need more than individual desire for happiness in order to choose well. Together, relationships, reason, and emotion help human beings engage in moral reasoning, which includes conversation that helps with decision-making and consideration of long-term consequences for actions as well as alternative actions,[27] not to mention the problems of moral relativism that follow from equating being true to yourself with satisfying your desires. What if what makes you happy and therefore what you want ("doing you") is bad for you or for other people? Americans love to say that everyone should be free to live their life in any way they choose, *as long as* it does not hurt anyone else. This presents two problems. The moment we say "as long as," we are actually saying we do not think people should be able to do whatever they want. Also, human beings have different ideas of what "hurt" means.

A fourth concern stems from what people are being rewarded for in this story—namely, living without regard for demands emanating from ties with others.[28] In this story, any negative effects of your convictions, choices, actions, and feelings on the environment, on political and social systems, and on other people are negligible. Similarly, the story presents self-love and neighbor love as mutually exclusive options, implying that we have to choose one or the other.[29]

26. Taylor, *Ethics of Authenticity*, 39.

27. Haidt, *Happiness Hypothesis*, 16, 18. Sometimes these "conversations" are internal, but all decisions are influenced by our relationships with other people, whether we are cognizant of this or not.

28. It is important to note that there are versions of moral relativism and the "narrative of authenticity" that do not necessarily devolve into moral nihilism.

29. "The ironic truth is that the conceptual resources of expressive individualism are able to sustain neither genuine self-love nor neighbor love." Pope, "Expressive Individualism," 386.

But we do not need to choose between loving ourselves and loving other people (Matt. 22:36–40) when this love is centered on God.[30]

Fifth, under the conditions of this world (i.e., the pervasiveness of false life), we need to make money and buy or trade things to live. At the very least, we need basic things like shelter and food to survive. I want to distinguish the unavoidable consumptive character (even when intentionally limited) of life in this age from this story's subplot, which suggests that consumption and the amassing of material goods are critical for giving life meaning. This is not true. We are *given* meaning by God, just as we are *given* life by God. Meaning is not something we have to achieve and certainly is not dependent on what we accumulate. It is also problematic to tightly connect the accumulation of material goods with happiness as the two are not always compatible, and attachment to material goods can actually make you less happy.[31] Moreover, when we consume without concern for who it affects, and when our consumption has no boundaries, it contributes to dehumanization, exploitation, violence, poverty, and suffering.

Sixth, happiness is a good feeling, but the entire spectrum of human emotions, including sorrow and even righteous anger, is integrally connected to embracing what it means to be fully human given the world's imperfect and fallen state.

Finally, this story also presents a troubling horizon. While living this story, you might wonder how to know when you have enough: enough self-expression to be considered authentic, enough options, enough money, enough consumption, enough material goods and access to cultural goods, enough happiness. Unfortunately, the story cannot answer that question. It is a story without an ending.[32]

---

30. Thomas Aquinas, *Summa Theologiae* II-II.25.4c. A strong line of Protestant thinkers believe you ought not to love yourself because loving oneself is incompatible with truly loving others. Nicholas Wolterstorff refers to this Protestant view as "benevolence-agapism" in *Justice in Love*, 37. However, it depends on how one defines self-love. Wolterstorff helpfully distinguishes between "self-love" and "advantage-love," which "consists of desiring that something come about because, so one believes, it would be to one's advantage, would enhance one's own good" (39). I am defining self-love as valuing who you are, your personhood, in light of God's love for you.

31. Muñiz-Velázquez, Gomez-Baya, and Lopez-Casquete write, "Excessive attachment to material goods is not only far from happiness, but close to depression" ("Implicit and Explicit Assessment of Materialism," 131). Cf. Wang et al., "Will Materialism Lead to Happiness?"; DeLeire and Kalil, "Does Consumption Buy Happiness?"; Polak and McCullough, "Is Gratitude an Alternative?"

32. We discover that the lack of ending is actually on purpose. You are never supposed to stop consuming or pursuing happiness; the idea is that you can never have enough of either. Miller explains that "consumer desire is not focused on particular objects but is instead stretched out across an endless series of potential objects. Seduction spurs consumption by prolonging desire

Always On: New Media and Cultural Stories

Regrettably, much of new media has been developed in light of this main story, its subplot, and its heroes and sheroes. Given that our culture at large values authentic self-expression, being happy, and making money, with the ultimate aim of ever-increasing personal preference–based choices, it should come as no surprise that new media designers and developers do their work with these values in mind. Indeed, new media has not only adopted this narrative but has added malformed convictions to it.

Getting Your Attention

New media is designed so that you will desire to be *always on*.[33] New media developers need you to want to always be connected to a device. Sean Parker, the founding president of Facebook, recently provided insight into the types of questions Facebook designers asked when building the platform. This included questions like, "How do we consume as much of your time and conscious attention as possible?"[34] It is vital to recognize that social media sites are designed to get and sustain your attention. In order to get your attention, social media platforms provide opportunities for you to engage in practices embedded with the values of the main story, values most of us have adopted. For example, social media sites give you opportunities to express yourself, make choices based on your personal preferences and feelings, and share your stories, especially remarkable experiences that display how happy you are. The first thing you do on a social media site is create a profile. Your identity online is self-defined. After creating a profile, you have the freedom to view, post, share, or respond to anything you desire and feel drawn to. You only have to reveal the feelings, interests, opinions, ideas, values, and beliefs that you want other people to associate you with. Participating on social media sites directly involves self-expression, so new media is branded as the ultimate conduit for you to share who you are and "do you," in the way you prefer, with anyone you choose.

When you create a social media profile you engage in a series of activities (depending on the platform), like choosing a photo or an avatar and

---

and channeling its inevitable disappointments into further desires" (*Consuming Religion*, 109). Graham Ward discusses endless desire in *Cities of God*, 52–78. See Hartmut Rosa's discussion of "dynamic stabilization" in *Social Acceleration*, where he argues that modern society requires growth, innovation, and acceleration in order to maintain the status quo.

33. Campbell and Garner use the phrase "always on" to discuss aspects and implications of constant contact in a new media culture. "Constant Contact" is a section within their description of the conditions of life in a network society. Campbell and Garner, *Networked Theology*, 54.

34. Allen, "'Exploiting' Human Psychology" and "'God Only Knows.'"

summarizing your passions, work life, and education. Thus, your value of personal preference–based choices is nurtured in new media's design as well. However, all of these choices are within a set of bounded choices that have been set up by the developers of new media. You can watch what you want *from a particular list*. You can post what you want *within certain boundaries of the platform*. You can choose your profile picture, but it goes *in this particular place on the page and has these dimensions*. So really, as in all of life, your personal preferences within a restricted scope are being managed by someone with more money and power than you. The choices online are endless. Display any photo you like. Post what you want. Watch what you desire. Friend and follow whomever you prefer.[35] If you become unhappy with your photo, change it. If you feel like what you posted or replied is not good, edit or remove it. If you do not want to be friends with someone anymore, delete them. Don't want to see someone's posts? Block them. In fact, changing the settings on your social media account is called "changing your preferences."

Not only do social media sites allow you to present who you are in whatever way you desire; they allow you to tell your stories—that is, the stories that you want to tell. On the world's most used platform, Facebook, a person's profile includes a timeline. Facebook's reformatting of users' profiles according to a "timeline" format in 2011 shifted "Facebook's content from a *database* structure into a *narrative* structure."[36] The narrative structure of Facebook "gives each member page the look and feel of a magazine—a slick publication, with you as the protagonist."[37] On Snapchat, currently one of the most popular social media sites for teenagers and young adults, you are invited to compile your videos and photos into a story, which is designed to tell your friends what you have been doing for the last twenty-four hours. Other platforms also integrate "stories" as well, icons you can click that provide short videos or images with words that tell you what other people have been doing recently. Given that human beings make sense of their experiences and make meaning of their lives by telling stories, these storytelling abilities on social media are important to people and encourage them to participate online.

Your values of authentic self-expression, personal preference, and storytelling are related to your participation in other cultural activities, like making art

35. Jaron Lanier discusses the ways social media platforms (by design) reduce personhood in *You Are Not a Gadget*, 1–45.
36. Van Dijck, *Culture of Connectivity*, 54 (emphasis original).
37. Van Dijck, *Culture of Connectivity*, 55.

and civic engagement, which have also become online activities. Henry Jenkins coined the term "participatory culture" in his first book, *Textual Poachers: Television Fans and Participatory Culture*.[38] While Jenkins recognizes that "participatory culture is not new—it has, in fact, multiple histories," his work explores the ways new media impacts participation—how and why people participate.[39] Jenkins and his collaborators provide the following list of the qualities of new media participatory culture:

- relatively low barriers to artistic expression and civic engagement
- strong support for creating and sharing creations with others
- some type of informal mentorship whereby what is known by the most experienced is passed along to novices
- members who believe that their contributions matter
- members who feel some degree of social connection with one another (at the least, they care what other people think about what they have created)[40]

As you reflect on the elements of participatory culture, you will notice that new media affords important opportunities, which I will come back to: active and communal engagement, creating, sharing, mentorship, belonging, and relationship. Opportunities to engage in these types of activities are other values new media draws on to get your attention.

Holding Your Attention

New media does not just want to get your attention though; it also wants to hold it. And it does this in several ways. Social media is designed to nurture your human desire for affirmation. In order to hold your attention, developers of social media platforms like Facebook work with human psychology in mind. For example, developers at Facebook built the platform with "liking" and "commenting" capabilities in the belief that users would get a dopamine "hit" every time someone else liked or commented on the content they posted.[41] They assumed users would enjoy being on Facebook so much that they would want to keep contributing content to the site and would desire to be on the site more and more.[42]

38. Jenkins, *Textual Poachers*.
39. Jenkins, Ford, and Green, *Spreadable Media*, 297.
40. Jenkins et al., *Confronting the Challenges*, 5–6.
41. Dopamine is one of the brain chemicals responsible for positive affect.
42. Allen, "'God Only Knows.'"

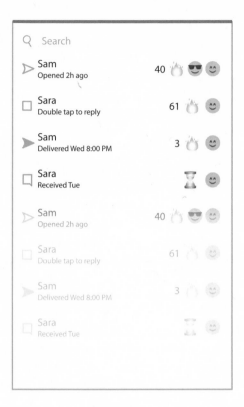

Similarly, Snapchat has what are known as "Snapstreaks" (see above). This is Snapchat's way of keeping users on their platform.[43] Snapstreaks occur when you and a friend have "snapped" (i.e., shared an image, video, message, etc.) each other within twenty-four hours for more than three consecutive days. A fire emoji appears next to your friend's name on your account when you have a Snapstreak going, and an emptying hourglass emoji appears if the streak is about to end. Ending a Snapstreak is supposed to give you the unpleasant sense that you are failing to connect with your friend, and since you are a relational creature who wants to feel connected to other people, you keep on snapping other people in order to feel associated with them.[44] In short, designers of social media platforms hope that you will find getting online so rewarding that you will be unable to resist coming back for more—more dopamine and more connection.

Meanwhile, as we keep getting online, social media sites are reshaping the nature of affirmation, recognition, and friendship. Affirmation and recognition

43. Shamsian, "Teens Are Obsessed."

44. I am analyzing platforms that are currently popular, but as new platforms are created, Christian communities can reflect on how they are designed as well.

are becoming associated with buttons that count clicks, and friendship is being represented by a fire emoji. Upon reflection, you could come up with historical examples of affirmation and recognition being quantified and of love and friendship being represented by signs. For example, in the recent past it was common for best friends to wear necklaces that each had half of a heart to represent their deep friendship. However, fire emojis on Snapchat have a much larger potential audience than a necklace. And as I said in chapter 2, new media hybrid living has marked differences from the past because of how often new media is being used (daily and for most people constantly), the quantity of modes of media people engage with (many more), and how quickly new media spreads information (much faster).[45]

New media also keeps you engaged with its pace. There are constant updates. Your newsfeed always looks different. What is trending is constantly changing. Unless you choose to turn off notifications (a good idea by the way), social media platforms relentlessly notify you of what's new: new posts, new replies, new likes, new shares, new messages, new stories, new news stories, new friend requests, new followers. Your streaming software even emails you when new shows or seasons of previously watched shows are available. Whether you turn off notifications or not, every time you get online or check your phone or email or turn on your streaming software, there are new things to view and to know, and new people to connect with.

New media is also built to give you access to more—more data and visuals—with simple clicks. Hypertext takes you between pages effortlessly, making it easy to stay online and keep clicking, reading, and watching. You may be able to remember a time when you got online merely to check the weather and ended up reading multiple news stories and watching several videos. Social media platforms have other embedded values that support the rapid pace of new media. For instance, Twitter values brevity. Posts ("tweets") must be 280 characters or less, which is about two or three sentences. This means you can read a lot of tweets quickly. Instagram, however, values expression through aesthetically pleasing images, and your brain can process images faster than it processes text. Users are encouraged to articulate who they are, communicate emotions, and share their experiences through photos or videos.

Constant updating, hypertext, brevity, and formats for faster processing have at least one thing in common: speed, which affects you in several ways. First, it influences what you value. Peter Horsfield explains that "speed in

45. This is part of the important work Christian communities need to engage in together—that is, thinking about how the hybrid new media landscape is changing the nature of affirmation, recognition, and friendship and what this has to do with Christian faith.

particular has become an important social value . . . ; cultural perceptions of time are changing from time as something ordered and following its own duration, to time as something immediate, fluid, and fast."[46] The social value for speed is felt during communication. When someone posts something to you online or texts or emails you, there is an underlying pressure to respond quickly. Likewise, appreciation and even expectation for speed is showing up in other cultural practices like cooking, eating, working out, and shopping. We like meals that can be made in under twenty minutes, fast food, quick workouts, and online shopping that will get us our items in two days or less, right on our front porch. In a culture that prefers a fast pace, what happens when something meaningful (e.g., spiritual direction) requires reflection, slowness, thorough description, and rest? Americans are forced to either transform the meaningful thing to assume the value of speed (e.g., church services in sixty minutes or less) or run the risk of the meaningful thing falling by the wayside and not being valued because it lacks speed. Additionally, the pace of media gives you the sense that if you are not in constant contact with your work, friends, family, or the news, you will miss something important. There is an acronym for this new media phenomenon: FOMO, or "fear of missing out." And while FOMO is affecting adults, it is having an even more dramatic impact on young people.

CNN's Anderson Cooper collaborated with child clinical psychologist Marion Underwood and sociologist Robert Faris to conduct a study of how thirteen-year-olds use social media and how involvement with social media relates to their social psychological adjustment.[47] The study included 216 eighth graders from six different states. These thirteen-year-olds completed an online survey and then enrolled with Smarsh, an online archiving service, which stored all their communications on Instagram, Twitter, and Facebook from September 2014 through April 2015 in a secure online archive. The study examined many aspects of teens' use of social media, one being compulsive checking of social media accounts. One of the chief complaints from adults about young people is that they are online too much and are always staring at their phones. Faris offers reasons why, explaining, "There's a lot of anxiety about what's going on online, when [youth] are not actually online, so that leads to compulsive checking."[48] This study found that compulsive checking can be attributed to a felt need by teens to monitor their own popularity status and defend themselves against those who challenge it. In fact, 61% of teens

46. Horsfield, *From Jesus to the Internet*, 265.
47. See the special report, "#Being Thirteen."
48. Hadad, "Why Some 13-Year-Olds."

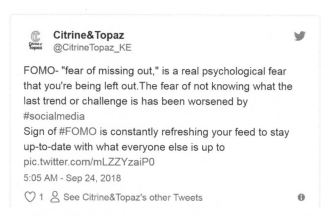

Citrine&Topaz
@CitrineTopaz_KE

FOMO- "fear of missing out," is a real psychological fear
that you're being left out. The fear of not knowing what the
last trend or challenge is has been worsened by
#socialmedia
Sign of #FOMO is constantly refreshing your feed to stay
up-to-date with what everyone else is up to
pic.twitter.com/mLZZYzaiP0
5:05 AM - Sep 24, 2018

♡ 1   See Citrine&Topaz's other Tweets

in the study said they wanted to see if their online posts are getting likes and comments; 36% said they often check social media to see if their friends are doing things without them; 22% wanted to use social media to see how well liked they are; and 21% said they wanted to make sure no one was saying mean things about them online.[49]

Unfortunately, new media does not just nurture the fear of missing out— missing out on connecting with other people, missing what is happening in the world, missing episodes of your favorite shows, missing what other people are doing without you, and missing what people are saying about you—it also cultivates the fear of not being seen. This is a legitimate fear because the less you are online, the less you are seen by your friends, not just because you are posting less but because of how social media platforms are *designed*. If you limit your engagement with social media, you actually decrease the likelihood of people seeing you, liking you, replying to you, and thus affirming you and connecting with you even when you do post. This is because social media platforms use algorithms to do two important things: (1) learn what you like in order to keep showing you what you like and (2) display the most liked, shared, and retweeted posts or videos first.[50]

First, when you like someone's post, and especially when you comment on a post, social media is configured to make sure you see that person's posts again. Social media imagines you prefer this person. Similarly, on streaming software or a site like YouTube, when you enjoy watching something, you are offered a list of other similar things to view. New media assumes that you

49. Underwood and Faris, "#Being Thirteen," 4. For the study's demographics, see p. 3. It is worth noting that the number one reason given for compulsive checking was boredom (80%), and the number two reason was the desire to connect with friends (71%).
50. Lua, "Decoding the Facebook Algorithm."

want to keep seeing what you "like" and reply to. Not only does this mean people only see things that reinforce what they enjoy and believe; it can have negative consequences for self-esteem. If your posts are not liked and replied to enough, the likelihood of your posts being shown to your friends goes down. The less you show up on people's newsfeeds, the less they will have the opportunity to like your posts and reply to you. It is a vicious cycle. To be seen and liked online, you need to regularly be online liking and replying and posting.

Similarly, social media displays the most liked, shared, and retweeted posts or videos first. If you are first or near the top of others' newsfeeds, even more people will be given the opportunity to see your post, like it, and comment on it. In short, always being on that particular platform translates to a higher likelihood of being seen and affirmed. Therefore, it is easy to excessively use new media and hard to let go of the desire to be always on, which, as we will see in chapter 5, is linked to increased mental distress.

New media holds your attention by offering short-term satisfaction of your desires for affirmation, happiness, and connection, as well as by cultivating fear. Combine this with the brain's habit-formation tendencies and, voilà, billions of people are on social media every day.

Making Money Off Your Attention

There is a primary reason social media designers and developers want you to value always being on: they want to make money. Have you noticed that when you search for something—a material good like shoes or a service like a massage—it often shows up in an advertisement on every other site you visit for the next few days? Google uses what you search for to target advertisements to you. Facebook tracks "loyal users as well as logged-off users and nonmembers by inserting cookies in your browsers. These cookies record the time and date you visit a website with a Like button or a Facebook plug-in, in addition to IP addresses,"[51] and are then used to market goods and services to you. Even if you are someone who only clicks "like" (rather than writing status updates, sharing content, posting photos, or searching for goods and services online), your likes express aspects of who you are—your personality and character traits—and are used to sell you goods and services. By monitoring the websites you visit and your likes, sites like Google, Facebook, Amazon, YouTube, and Instagram try to accurately predict who you are (age, gender, education level, location, etc.) and what you want, so that they can advertise

51. Van Dijck, *Culture of Connectivity*, 53.

things to you that you will be interested in purchasing; this is called targeted advertising.[52] For example, Apply Magic Sauce is a predictive technology that claims to accurately determine psychological traits simply by reviewing your likes on your profile.[53] Apply Magic Sauce is supposed to be able to predict, with a high rate of accuracy, your gender, relationship status, extroversion or introversion, whether you are spontaneous or organized, and whether your parents are married or divorced.[54]

This information is compelling to companies that are trying to sell products. Specifically, companies like Facebook will market their products to targeted audiences who are most likely to purchase what they are selling. This is why Facebook makes most of its money, billions of dollars, through digital ads.[55] Many social media sites have evolved "from nonprofit, collectively owned, user-centered organizations to for-profit, corporate owner-centered enterprises."[56] Digital newspapers, streamed TV shows, digital music channels, and social media platforms all aim to make money by advertising.

Developers of new media and mass media believe, first and foremost, that *you are a consumer*. And they want you to believe it too. In addition to satisfying your desire to be liked, social media sites are designed to fulfill your desire to consume—more information, more sensational stories, more humor, more material goods, more music, more videos, and more gossip. New media is often telling you to believe something else too: *you do not have enough*. Scarcity is the basis of the market and trade.[57] Scarcity highlights dissatisfaction, encourages detachment and pleasure in the *pursuit* of objects rather than in the objects themselves, and assumes that what I own is *mine* not *ours*. Scarcity discourages sharing while establishing that no one ever has enough. In order for the marketplace to do well, you need to be convinced of your lack. Indeed, every day you will be encouraged to believe with every click that what you have is inadequate. You will see banners and images and GIFs and videos, all trying to convince you that you need more.

Social media is constantly educating your desires and telling you what is worth wanting, pursuing, and loving. Jenkins and his coauthors explain: "Increasingly, content comes to us already branded, already shaped through an economics of sponsorship, if not overt advertising. . . . Commercial interests even shape the order of listings on search engines in ways that are

52. Van Dijck, *Culture of Connectivity*, 19.
53. "You."
54. Goodfellow, "How Your Facebook 'Likes.'"
55. Sharma, "How Does Facebook Make Money?"
56. Van Dijck, *Culture of Connectivity*, 36.
57. Cavanaugh, *Being Consumed*, 90–91.

often invisible to those who use them."[58] In case you cannot be convinced that you do not have enough, the market will do its best through new media engagement to make you believe that *what you have is not good enough*. Sure, you have clothes, beauty products, furniture, decorations, devices, sports equipment, but you know what? It could all be *better*. We throw away stuff that is perfectly useful simply because we have been made to perceive that what we have is old and so we need to get to new stuff. In fact, 99% of the stuff created in the "materials economy" is no longer used after just six months.[59]

Buying things online shapes you in other ways too. Like most in-person shopping experiences, online shopping distances you from the people who make the goods you are purchasing. You do not see where goods are made or the work that went into making them or the sacrifice of the people who made them. This means we often lack appreciation for the goods we buy, which also contributes to reasons Americans easily discard and replace goods. Too often, when we purchase online, as with in-person purchases, we don't realize that the goods were made without care for the environment or for the people creating and packaging them. For example, we can buy shoes online that were made in a factory in a developing nation by someone who works fourteen-hour days for little money and no access to a bathroom, and we never even know it. (This is mostly because we do not care where what we buy is made or how it is made. We just want it, preferably *now*.)

Spending is easier online than posting a status update on Facebook. You can buy shoes with a few clicks. You do not even have to get off your couch. Perhaps this is one of the reasons Americans' total credit card debt continues to increase and presently totals an estimated $905 billion.[60] In an online survey of over two thousand people, the number one reason people gave for credit card debt was purchasing things they did not need with money they did not have.[61] Meanwhile, every second, Amazon makes $1,084 and Google makes $929.[62] Because shopping in stores requires physically loading a cart, we are able to feel and see in a visually compelling way just how much we have gathered and how much we are buying. It is more difficult to see and thus feel the effects of how much we are buying online because webpages are

58. Jenkins et al., *Confronting the Challenges*, 23.
59. "Story of Stuff."
60. El Issa, "American Household Credit Card Debt." Since the 1970s, there have been other macroeconomic structural shifts, like stagnating wages and rising health care costs, that contribute to credit card debt.
61. El Issa, "American Household Credit Card Debt."
62. Dunlop, "20 Websites."

flat and because we do not hand over cash or a credit card, which means it is even easier to purchase more and more goods.

New media developers do not only want to make money off advertising; they want to make money by inspiring *you* to make money online too. On social media platforms, your social interactions and cultural activities can be packaged and sold as commercial products.[63] For example, friending, posting, and replying on Facebook can help you build a network of people who will purchase the makeup you sell. While liking friends' posts and following people's lives on Pinterest or Instagram, you can also promote products to make money. You can create videos and upload them to YouTube. If you get enough people following your YouTube channel, you can sell video advertisements that are shown before your videos play. You can blog to earn an income. Top-earning bloggers make anywhere from $9,000 to over $14 million per month.[64] However, the top earners on social media are not individuals like you and me. They are the Mark Zuckerbergs (cofounder of Facebook) of the world. Zuckerberg's net worth is over $74 billion.[65]

Changing Your Beliefs, Desires, and Practices

New media has not only adopted the convictions of our culture's main story and subplot; it has added malformed convictions to the story. New media associates authentic self-expression and pursuit of your desires online with accumulating attention and accruing social capital.[66] As you engage with new media, creating an exhibit of yourself and expressing yourself through posting, liking, replying, tweeting, pinning, and so forth, other people have an opportunity to recognize and validate your self-expression. People can choose to respond to your online self-presentation by liking your posts, clicking emojis, writing a reply, or sharing your content. Friends and followers can supply positive feedback to what you do and say online. On the other hand, friends

63. Horsfield, *From Jesus to the Internet*, 263.
64. Adams, "10 Wildly-Successful Blogs."
65. "Forbes Profile: Mark Zuckerberg."
66. Van Dijck explains that "a platform is a *mediator* rather than an intermediary: it shapes the performance of social acts instead of merely facilitating them" (*Culture of Connectivity*, 29, emphasis original). In order to use a platform, people must use online protocols that "provide a set of instructions that users are forced to obey if they want to partake in the mediated flow of interaction." These protocols are hidden "behind invisible or visible *interfaces*" (31, emphasis original). Platform owners control these interfaces, which are defined, at least in part, by their default settings, and so these interfaces have a profound influence on norms, social culture, and expectations on each platform.

and followers can also respond negatively to your online self-expression by replying with harsh words, arguing with you, or choosing not to respond at all. People can ignore your posts, decide not to view your snaps, refuse your friend requests, or even block you as a follower.

Social media sites numerically keep track of the attention you have received online and thus encourage you to assess the success of your online self-expression by monitoring and reflecting on numbers: the number of friends or followers you have, the number of likes or other types of replies you have acquired, the number of snaps that you have sent and received, the number of times your video has been viewed, the number of total engagements with your pins, the number of retweets, the number of times your content has been shared, and so on. Given that these numbers are always on display, it is difficult to ignore them.[67] Social media not only deepens your desire for attention but also *quantifies* the attention you receive.[68] Attention online is not elusive; rather, it is conclusive. There is evidence. You know exactly how much (or how little) you are friended, followed, liked, retweeted, shared, and trending. And so does everyone else.

When people respond to you online, an audience is watching. Others can see the numbers just as well as you can. Shares, likes, replies, friends, and followers: all your tallies are visible. And on Snapchat, other people can view your Snapchat score, the number of snaps you have sent and received. In person, there are usually only a few people who see how your self-presentation is received and then responded to, unless you perform in front of large audiences on a regular basis. But online, people can always see whether you are being recognized, how much, and how good or bad the recognition is. Additionally, your online actions become exhibitions. If you say something embarrassing in person, it generally cannot be accessed again (apart from human memory). If you say something embarrassing online, it is immediately on display and is viewable for longer than in-person actions. Worst-case scenario: other people may be able to access it forever, even if you delete it.

There is more. In this new media milieu, the word "network" typically describes a connected group of computers, mobile phones, or people. Increasingly, it refers to people using computers and mobile phones to network with each other. Networks consist of relationships and groups of relationships with

67. There are loads of advice articles about how to get more likes, comments, and shares on social media. For example, one article I found provides twenty-six tips for more Facebook engagement, including ideas like posting an appealing photo with a question and creating a post that will make an emotional connection with the audience. Cromwell, "26 Tips."

68. Ryan McAnnally-Linz discusses quantitative recognition in his dissertation, "Unrecognizable Glory," 154–55.

no clear starting place or gatekeeper.[69] The term "networked individualism" describes the nature of these networks of people. "In generations past, people usually had small, tight social networks—in rural areas or urban villages— where a few important family members, close friends, neighbors, leaders and community groups (churches and the like) constituted the safety net and support system for individuals."[70] Since the 1950s, people instead "have become increasingly networked as individuals, rather than embedded in groups. In the world of networked individuals, it is the person who is the focus: not the family, not the work unit, not the neighborhood, and not the social group."[71] Networks are characterized by "needs and preference" and thus change over time.[72] Individuals are "oriented around looser, more fragmented networks that provide succor," and they have "been powerfully advanced by the widespread use of the internet and mobile phones."[73] These newer social networks are more diverse and far-reaching, which provides some new opportunities, but means they are also less tight-knit.[74]

The reality of networked individualism requires people to network for multiple reasons, a major one being to solve problems. Solving problems through networking necessitates remembering things, like which members of your network are useful for what sorts of things, and maintaining relationships with people both near and far, as well as actively forging useful alliances within your network.[75] Networking, as the word implies, requires *work* and is especially difficult in the midst of difficult circumstances. In order to cultivate a network (so you have people to connect with, help you, and meet your needs), you need social capital.[76] Social capital is key to getting information, a job, advice, mentorship—in short, it is the key to survival in contemporary

69. Campbell and Garner, *Networked Theology*, 5. On the concept of "network," see their discussion on pp. 3–10.

70. Rainie and Wellman, *Networked*, 8. When working at their best, these groups nurtured safety and support for privileged individuals.

71. Rainie and Wellman, *Networked*, 6. Campbell and Garner explain: "Beginning in the 1950's, sociologists began to document changes in the nature of community. . . . Modern society, instead of being made up of homogenous, small-scale relationship networks defined by geographical and familial relations, was marked by fluid boundaries, changing interactions, and diverse, large-scale associations based on needs" (*Networked Theology*, 6–7). Campbell and Garner also write that these networks are "defined by commonality and select needs or interests" rather than by "familial, institutional, and other tightly bound relations." *Networked Theology*, 7.

72. Campbell and Gardner, *Networked Theology*, 7, 64.

73. Rainie and Wellman, *Networked*, 8.

74. Rainie and Wellman, *Networked*, 9, 11.

75. Rainie and Wellman, *Networked*, 9.

76. Rainie and Wellman, *Networked*, 56. While you are gaining social capital, owners of social media platforms are amassing *economic* capital.

culture. Social media platforms implicitly inspire you to not only accumulate attention but also accrue people. Of course, this is not called "collecting people"; it is called friending and following. When you consider that social media sites implicitly encourage you to turn your social interactions and cultural activities into products, nurture your desire for affirmation, cultivate your fear of not being seen, accumulate positive attention, consistently monitor the quantity of your attention, and collect social capital by networking, it makes sense that you would begin to think of yourself not just as a consumer but also as a *brand*.[77]

You Are a Brand

At the beginning of this chapter, I described an exercise I did with college students to discuss contemporary ideas of branding. I mentioned that after the exercise I reminded students that they are human beings, not brands. Even though they agreed with me, they still insisted that they *had* a brand and that it was their responsibility to thoughtfully create, monitor, and nurture it. The college students I have had the privilege of teaching are not unlike the college students Donna Freitas interviewed and surveyed, 79% of whom responded "yes" to the statement, "I'm aware that my name is a brand and I need to cultivate it carefully."[78] Freitas discovered that the college students she interviewed felt they were constantly being monitored and evaluated. Freitas explains:

> College students are acutely aware they have an image not only to protect but to *create*. Doing so is important because a vast potential audience is out there waiting—waiting to be entertained but also to pounce when they see something they don't like. . . . Most college students are highly aware of how to navigate the new public construction of self on social media, and many of them are incredibly savvy about negotiating exactly how they are seen by others. They worry about their image like celebrities and politicians with teams of handlers might.[79]

Like the students Freitas interviewed, when you post, like, and share online, it is natural to imagine the audience you are performing for and try to win over that audience.

77. To explore the development of the cultural phenomenon of personal branding, see McAnnally-Linz, "Unrecognizable Glory," 124–60. Personal branding did not begin because of social media. However, the internet, especially Web 2.0, provides resources that make personal branding possible, like access to an audience and new capabilities for marketing and making money.
78. Freitas, *Happiness Effect*, 80.
79. Freitas, *Happiness Effect*, 73 (emphasis original).

Social media creates the perfect conditions for branding because being online requires accepting that you have an audience, and participating online demands *curation*. For example, on some platforms you are given only a few characters under your profile picture to introduce yourself. The limited word count encourages you to make careful decisions. What aspects of yourself do you want to expose? What parts do you want to highlight?[80] You curate a set of facts and photos and experiences about yourself for other people to view, an act similar to that performed by a museum curator who chooses objects for an exhibit or a curate in a church who assists with the organization of the worship service. James Cohen and Paul Mihailidis explain: "The goal of a curator is to tell a story, or perhaps to create an environment that communicates a narrative. Curation is a skill that is utilized based on the specific material or media being organized."[81]

Curators tell stories by organizing objects or information in particular ways. Comparably, social media users reflect on life events, post feelings, snap photos, and pin objects in a particular order on specific sites to share their stories.[82] From a personal branding perspective, these curated online activities are not only related to storytelling though: they are commercials for who you are. Therefore, you will want to curate yourself online in ways that market your importance. Like a good brand, you should describe yourself and write storylines that support how you want your audience to perceive you. Why are you important? What sort of value do you add? Why are you unique? Other online activities, like tagging, signifying location, filtering, and editing, also help you curate your brand. You can tag certain people that you want your brand to be affiliated with, people who will raise the value of your brand. You can check in to locations and events that support the ways you describe yourself and the stories you tell. You can filter your photos and edit your videos to present yourself to your audience. Effective personal branding results in standing out and gaining lucrative public recognition through positive attention.[83]

If you want to have a popular personal brand online and positive attention, you will need good marketing strategies like this one: "The number

---

80. It is important to note that people also curate themselves offline and thus express different aspects of who they are in various settings, depending on who is present, the circumstances, and the environment's social norms. Offline, people also make choices about what to say to other people, what circumstances to react to and what emotions to show when reacting, and what aspects of their personality to exhibit. However, offline they have less control over how they are perceived.

81. Cohen and Mihailidis, "Conducting Research Utilizing Social Media," 89.

82. However, social media users are not the only curators of their online profiles. It is important to recognize that social media developers are sort of "second curators," comparable to a museum curator's manager who comes in after the curator has done their work and further rearranges the exhibit and directs people to pay attention to particular parts of the exhibition.

83. McAnnally-Linz, "Unrecognizable Glory," 131.

one characteristic of the most liked Instagram photos is their ability to relate to its audience. Ideally, your audience should want to involve itself in the life that you set forth in your photographs. The more that you can make an individual want to participate in your life, the more likeable your photos become."[84]

Relatability and likeability are what helps a brand receive value recognition, which is also integral to successful personal branding. Ryan McAnnally-Linz describes value recognition "as a qualification or modulation of the broader category of esteem. Unlike bare esteem, it builds in the conjunction of a positive assessment and its correspondence to something real. Esteem might be misplaced without ceasing to be genuine esteem."[85] Value recognition is often received for accomplishments, but it can also be ascribed to identities when an aspect of someone's personal identity (i.e., a characteristic) is seen as valuable or when someone's achievements are recognized as directly connected to who they are.[86]

If you want your personal brand to receive value recognition, you will need to project a valuable personal identity and advertise your accomplishments, but in a way that demonstrates you are being true to yourself.[87] To summarize, authentically expressing yourself by pursuing your desires online is connected to personal branding online, which involves accumulating remarkable experiences, positive attention, social capital, and value recognition. The aims of personal branding, like the aims of product branding, are marketing value, increasing value recognition, and acquiring success by making money and/or becoming well known, followed, and sought after. A person's practices should support these aims, and anything that does not support them is perceived as either subservient to these goals or "off brand."

Subliminal Messages

Social media sites often have well-intentioned ambitions, and many have meaningful mission statements. For example, Facebook's mission is to "give people

84. Donovan, "5 Things."
85. McAnnally-Linz, "Unrecognizable Glory," 114.
86. "Value recognition of identities occurs in at least two ways. First, the identities ascribed in identity recognition are regularly freighted with evaluations. . . . Second, the recognition of *accomplishments* can itself be a form of value recognition of identities when accomplishments are taken to express an identity." McAnnally-Linz, "Unrecognizable Glory," 114–15 (emphasis original).
87. "Personal branding reveals the ways in which the ideal of authenticity collapses the distinction between value recognition of accomplishments and value recognition of identities and illustrates the extent to which contemporary economies of recognition are imbricated with capitalist markets, labor and otherwise." McAnnally-Linz, "Unrecognizable Glory," 125.

the power to build community and bring the world closer together."[88] YouTube's mission states: "We believe that everyone deserves to have a voice, and that the world is a better place when we listen, share and build community through our stories."[89] The problem is that the designers of social media are often guided by less-praiseworthy aims, such as that of exploiting their sites' hold on people's attention in order to make money and, consequently, designing online platforms that, in their material architecture, fall short of the lofty principles upon which those sites were ostensibly founded.

New media is often designed to get your attention and hold your attention so that new media companies can make money off of your attention. When the ultimate aim is making money and there is little regard for what it takes to do so, new media developers not only spread malformed convictions, values, and practices but also create new media that contribute additional malformed convictions, values, and practices to humans' visions of the good life. An example is the belief that people *are* brands. The result of constantly using new media with little to no critical and theological reflection is the transformation of desires—namely, an obsession with excellent personal branding through accumulation of remarkable experiences, positive attention, social capital, and value recognition.

When you use new media, you are implicitly being told what is worth believing, doing, desiring, and feeling. As you engage with new media, its embedded values and practices are tacitly telling you: Of course you need to do whatever you want to feel happy; define yourself by telling everyone how successful you are; consume as much as possible; make money; accumulate attention and social capital; and be "on brand." All of these activities are connected and meaningful and they are the right actions for getting the good life. It is just the way things are in a new media landscape.

Given the amount of new media that we engage with and how often we are online, it is difficult not to buy into the convictions of the dominant narrative and subplot described in this chapter, and it is therefore equally difficult not to live toward the malformed vision this story nurtures. Christian communities should engage in discerning conversation about the ways the cultural stories, and new media developed in light of these stories, are shaping human beings. This requires interest in telling these stories and in talking with your community about the content of these stories. Christian communities need to be invested in exploring why the aims, convictions, practices, and values of these stories are different from those of Christian visions of true life. Unearthing the

88. "About," Facebook.
89. "YouTube: Our Brand Mission."

values and practices embedded in new media and discovering why new media is compelling, how it holds our attention, why it wants our attention, and how it changes our values and self-understanding is empowering. Interested conversation that empowers through discernment will assist Christian communities in articulating a counter-vision, a Christian vision for embodying the true life in a new media–saturated culture.

In view of malformed visions of human flourishing, like the one described in this chapter, new media is developed and used for damaging purposes, which only intensifies the false life: malign circumstances, harmful practices, and destructive feelings. You may be feeling overwhelmed by the content of this chapter and wondering what Christian communities can do in response to malformed visions of the good life. I believe the best way to counteract malformed visions is to *communicate a more compelling vision and live it well*. The next chapter imagines Jesus's life and ministry as a methodology for articulating Christian visions of true life.

interested conversation in practice

Discussion Questions

1. The main story in American culture is "Be true to yourself. You do you. Do what you want, whatever feels right to you. Be happy." Do you resonate with this story? Why or why not?
2. What does "you do you" mean?
3. In what ways do the convictions of this main story contradict Christian convictions?
4. The subplot suggests that what will give you significance, and thus what you *really* should desire and what will *really* make you happy, is making money and consuming. Do you feel like it is your duty to make money and consume? Why or why not?
5. How does social media get your attention, hold your attention, and make money off of your attention? How does this make you feel about using social media?
6. Do you believe you *are* a brand or you *have* a brand, or neither? Why or why not? What are possible implications of believing you *are* or even *have* a brand?
7. How might the aims of product branding—namely, marketing value, increasing value recognition, and acquiring success—defy the aims of Christianity?
8. Is there a way to maintain a personal brand that supports the aims of the gospel rather than the aims of product branding? If not, what do you do in a culture that insists on encouraging personal branding and reputation management?

four

online jesus

It is quite strange in a technologically advanced world to watch someone die and not be able to do anything about it. In tears, I sent the email above to my colleagues an hour after my dad passed away. I needed people to know and share in my pain. My colleagues are not aware of this, but I saved their beautiful responses to my email in a folder in my email account. I went back to their emails several times over the next few days as I was preparing for my dad's funeral. My friend and colleague Drew wrote, "There are no words. Even in my prayers for you I find it impossible to articulate what I'm asking of God. The only thing that comes close are tears. I am crying for you and with you." Even through email, Drew's words comforted me. We were unable to talk in person at that time; I needed to plan my dad's funeral and go to his house and choose some of his things to remember him by. I had no energy to talk on the phone anyway. I felt empty and at the end of myself. My colleagues' emails helped me sense God's presence and feel the compassion of Jesus during this difficult time. Emails can be powerful forms of communion.

It may be tempting to reflect on the malformed visions of the good life that have largely shaped our hybrid new media milieu and decide that new media design and use only contributes to profound brokenness. However, throughout this book I am arguing that our hybrid new media landscape also has glorious possibilities. Such possibilities are conceivable and achievable when new media design and use is shaped by Christian visions of flourishing life. Therefore, interested conversation includes *interest in articulating a Christian vision of the good life in a new media landscape*. To articulate such a vision, one must discern within a Christian community how a person formed in the image of God, which is Jesus Christ, would act and feel when using new media, and what kinds of new media circumstances Jesus would seek to create. This chapter provides a methodology for articulating Christian visions of true life by imagining Jesus's life and ministry.

For Christians, revelation about true life is offered through Jesus since "Jesus Christ—in his person, his life, and his mission—is both the embodiment of God's home among mortals and the promise of its full and universal realization."[1] All of the aspects of Jesus's life as recounted in Scripture—birth narrative, relationships, social and public interactions, sermons, parables, healings, death on a cross, and resurrection—are part of God's mission of presence, and all are acts of nesting, transforming and preparing the world, realizing its eternal intention to become God's home.[2] By considering how Jesus saw and related to others in the Gospel narratives, we can learn about Jesus's vision of flourishing life, specifically the sorts of circumstances that Jesus sought to nurture and the habits that he cultivated.

1. Volf and Croasmun, *Life of the World*, 75.
2. Nesting is the act of preparing a home for the arrival of a new child. "Human beings and the world come to fulfillment when they become in actuality what they have always been in intention: when God rules the world in such a way that God and the world are 'at home' with each other." Volf and Croasmun, *Life of the World*, 68.

I will demonstrate one way of articulating a Christian vision of true life for our new media milieu by reflecting on chapters 4 and 7 of the Gospel of Luke. In so doing, I will sketch the contours of a theology of truthful seeing and relating in the kingdom of God.

Jesus's Life and Ministry

As a Christian community attempts to get a basic understanding of hybrid living and the new media landscape (chap. 2) and to analyze cultural stories (chap. 3), members of the community must fix their eyes on Jesus (Heb. 12:2).[3] Christian communities attend to Jesus's enactment of God's relationship with the world and the world's relationship with God, an interactive, dynamic interconnection.[4] In Jesus, Christian communities glimpse what it looks like to share in God's love in actualized ways in the world.

Jesus's ministry is like a pair of glasses that we wear.[5] Members of Christian communities reflect on the accounts of Jesus's life and ministry to discern Christian norms. Jesus is the standard by which humans judge our participation in the kingdom of God. We read the rest of Scripture, our own lives, and our communal life together in view of how Jesus lived, with special attention to how Jesus listened and yielded to the Spirit. Jesus helps us to imagine what is possible. Parker Palmer explains, "Jesus is a paradigm, a model of this personal truth. In him, truth, once understood as abstract, principled, propositional, suddenly takes on a human face and a human frame. In Jesus, the disembodied 'word' takes flesh and walks among us. Jesus calls us to truth, but not in the form of creeds or theologies or world-views. His call to truth is a call to community—with him, with each other, with creation and its Creator."[6]

Jesus's life and ministry help nurture our imaginations to see the glorious possibilities of human relationships. As a Christian community examines Jesus's circumstances and the conditions he sought to create—which were material, social, political, and economic—and considers the ways he identified himself, used technology, interacted with other people and built his social

---

3. Kathryn Tanner explains that human beings "are the mirror of whatever it is upon which they gaze." Tanner, "In the Image," 123.

4. "The kingdom of God that Jesus proclaimed and enacted is a particular kind of *dynamic relation* between God and the world: it is 'the world-with-God' and 'God-with-the-world.'" Volf and Croasmun, *Life of the World*, 68.

5. Volf, "Theology for a Way of Life," 250–51. I especially appreciate Volf's attention to the way the story and life of Christ provide an external norm for Christian practice.

6. Palmer, *To Know*, 49.

network, and navigated social and power structures, the community discovers guiding norms.

True Seeing and Relating

Jesus's life was a complex whole, and its contents have been mediated to us by the writers of the Gospels and other books of the New Testament. Each Gospel writer emphasized different aspects of Jesus's life. I have chosen to focus on the Gospel of Luke—in particular, chapters 4 and 7—which significantly influences my articulation of a Christian vision of true life. I chose Luke 4 because it contains a summary of Jesus's vision for his ministry. This is one of the instances within the Gospels where Jesus explained what he would do and whom his ministry was for. Joel Green points out in his commentary on Luke that Jesus embodied his vision in three stories in chapter 7 (vv. 1–10, 11–17, 36–50).[7] Together, Luke 4 and 7 demonstrate how Jesus's vision—the conditions he sought to nurture because of his desires and beliefs—shaped his practices. Keeping in mind that new media activities involve larger themes of seeing and relating (chap. 2), Christian communities ought to reflect on the way Jesus's desires, beliefs, and practices coalesce in the Gospel narratives, together informing Jesus's distinct ways of seeing and relating.[8] Theological reflection about truthful seeing and relating can help Christian communities discern Christian norms for seeing and relating in a new media milieu.

Seeing and Relating to God

In Luke's Gospel, God is portrayed as an agent who is active in places and in people. In Luke 1, God favored Elizabeth and helped her become pregnant (v. 25). God sent the angel Gabriel to Mary in Nazareth to explain to Mary that God was with her. Gabriel explained to Mary that she was being honored by God and that the power of God would overshadow her. The Holy Spirit led Simeon to Jesus (2:27). A couple of chapters later, the Spirit led Jesus into the wilderness (4:1). As Jesus grew up, observers recognized that God's favor was on him (2:40, 52). Later in Luke, Jesus commanded an unclean spirit to

---

7. Green, *Gospel of Luke*, 281.

8. I contend that the Gospels are reliable sources for considering the historical and cultural context in which Jesus lived and for reflecting on the life and ministry of Jesus. When contemporary Christian communities consider the context in which Jesus lived and imagine the stories described in the Gospels, the Holy Spirit helps them discern and articulate normative visions of the good life that community members can, by the grace of God, live toward.

come out of a man and then told him to tell everyone what *God had done for him* (8:26–39). Throughout Luke's Gospel, Jesus is on the move—healing, reconciling, teaching in all sorts of places among many different types of people. The God of Luke's Gospel is a God who is out ahead of God's people and a God who is always up to something.[9] To rightly see God, according to Luke, is to recognize God's dynamic presence. One can interpret from Luke that God is also active in our hybrid lives.

The Gospel of Luke also helps readers to rightly see attributes of God. According to Zechariah, God has deep compassion (Luke 1:78), and from John the Baptist we learn that God forgives sin (3:3). In Luke 7, the tax collectors affirm God's justice. Furthermore, in Luke 11, Jesus talks to the disciples about God's generosity, telling them that God would give to them what they needed. Jesus embodied these attributes in the narratives described in Luke 7, which I will consider later in this chapter. To rightly see God is to see God's compassion, forgiveness, justice, and generosity.

Ultimately, Jesus saw God as a God of unconditional love. Jesus described God as the shepherd who leaves the ninety-nine to look for the one, as the woman who searches carefully and celebrates when what was lost is found, and as the compassionate father who runs to embrace his child (Luke 15). Through these stories, Jesus depicted God's love as relentless in the most beautiful way. Jesus explained to people gathered around him in Luke 15 that God rejoices over people who, once lost, are found and who, once dead, become alive. At the heart of Luke's Gospel is the invitation to readers to embrace the incredible revelation that God is love. Jesus's life and ministry demonstrates that once human beings truly see God's unconditional love, they understand that meaning and purpose is found in experiencing and sharing in God's love. One can imagine that in our new media milieu, Jesus's attention would continue to be focused on participating in God's unconditional love, as he was throughout Luke's Gospel narratives.

Seeing and Relating to Self

During the account of Jesus's baptism, readers learn that the Spirit came down on Jesus while he prayed, with a voice from heaven saying, "You are my Son, whom I dearly love; in you I find happiness" (Luke 3:22). God clearly told Jesus that he belonged, was loved, and was rejoiced over. Before his ministry started, Jesus's identity was well defined; he had a relationship with God, which is clear throughout the annunciation and infancy narratives (1:32–35;

9. Richard Osmer writes, "God is already out there in the world ahead of us." Osmer, *Teaching Ministry*, 212.

2:11).[10] Jesus recognized this relationship, and it shaped the way he saw himself and the way he lived. Jesus saw connections between God's love and his identity. It seems, then, that while using new media, Jesus would not feel the need to search for self-fulfillment or meaning by cultivating an excellent brand; rather, the source of his identity would be God's unchanging, unconditional, relentless love.

In Luke's account of Jesus's temptation, Jesus was filled with the Holy Spirit at his baptism and then led by the Spirit into the wilderness (4:1). Satan tested Jesus by poking at his status as Son of God (v. 3). Satan wanted Jesus to prove he was the Son of God by successfully turning stones into bread (v. 3). Henri Nouwen explains: "There are many other voices, voices that are loud, full of promises and very seductive. These voices say, 'Go out and prove that you are worth something.' . . . They want me to prove to myself and others that I am worth being loved, and they keep pushing me to do everything possible to gain acceptance. They deny loudly that love is a totally free gift."[11] Jesus did not deny God's love and did not give in to Satan's test because Jesus did not feel the need to perform for Satan. In the wilderness, Jesus demonstrated that those who comport themselves according to the principles of the true life recognize that they do not have to work either to be seen or to be recognized as valuable. Though Jesus found himself alone and being tempted, Jesus passed up Satan's offers of power and glory (vv. 5–8), as well as the opportunity to test God's love for him (vv. 9–12). Similarly, I can imagine that in a new media milieu, Jesus would not feel the need to prove his status or worthiness by promoting himself and posting about his remarkable experiences or his successes.

Human beings are seen and recognized as valuable by God, without any work necessary. Marcus Borg explains: "The path of transformation of which Jesus spoke leads from a life of requirements and measuring up (whether to culture or to God) to a life of relationship with God. It leads from a life of anxiety to a life of peace and trust. It leads from the bondage of self-preoccupation to the freedom of self-forgetfulness."[12] Self-forgetfulness is not rooted in self-hatred or self-neglect; rather, it is rooted in the understanding that God's love ensures that one does not need to seek or market one's value. The problem is that "in the complexity of life's journey, we all

10. God's declaration and anointing of the Spirit is a pivotal moment that "sets the course of [Jesus's] entire mission (cf. 4:1, 14, 18–19)" and "determines his understanding of his divine mission and empowers him to perform accordingly," as well as "anticipates the analogous empowering of Jesus's followers in Acts (e.g., Acts 1:8)." Green, *Gospel of Luke*, 186.

11. Nouwen, *Return of the Prodigal*, 40.

12. Borg, *Meeting Jesus Again*, 88.

begin to forget [especially in a new media landscape]. It grows harder and harder to remember our original identity in God. Many of us experience a crisis of meaning and hope that keeps us scrambling for external power, perks, and possessions, trying to fill the void."[13] I think we are so used to conditional love, conditional worthiness, and conditional relationships that it is hard for us to fathom, as Jesus did, the idea that we are unconditionally loved. The quest during hybrid living (as in any other context or time) is continual surrender, receptivity, and acceptance of this love, which could be summarized as *abiding in God's love.*

In the Gospel of Luke, Jesus's life provides an example of how to abide in God's love and continually see our identity and meaning in view of God's love. Jesus exhibited a regular practice of prayer. Instead of being "always on," the Gospels tell us that Jesus often disrupted his ministry tasks in order to go away and pray. Sometimes he did this alone. For example, Luke 5:16 tells readers that Jesus often withdrew "to deserted places for prayer." At one point in Luke's Gospel, Jesus prayed all night long (6:12). Other times, Jesus prayed with his community. Prayer and fasting were frequent practices for Jesus and his disciples (5:33).[14] In chapter 9, Luke describes how prayer transformed Jesus in front of the disciples. That Jesus took time to be alone and to pray even while engaged in a very public ministry is instructive: it suggests that in a hybrid new media landscape, being active in the public square (including social media sites) ought to be coupled with taking time away from crowds (and screens) to be alone with God, praying and fasting.

It is clear in Luke's Gospel that Jesus knew who he was and knew that he was invested in being true to his identity in God's love. Jesus was not interested in managing his reputation or accumulating positive attention and value recognition; rather, he was interested in doing what the Lord appointed him to do—the vision God anointed him for and the things the Spirit was leading him to do.

Seeing and Relating to Others

In the Gospel of Luke, Jesus had a vision for his ministry. In Luke 4:16–21, Jesus opened the scroll of Isaiah and stated that *the Lord had anointed him* for specific tasks: to preach good news to the poor, to proclaim release to the prisoners, to proclaim recovery of sight to the blind, and to liberate the oppressed. Throughout the rest of Luke's Gospel, readers discover that these tasks represent the sorts of circumstances Jesus sought to nurture during

13. Rohr, "Returning to Union."
14. To learn with your community about the Christian tradition of fasting and approaches to fasting, read Baab, *Fasting.*

his ministry: *compassion* for the poor, *forgiveness* and *relief* for imprisoned people, *vision* for the blind, and *freedom* for the oppressed.

Recognizing the people Jesus ministered to gives further context to his vision of the good life. It is important to understand *who* Jesus was inviting his listeners to see in Luke's description of his vision. By reading the rest of Luke's Gospel, it becomes clear that when Jesus addressed "the poor" (4:18), he was talking about people who could be labeled as poor for numerous reasons. Therefore, Jesus's good news was for those "poor" in social status, regardless of whether that social status was linked to their finances, education, gender, family heritage, vocation, or, as was often the case, some combination of these.[15] Jesus's good news did not merely speak to people's spiritual condition but "very much concerned the 'outer person' as well and the circumstances of human life: ordinary poverty, hunger, sickness, oppression, captivity, and so on (see Matt. 5:3–12; Luke 4:18–19; 6:20–26)."[16] According to Luke, Jesus did not just minister to the poor; rather, Jesus *was* poor.

Jesus was a poor Jewish man who had humble beginnings. Jesus was born and laid in a manger (Luke 2:7), an object used to feed animals. In Luke 2:24, Jesus's parents brought two pigeons as their sacrifice for ritual cleansing. Leviticus 5:7 teaches that people who cannot afford to bring an animal from their flock for ritual sacrifice should bring two doves or two pigeons instead.[17] Therefore, by describing what Jesus's parents brought to sacrifice, Luke further defines Jesus's low-income status. Likewise, Jesus was homeless (Luke 9:58) during his earthly ministry and had few material possessions. Jesus lived in solidarity and in community with the poor.[18] I can imagine that by seeing the poor, we see Jesus.

The prisoners Jesus refers to are people confined by personal sin as well as by political and economic systems and institutional visions that keep people poor.[19] The sort of release Jesus offered and invited followers to participate in is multifold: release in the form of forgiveness (Luke 5:24; 15:11–32); release from powers of evil (8:26–39; 19:45–46); and release from debt (4:19).[20] Leonardo Boff describes the kingdom of God as "all-embracing, proclaiming the deliverance of every human and cosmic reality from all sin."[21] Jesus's vision

15. Green, *Gospel of Luke*, 211.
16. Volf and Croasmun, *Life of the World*, 72.
17. Thurman, *Jesus and the Disinherited*, 17.
18. Christian, *God of the Empty-Handed*, 186.
19. For more about Jesus's love for people who are poor and about structural and institutional violence that keeps people poor, see Cone, *God of the Oppressed*; Gutiérrez, *Theology of Liberation*; and Myers, *Walking with the Poor*.
20. Green, *Gospel of Luke*, 211–12.
21. Boff, *When Theology Listens*, 2.

also specifically addressed the oppressed. The oppressed are those who live in fear because they lack economic, social, or political power, and so the poor are often those who are oppressed.[22] In short, Jesus's ministry is *for* and *to* the poor: the ignored, the marginalized, the hated, the incarcerated, and the powerless.

Jesus's Vision in a New Media Landscape

In light of Luke's description of Jesus's life and ministry, it is not hard to imagine that online Jesus would seek to cultivate conditions in our new media landscape that support people who are poor, imprisoned, and oppressed. Given that new media use helps people meet basic needs, have access to meaningful information (e.g., weather patterns, maps), apply to schools, find work and health care, participate in civic engagement, and have a voice in their community, I can picture Jesus advocating for all people to have access to technological resources and the internet, as well as the skills to use devices and participate online.

Jesus would also challenge ways new media design and use contributes to various forms of inequality, injustice, and hardship in people's lives. Jurgenson explains that the augmented reality of our hybrid existence "is one where the politics, structures and inequalities of the physical world are part of the very essence of the digital domain: a domain built by human beings with histories, standpoints, interests, morals and biases." It is critical to recognize that new media spaces are not neutral spaces where everyone has equality of access, ability, power, or representation, for instance. "Technology never removes humanity from itself, . . . never creates a space outside of fundamental social structures."[23] In view of Luke's depiction of Jesus's ministry in Luke 4, Jesus would address digital conditions that keep people poor and oppressed, recognizing the ways access to new media and characteristics of the digital domain contribute to new forms of poverty and oppression.

According to Luke, Jesus constantly talked about the kingdom of God. Jesus saw and related to God, himself, and others in view of this already-but-not-fully-realized true life. The dominant and all-encompassing sign of God's kingdom in Luke's Gospel is healing (10:9). Jesus saw that in the kingdom of God, true life is found by belonging to a healing community marked by compassion, forgiveness, relief, vision, and freedom. Jesus offered these gifts wherever he went. In other words, the circumstances Jesus sought to nurture— the alternative reality of the kingdom of God described in Luke 4—shaped the way he led his life, and specifically how he saw and related to others.

22. Thurman, *Jesus and the Disinherited*, 37–38.
23. Jurgenson, "Digital Dualism and the Fallacy of Web Objectivity."

Seeing Others

Jesus seemed to see in people what others failed to see, and he helped people to see themselves as God does. Jesus welcomed and ate with sinners and tax collectors (Luke 5:30), actions commonly viewed by his contemporaries as "unclean" and, for some, even appalling.

In Luke 7:36–50, Jesus ate with a self-righteous Pharisee, Simon, and a woman who was marginalized in her community. As an expert in the law, Simon was someone of high stature and holiness. During dinner, a woman of low social status courageously entered Simon's home. We do not know why. Perhaps it is because she had heard that Jesus was a friend to people like her. Her reasoning did not matter to Simon though. Everything about her being at that dinner was wrong.[24] She was an uninvited, "unclean sinner," and the actions she performed—touching and kissing Jesus's feet, letting down her hair, and then wiping his feet with her hair—were viewed as inappropriate by the dinner's host (and presumably by guests).[25] Simon said to himself, "If this man were a prophet, he would know what kind of woman is touching him. He would know that she is a sinner" (v. 39).

Simon judged not only this woman but also Jesus. Simon's inability to see this woman was related to his inability to see Jesus; the two were interconnected.[26] This woman was recognized as a sinner by others in her community. Although she held an expensive alabaster jar, she was poor, both in relationships and in possibilities.[27] Perhaps surprising Simon, Jesus replied by telling him a simple parable about two debtors: One owes less than the other, but they are both released from their debts. Jesus wanted to know who would love the lender more. Simon answered correctly that it was the debtor with the greatest debt. For Jesus, "much love follows much forgiveness."[28] What happens next is even more surprising: Jesus turned toward the woman but asked Simon, "Do you *see* this woman?" (v. 44).

By asking this question, Jesus suggested that Simon had not actually *seen* her. In Luke 4:18 Jesus stated that he had been sent to recover sight for the blind. Recovery of sight for the blind was both a literal part of Jesus's ministry (his was a ministry of physical healing) and "a metaphor for receiving revelation and experiencing salvation, and inclusion in God's family."[29] In Luke's

24. Green, *Gospel of Luke*, 309.
25. Green, *Gospel of Luke*, 310. Unlike Green, I do not think readers of Luke should assume she had a reputation as a prostitute.
26. Reid, "'Do You See This Woman?,'" 110.
27. Green, *Gospel of Luke*, 309.
28. Reid, "'Do You See This Woman?,'" 110.
29. Green, *Gospel of Luke*, 211.

Gospel, "'seeing' is related to the ability to perceive and respond properly to Jesus."[30] Note that the passage does not tell us how Simon responded. The text seemingly invites listeners to take up the challenge presented to Simon—namely, to see Jesus rightly and also to see as Jesus did, with forgiveness and extravagant love.[31] Jesus compared the woman's and Simon's versions of hospitality and explained how the woman "has shown great love." Conceivably, the text is also an invitation to respond to Jesus as this courageous woman did.[32]

Throughout the Gospel of Luke, Jesus is remembered for the sort of recognizing that is not related to standard worldly accomplishments. Instead, Jesus recognized things like faith (7:9, 50; 17:19; 18:42). Jesus embodied an alternative action to seeking positive attention and value recognition, demonstrating that Christian visions of true life invite us to focus on leading our lives well by instead *giving* positive attention and recognition.[33] I can imagine Jesus going online looking for people to recognize and affirm, helping people to see in themselves what he sees, recognizing the practice of faith in digital spaces. Likewise, Jesus would probably post status updates and replies that would tell important stories of people who are being excluded, and he would consistently ask, "Do you *see* this person, this group?" I can also envision Jesus advocating for design features of new media that encourage users to love and recognize one another rather than compete with one another.

Relating to Others

Jesus's sense of responsibility always went beyond his family and his friends. Jesus related to God's extravagant love by how he loved those whom society tried to implicitly and explicitly say he should not be associated with. For example, in Luke 7:1–10 a centurion's slave needed healing. Believing that Jesus could heal his slave, the centurion activated his social network—that is, members of the local Sanhedrin—and asked them to speak to Jesus on his behalf. Jesus was a Jew and the centurion was a gentile—and a representative of imperial Rome at that—so we know right away that they should not associate with each other. Green explains: "The principal issue of this account was raised with Jesus's sermon [Luke 6:35]: If love is to be extended even to

30. Reid, "'Do You See This Woman?,'" 106–7.
31. Reid, "'Do You See This Woman?,'" 112; Green, *Gospel of Luke*, 308.
32. The fact that this woman remains nameless in Luke's Gospel illustrates how women were viewed in ancient Palestine. Women were typically viewed as objects and seen as inferior to men.
33. McAnnally-Linz, "Unrecognizable Glory," 264–65.

enemies, are there any functional perimeters for the reach of Jesus's gracious ministry?"[34] In this story the answer was no. Jesus demonstrated that the scope of responsibility and generosity in Christian visions of true life is not limited to those we love but extends to those we may not like and perhaps even hate. Jesus did not draw "insider-outsider lines"; he saw his responsibility to both the centurion and the slave and related to them accordingly. After Jesus was asked to help, he was willing to enter the centurion's home and heal his slave. The centurion saw who Jesus was, humbled himself, and told Jesus, "Just say the word, and my servant will be healed" (Luke 7:7). I imagine online Jesus would embody this type of love, generosity, and healing in his mediated relating too, even with potential enemies.

A story about a widow and her dead son further teaches how Jesus's seeing and relating were connected to his participation in God's love (Luke 7:11–17). Jesus, surrounded by a great crowd, saw a woman, also in the midst of a crowd, mourning the death of her only son as his body was being carried out of the city. As readers, we should understand from Luke's description of the woman that she was vulnerable, lacking both substantive means of personal support as well as visual markers of social prominence within her community.[35] Luke describes how Jesus, when he saw this woman, immediately had compassion for her. This woman, "who epitomizes the 'poor' to whom Jesus has come to bring good news,"[36] became the focus of Jesus's compassion. This feeling of compassion moved Jesus to go toward her pain and to speak gentle words to her, even though they were both surrounded by people.

Jesus said, "Don't cry," and then touched the wooden plank that her son was lying on, thereby crossing a boundary of ritual purity.[37] Jesus was willing to touch the plank, something viewed as "unclean," and therefore be seen as unclean himself. In other words, Jesus did not just acknowledge her pain; he allowed her suffering to impact him and how others viewed him. Next, Jesus commanded the widow's dead son to rise. Her son sat up and spoke, and Jesus gave him to his mother. With each movement of the text—from seeing, to extending compassion, to speaking, to touching the stretcher, to healing—Jesus expressed a deeper form of concern for this woman. It is one thing to see pain; it is another to feel compassion for someone else's pain; and it is even a further step to get close to their pain and acknowledge it directly with words. And it is something entirely different *to lessen that pain* either by actually stopping it or by sharing in it.

34. Green, *Gospel of Luke*, 283.
35. Green, *Gospel of Luke*, 289.
36. Green, *Gospel of Luke*, 289–90.
37. Green, *Gospel of Luke*, 292.

When my colleagues acknowledged and shared in my pain following my dad's death, it felt as if Jesus himself was speaking to me through their emails. Their compassion mirrored the compassion of Jesus in Luke 7.

While some would argue that the internet is a place of distraction and avoidance, Vincent Miller insists that "it can take us closer to need and suffering in places where we could not easily be physically present" and "lift us from insulated spaces of privileged safety and place us in the midst of violence and atrocity."[38] I imagine Jesus would see social media sites in a way similar to Miller, who describes the internet as "moral space." Miller explains: "When space becomes a matter of choice, our decision about where to place our attention becomes a moral matter. Do we engage and attend to needs and opinions outside our comfort zone? Or do we allow this new power of choice to further insulate us from the world and responsibility?"[39] If Jesus were to see a crisis online or hear a story of suffering, he would attend to people's pain. He would do something meaningful and respond to any suffering he encountered online.

In Luke's description of Jesus's sermon in Luke 6, Jesus invited his disciples to lead their lives well by loving their enemies, being compassionate, and participating in God's forgiveness. Throughout Luke 7, we see Jesus practicing what he preached. We notice that he invested in a ministry of holistic healing— that is, one that healed not only people's bodies (vv. 21–22) but also how people were seen by their communities and themselves, as well as the broken relationships and circumstances in which people were entangled. In short, his was a ministry where others were invited to enter into Jesus's community of healing. Similarly, Jesus's "social network"—his disciples—was built to teach people about God's peace by bringing people healing (9:1–6; 10:1–12). Such is the home of God: It is a place where people do not have to strive to be seen or included or valued; a household with space for all; a community where people find belonging, wholeness, and relationship with God and others.

The Cross

The sort of seeing and relating that marked Jesus's ministry caused fear in people in authority, and they looked for a way to kill Jesus (Luke 22:2). The cross was a technology that was designed to subject people to indignity, humiliation, and shame.[40] It was a penalty for serious crimes committed

38. Miller, "Online."
39. Miller, "Online."
40. Hengel, *Crucifixion*, 24, 62.

against the state, serving as a "religious-political punishment, with the emphasis falling on the political side."[41] Crucifixions of this nature were meant to be a deterrent and to pacify rebelliousness in order to make sure people maintained the status quo. However, these are the sorts of barriers Jesus constantly crossed, the categories of people Jesus refused to abide by, and the types of laws Jesus consistently challenged.[42]

Jesus's death involved suffering, surrender, and love rather than redemptive violence: "The cross *breaks the cycle of violence.*"[43] Rohr explains that the cross "moves history from the persistent myth of redemptive violence to the divine plan of redemptive suffering."[44] Jesus told his disciples that he was going to suffer (Luke 22:15). However, it was not merely his suffering that overcame violence; rather, as Volf points out in *Exclusion and Embrace*, it was his *active opposition to oppression* (an act of great love) that gave meaning to his nonviolence.[45] Jürgen Moltmann clarifies, "The crucified God is in fact a stateless and classless God. But that does not mean that He is an unpolitical God. He is the God of the poor, the oppressed and the humiliated."[46] Jesus allowed himself to be arrested and prohibited his disciples from defending him (22:49–52). Jesus overcame evil with love. Jesus transformed the cross from a technology of violence to a technology of love.[47]

Jesus took the cross—a technology meant to shame—and did something new and unexpected with it. In *God of the Empty-Handed*, Jayakumar Christian writes, "The cross was Jesus's decisive criticism of the world's understanding of power. . . . The cross redefined the very concept of power and made powerlessness an authentic expression of power, albeit a strange form of power."[48] Jesus demonstrated how God's love "challenges the distorted values that have ruled the world."[49] Jesus's life and death invited self-transcendence and challenged the value of happiness and whether it is a good to be pursued. At the end of his life, Jesus was not with the thriving "brands"—he was not with popular religious people or with wealthy or powerful people. Jesus was

---

41. Hengel, *Crucifixion*, 46.
42. Hengel, *Crucifixion*, 47.
43. Volf, *Exclusion and Embrace*, 291.
44. Rohr, *Things Hidden*, 142.
45. Volf, *Exclusion and Embrace*, 293.
46. Moltmann, *Crucified God*, 329.
47. If you are wondering what transforming technologies of violence could look like in contemporary culture, consider the example of RAWtools, Inc., which takes its motivation from Isa. 2:4 and Mic. 4:3 ("They will beat their swords into iron plows and their spears into pruning tools") and physically transforms weapons into garden tools and other hand tools. Learn more about their work here: https://rawtools.org/about-us/.
48. Christian, *God of the Empty-Handed*, 182.
49. Christian, *God of the Empty-Handed*, 190.

with those who were forgotten, those who were deemed worthless and disposable because of their sin. Jesus's death reveals the gospel as radical love and forgiveness that liberates.

Malformed visions of the good life are focused on actions that make us feel happy and help us appear successful. However, for the sake of preparing the world to be God's home, we must be willing to embrace hardship and even to bear things in faithfulness that are contrary to feeling happy and appearing successful on social media—like practicing active opposition to oppression, telling the truth, suffering, and being unpopular, unfriended, humbled. Sometimes God's will and desire for us requires being uncomfortable and exposed, especially if, like Jesus, we challenge the status quo.

On the cross, Jesus was willing to forgive not only those to his right and left but also those who were crucifying him (Luke 23:34). In words worth quoting at length, Martin Luther King Jr. describes this forceful, beautiful combination of forgiveness, love, and nonviolence as the very essence of *agape* love:

> *Agape* is not a weak, passive love. It is love in action. *Agape* is love seeking to preserve and create community. It is insistence on community even when one seeks to break it. *Agape* is a willingness to sacrifice in the interest of mutuality. *Agape* is a willingness to go to any length to restore community. It doesn't stop at the first mile, but it goes the second mile to restore community. It is a willingness to forgive, not seven times, but seventy times seven to restore community. The cross is the eternal expression of the length to which God will go in order to restore broken community.[50]

The ways Jesus saw and related to God, himself, and others shaped his participation in the kingdom of God. Jesus's passion for the kingdom shaped what he desired and the way he lived, and it had implications for the emotions that marked his life.

Joy in the Holy Spirit

As Jesus lived toward the vision he felt called to in Luke's Gospel, Jesus experienced a range of human emotions.[51] Jesus admired the centurion's faith

50. King, *Stride toward Freedom*, 94.
51. I am grateful to my friend and colleague Sarah Farmer for encouraging me to consider the importance of human beings allowing themselves to feel a whole range of human emotions. Upon reflection, I recognized how Jesus embraced all types of emotions in Luke's Gospel.

(Luke 7:9). In Luke 12, Jesus is described as distressed (v. 50). And in chapter 19 Jesus wept over the city of Jerusalem (v. 41). Moments later, in righteous anger, Jesus threw out people who were selling things in the temple because it was to be a house of prayer and instead had become a hideout for crooks (vv. 45–46). In Luke 10, Jesus is described as overflowing with joy from the Holy Spirit (v. 21).

What may be surprising to readers of Luke is that joy is discussed quite often. When Elizabeth was greeted by Mary, pregnant with Jesus, Elizabeth told Mary that the baby in her own womb, John the Baptist, jumped for joy (1:44). Strangely, Jesus uses a similar phrase in his sermon on the plain: he encourages listeners to leap for joy when others hate, reject, insult, and condemn them (6:22–23). It appears Jesus's account of joy was that it can be an act of resistance against despair.[52] In Luke 10, the seventy-two returned joyously (v. 17). When Jesus described God's love in Luke 15 through parables, Jesus also discussed God's joy: the shepherd, the woman, and the father rejoiced and celebrated (vv. 7, 10, 32). Finally, after seeing Jesus ascend into heaven, the disciples returned to Jerusalem overwhelmed with joy (24:52). Joy is discussed throughout the book of Luke. Seemingly, living Christian visions of true life entails experiencing a range of human emotions, and in Luke's Gospel, there is particular emphasis on feeling joy. On reflection, it seems online Jesus would not be focused on feeling happy (i.e., pleasure or the absence of pain); rather, Jesus would concentrate on belonging to a healing community and on seeing and relating truthfully. The outcome of Jesus's pursuit of such flourishing life would be Jesus regularly feeling deep joy and choosing to rejoice.

Christian visions of the good life have implications for our actions, as well as the circumstances we pursue and the emotions that mark our lives. Paul described the kingdom as being about "righteousness, peace, and joy in the Holy Spirit" (Rom. 14:17), key characteristics of Jesus's life and ministry in Luke.[53] Jesus's good news was not just for another age; rather, Jesus was invested in challenging the status quo of the false life and inviting true life in the present.[54] As we share in the true seeing and relating of Jesus, we too participate in the kingdom of God and experience God's love and the peace of God's kingdom. Ultimately, to participate in preparing the world to be God's home is to feel joy, which remarkably is listed between "love" and "peace" in Paul's description of the fruit of the Spirit (Gal. 5:22–23).[55]

52. Jennings, "Theology of Joy."
53. Volf and Croasmun, *Life of the World*, 179, 182.
54. Volf and Croasmun, *Life of the World*, 70–80.
55. Volf and Croasmun, *Life of the World*, 166.

Competing Visions of the Good Life

The Christian vision of true life developed in Luke 4 and 7 is not only different from the malformed visions I described in chapter 3 but is fundamentally at odds with them, as table 4.1 illustrates (see next page). As I discussed in chapter 3, it can be difficult to delineate differences between dominant cultural visions of flourishing and Christian visions of flourishing. This table reveals explicit differences between visions of the good life that have been presented. Members of Christian communities need to reflect together on such differences and ask for God's guidance in pursuing the true life, rather than blindly integrating desires of malformed visions into Christian visions of the good life and thus allowing malformed visions to thwart our practice of faith.

Imagining Jesus's Ministry

In this chapter, I have offered a glimpse into what a vision of Christ looks like in a new media landscape. In so doing, I have provided you and your community with an example for imagining Jesus's life and ministry and a framework for describing visions of the good life (right actions, right circumstances, right feelings) in the hope that, together, your community might discern and articulate a Christian vision for faithful living in a new media landscape.

There are many ways a community can imagine Jesus's life and ministry. One of the most common is to retell stories from the Gospels and talk about them together as a community, asking particular questions. As a Christian community reads about Jesus's life in the Gospels, members could ask each other, "Given that Jesus is led by the Spirit, how does his ministry engender actions, habits, practices, and feelings that demonstrate the fruit of the Spirit?" As members describe such actions, habits, practices, and feelings, your community can discuss what a person formed in the image of God acts and feels like online. Your community could also ask, "What might Jesus teach us about how to see and relate truthfully, in light of the Spirit's leading?" And, "What sorts of circumstances (material, political, social) did Jesus pursue?" And, "What circumstances should we seek in a new media landscape?" As we ask these kinds of questions and imagine Jesus's life and ministry, we will be given inspiration and vision for what is possible, for what it could look like to live by the Spirit in a new media milieu.

I was involved in youth ministry for fourteen years prior to teaching at Fuller Theological Seminary. Youth ministry is amazing for many reasons, one of which is that it typically includes imagining and entering the stories of the Bible through role-playing and acting. When I was the children, youth,

Table 4.1 Comparing Visions of the Good Life

Vision of the Good Life (what is viewed as worth doing, wanting, and feeling)	Right Actions (life led well)	Right Circumstances (life going well)	Right Feeling (life feeling well)
A Dominant Vision (convictions shaped by expressive individualism, utilitarianism, and capitalism)	Authentic self-expression: Be true to yourself (only). You do you. Make money. Consume.	Individual has self-fulfillment because of ever-increasing status, success, power, and wealth.	Happiness
A Dominant New Media Vision (convictions shaped by the vision described above as well as branding and marketing strategies)	Be always on. Make money off your cultural activities and social interactions. Constantly share remarkable experiences you have. Stand out from the crowd. Obtain friends and followers. Market your value. Post how successful you are. Filter as needed.	Individual has an excellent personal brand because of ever-increasing remarkable experiences, positive attention, social capital, and value recognition.	Happiness
A Christian Vision[1] (convictions shaped by the life and ministry of Jesus as reflected, e.g., in the Gospel of Luke)	Righteousness: Abide in God's love. Respond to the Spirit's leading. Participate in truthful seeing and relating. Pray and fast. Provide relief for people who are poor, incarcerated, and oppressed. Practice holistic healing. Recognize others. Be compassionate and generous. Forgive. Break cycles of violence.	Peace: Individual belongs to a healing community, marked by ever-increasing love, compassion, forgiveness, relief, vision, and freedom.	Joy in the Holy Spirit[2]

1. Volf and Croasmun explain, "Righteousness (or justice) is the substance of life led well. Peace is the substance of life going well. Joy is the substance of life feeling as it should." *Life of the World*, 153.

2. Volf and Croasmun, *Life of the World*, 166, 170, 176–77. Each aspect of a Christian vision of true life has an affective component. Righteousness is acted out and felt as love. Peace is a condition and it is felt. And as we belong to a healing community, we experience and participate in God's joy.

and family pastor at Pasadena Mennonite Church in Pasadena, California, this happened on a regular basis. Youth were often put into small groups and sent to various rooms in the church to read and discuss Bible stories. Then we would all come back together, and each group would act out the scene. Usually, the youth leaders and I would give the same story to every group. This allowed everyone to really learn the stories through repetition, and it allowed us all to see the variety of ways the same story—the characters, actions, and themes—was interpreted differently by each group. It was especially wonderful when the youth (and youth leaders) would add clothing or props from the church dress-up closet (even without being encouraged to do this). I often wonder why churches encourage this sort of imaginative play in children and youth ministry but do not make it a regular part of adult worship or education.

Other ways to envision and contemplate Jesus's teachings and social interactions are through imaginative prayer and *lectio divina*.[56] Imaginative prayer is part of the spiritual exercises that were developed by St. Ignatius of Loyola to help people deepen their relationships with God.[57] After being wounded in battle, Ignatius found joy in reading about the life of Jesus and the lives of saints. He collected his insights, prayers, and suggestions in *The Spiritual Exercises*.[58] Imaginative prayer is a way to help individuals or groups imagine being a part of the stories in the Bible. *Lectio divina* is a way of reading Scripture in which people listen attentively to a passage as a way of opening themselves to what God might want to say. The practice involves repeated listening and silence, trusting that God will meet the listener during the reading. *Lectio divina*, which means "divine reading," has roots in Judaism and was later widely practiced in the desert monastic tradition from the third to the fifth centuries CE. However, "Saint Benedict of Nursia, who lived at the turn of the sixth century, is credited with promoting and refining its use."[59] Imaginative prayer and *lectio divina* are excellent spiritual disciplines for entering into the stories about Jesus and inviting the Spirit to guide our reading and listening. The following section, "Interested Conversation in Practice," provides guidelines for engaging in imaginative prayer and *lectio divina*.

56. For more information on Ignatian exercises, including imaginative prayer, see O'Brien, *Ignatian Adventure*; and Fleming, *What Is Ignatian Spirituality?* For ways to engage in imaginative prayer with children, see J. Boyd, *Imaginative Prayer*. For more information on *lectio divina*, see Painter, *Lectio Divina*.

57. You can read more about St. Ignatius, a priest and theologian who lived from 1491 to 1556, and about his spiritual exercises on this website: "St. Ignatius Loyola," Ignatian Spirituality, https://www.ignatianspirituality.com/ignatian-voices/st-ignatius-loyola.

58. Ignatius of Loyola, *Spiritual Exercises*.

59. Painter, *Lectio Divina*, 4.

As you consider Jesus's life, ministry, death, and resurrection, reflect on his identity, reputation, values, and beliefs and how these were embodied in his actions. Think about how he nurtured relationships with other people, built his social network, and used technology. And as you do so, invite the Spirit to teach your community how Jesus might act and feel in a new media landscape and what sorts of conditions Jesus would seek. In chapter 5, I explore how various visions of the good life—both malformed and Christian—converge in a new media landscape.

interested conversation in practice

Imaginative Prayer

Choose one of the stories from Luke 7, focusing on one of the following: vv. 1–10, 11–17, or 36–50.[60]

1. Invite everyone to close their eyes and get into a comfortable position.

2. Invite participants to pay attention to the details—the sights, sounds, tastes, smells, and feelings of the event—as they are listening to the story.

3. Read the story aloud. Ask participants to silently reflect on questions like

   ➤ What do you see in your surroundings?

   ➤ What do you smell?

   ➤ What sounds are you hearing?

   ➤ What can you taste?

4. Read the story aloud again. Ask participants to silently reflect on questions like

   ➤ Who are you in the story?

   ➤ Is anyone or anything near you?

   ➤ What are you feeling?

   ➤ Do you want to say something that has not been said in the story? If so, what do you want to say and whom are you talking to?

5. Read the story aloud a third time. Ask participants to silently reflect on questions like

60. I learned the steps of this version of imaginative prayer as part of my training as a Vocation and Formation Group leader at Fuller Theological Seminary in the fall of 2015. These practices can be engaged in with any biblical story or passage.

➤ What happened before this?

➤ What is going to happen next?

6. Invite the group to share aloud what they experienced.

Individual *Lectio Divina*

Choose Luke 4:16–21 or one of the stories from Luke 7, focusing on one of the following: vv. 1–10, 11–17, or 36–50.[61]

1. Move into a time of silence to prepare to hear from God. Make sure you are in a comfortable, relaxed position.
2. After a few minutes of silence, ask God to help you listen for a word or a phrase that catches your attention, and then begin reading the passage.
3. When you are finished reading, spend time in silence reflecting on the word or phrase that caught your attention.
4. Read the passage a second time. In silence, ask God for deeper understanding or clarity about this word or phrase. If a question arises, offer your question to God.
5. After another brief time of silence, read the passage a third time. After reading, ask God for an image or an invitation that God is offering to you in relation to this reading.
6. Consider connections between the reading, practicing faith, and new media use.
7. Consider writing your reflections in a personal journal.

Group *Lectio Divina*

If you want to have a group discussion about a passage, after engaging in steps one through six of this practice, put people into groups of two and have them share their reflections with their partner. Next, invite the participants to share in the larger group what they heard their partner say. If you have a really large group, participants could first share their reflections in a small group, and then you can ask to hear from a representative of each group.

---

61. Branson and Martínez, *Churches, Cultures, and Leadership*, 72–73. Branson notes that he was influenced by the approach of Ellison and Keifert, *Dwelling in the Word*.

five

the convergence

Let us know the power for life that is in us, the life-force that is in our senses and the might that is in our heart. Let us know you as the source of such force and be wise to its true streams and false currents.

J. Phillip Newell, *Sounds of the Eternal*

A (male) Facebook friend posted a status saying that women needed to be modest and think twice about wearing yoga pants in public because yoga pants can cause men to lust and "stumble." I read the post and was immediately infuriated. Comments like these shift the blame of lusting and sexual harassment *away from* the people who are actually doing the lusting and harassing *to* the victims of these actions. His post reminded me of multiple discriminatory comments I've received about my gender or my appearance. For example, "You're a pastor? You don't *look* like a pastor." Or, "Did you consider what men would think about while you were preaching in *that* dress?"

I had not talked to this Facebook friend since high school, but I wanted to make sure he knew how I felt about his post and why it was wrong, logically and theologically, so I wrote a detailed reply. I refuted his arguments one by one. I was not kind, and I did not invite dialogue. I wanted him to feel as small as possible—the way his post made me feel and how other unfair remarks about my appearance and gender have made me feel. For me, this post represented everything that I despise about misogyny. *This post was a justice issue, and I was going to change his mind.*

I imagined my reply would get likes from other people, and I eagerly awaited my high school friend's response. I thought that other people might reply too, either agreeing or disagreeing with me. I was prepared for multiple people to explain how enlightening my reply had been for them, but I was also ready for a Facebook debate. I checked back several times to find that no one had responded to my reply: no emojis, no replies, no arguments, no support, no awakenings, nothing.

Visions of the good life—both malformed and Christian—converge in a new media landscape. Various visions are revealed in and shaped by new media design (chap. 3) and new media use. For example, when new media users seek desires rooted in malformed visions of the good life, such seeking is exposed in their wounding actions. Members of Christian communities participate in wounding actions when the Spirit's voice is thwarted and our imaginations are captured by malformed visions such that we become practiced at living out beliefs and values that are contrary to Christian visions of the good life.[1] Living Christian visions of true life in a new media landscape does not merely mean using media well or not participating in wounding actions. The hard work of faithful living in a new media milieu is about practicing discernment. For Christian visions of true life to make a difference, interested conversation requires *interest in hybrid faithful living*.

Hybrid faithful living—righteousness, peace, and joy in the Holy Spirit during mediated conversation and other activities in both physical and digital spaces—is challenging since malformed visions of the good life can be seductive and subliminal. However, we do not rely on human wisdom; rather, God's grace helps us know what to do and strengthens us (2 Cor. 1:12; 12:9; Heb. 4:16; 13:9). The Spirit of God lives in us, and so "the way we live is based on the Spirit" (Rom. 8:4; see also vv. 9, 13). By the grace of God (2 Cor. 9:8), we can be receptive to the Spirit's voice and participate in the Spirit's work in the world, in person and online (1 Cor. 15:10). Hybrid faithful living demands receptivity to God's grace and the Spirit. Such receptivity requires commitment to *regularly practicing discernment* (this chapter) and *dedication to nurturing a hybrid, healing Christian community* (chap. 6). Christian communities need to practice discernment in order to advocate for new media to be designed for flourishing, to make critical decisions about new media, and to theologically reflect on community members' new media experiences.

---

1. My use of the concepts "receptivity to the Spirit" and "thwarting the Spirit's voice" in this book is thanks to an in-person conversation with Willie Jennings, who helped me think about connections between sharing in Christlikeness and being receptive to the Spirit. Additionally, he described responding to the Spirit's leading as an art and not a science, which I also borrow in chap. 6.

The Flattening

Given that mediated communication presents the challenge of diminished humanness (chap. 1) and that, by design, social media sites often encourage their users to desire remarkable experiences, positive attention, social capital, and value recognition (chap. 3), social media use can flatten the way users see and relate to and, therefore, experience the presence of God's love. I borrow the term "flatten" from Charles Taylor. In *A Secular Age*, Taylor defines "flattening" in terms of things being stripped of meaning, emptied, reduced, and impoverished.[2] In a manner similar to Taylor's usage, I employ the term "flattening" to describe the temptation, especially acute in our new media milieu, to diminish the humanness of others (a form of deficient seeing) and then to treat other people as commodities (a form of deficient relating). Deficient seeing and relating leads people to participate in wounding actions rather than in God's love.

Deficient seeing and deficient relating are connected. The way new media users see themselves impacts the way they see others. If users see themselves as brands, they are likely to see other people as brands too—products to be consumed, affiliated with, or exchanged.[3] Commodities are objects—useful or not—with economic value. Social media, by design, makes it easier to treat other people as commodities. Users can delete friends, add friends, block friends, follow new people, allow new followers, swipe left or right, and so on.[4] These options allow social media users to think of friends or followers as entities to be acquired or, when those friends no longer serve them well, to be disposed of. For example, a wounding action related to online dating is "ghosting," when a person suddenly no longer responds to a romantic partner or friend (on social media or through a device).[5] The person disappears with no explanation, which can be quite painful.

When socializing online becomes mainly about marketing remarkable experiences, and getting attention, social capital, and value recognition, socializing

2. Taylor, *Secular Age*, 372, 758, 761.

3. Similar to Diane P. Michelfelder, who argues that the web *can* "conspire" more with community than with commodity and, in so doing, make a positive contribution to human flourishing under some conditions, though not all. I think new media can contribute to human flourishing, but it also contributes to flattened relating, when relationships are seen as a means to an end. Michelfelder, "Web 2.0," 204.

4. A popular dating app, Tinder, has users "swipe right to like someone or swipe left to pass." If two people "swipe right," they can message one another and, if they so desire, arrange to meet in person.

5. "Ghosting, for those of you who haven't yet experienced it, is having someone that you believe cares about you, whether it be a friend or someone you are dating, disappear from contact without any explanation at all. No phone call or email, not even a text." Vilhauer, "This Is Why Ghosting Hurts."

is reduced to being simply a means to an end. In other words, users begin to think of relating in terms of what it can do for them and how it can serve their desires. Rather than treating human beings as ends in themselves,[6] users commodify relating and think about others in terms of their value and usefulness.[7] In a new media landscape, this is reflected in the drive among social media users to relate to people in person in ways that are "post-able." With personal desires in view, before friending or following someone, a social media user might wonder, "Is it beneficial to me to friend or follow this person?" As Taylor explains, "The dark side of individualism is a centering on the self, which both flattens and narrows our lives, makes them poorer in meaning, and less concerned with others or society."[8] To say that social media contributes to the flattening of relationships is to say that it has the capacity to empty true relating of its meaning, which I have defined in terms of love, generosity, healing, and compassion.

Despite efforts to lead our lives well, we often fail. When we reject God's grace, fail to abide in God's love, and thwart the Spirit's voice in our lives, we participate in wounding actions. Diminishing humanness and thinking about other people as commodities manifests itself through a number of wounding actions that nurture destructive feelings and perpetuate malformed beliefs. When social media users participate in wounding actions, new media spaces and devices can be sites and instruments that cause profound brokenness. Wounding actions nurture destructive feelings like anxiety, jealousy, and despondency. It is critical that pastors and other Christian religious educators and the communities they lead become aware of the wounding actions related to new media use. Awareness makes it more likely that Christian communities will create spaces for dialogue about people's experiences with new media, provide help for navigating the profound brokenness of the new media milieu through concrete practices and resources, and nurture a Christian community that is oriented toward living into new media's glorious possibilities.

As you read about wounding actions, I hope you will keep a few things in mind. First, although I am going to focus on how wounding actions take shape in mediated communication, specifically through social media, the wounding actions that are described here happen in person too; and in-person actions impact mediated actions even as mediated actions impact in-person actions. Therefore, in-person and mediated actions are connected and seep into one

6. An element of Immanuel Kant's moral philosophy is the categorical imperative. One of Kant's tests for morally acceptable actions is whether the action treats humanity as an end in itself or as a mere means, which is morally wrong. Kant, *Groundwork of the Metaphysics*, 102–3.

7. Baab, "Theology of the Internet," 284–85.

8. Taylor, *Ethics of Authenticity*, 4.

another. Second, rather than focusing on how other people participate in wounding actions, I invite you to reflect on how you participate in them. Finally, I hope you will be motivated to consider how your Christian community might show love amidst the profound brokenness of new media settings.

Flattened New Media Use

The profound brokenness of the new media milieu is evident in *how* people spend time using new media—namely, in passive, unreflective, and negative ways. These types of engagement with new media often become or are forms of flattened new media use and, thus, nurture deficient seeing and relating. In other words, people's passive, unreflective, and negative media use cause users to reduce human beings to their social media profiles. Flattened new media use contributes to both diminishing the humanness of others and commodifying, weakening, or otherwise destroying relationships.

Envy

Passive internet use is getting increasing attention in research about social media. "Passive scrolling" refers to the practice of getting online and viewing content or conversations without actively participating in them. Passive social media use can negatively affect people's perception of the quality of their lives.[9] In a study of 584 Facebook users, a group of researchers discovered one reason users may have a negative perception of their lives is because passive internet use is linked to envy, which "can lead to frustration and exhaustion, damaging individual life satisfaction—a critical indicator of users' well-being."[10] Envy is flattened seeing because it involves looking at someone else but seeing yourself instead and, hence, not actually seeing that other person.

You are more likely to experience envy while engaged in "passive following" of other people online—that is, viewing multiple posts of someone you do not regularly talk to online or in person.[11] It could be someone you do not know very well or someone you do not know at all (e.g., a celebrity you follow but do not know personally). Envy occurs because the less you know about someone's life, the more likely you are to reduce their life experiences

9. Chen et al., "Passive Social Network."
10. Krasnova et al., "Envy on Facebook," 7.
11. Krasnova et al., "Envy on Facebook," 11. Researchers explain that "intensity of passive following is likely to reduce users' life satisfaction in the long-run, as it triggers upward social comparison and invidious emotions."

to their curated social media posts.[12] Envy is most often induced when social media users see posts about three particular themes: travel and leisure, social interactions, and happiness.[13]

Social Comparison

In a humorous but sobering article for the *New York Times* titled "Don't Let Facebook Make You Miserable," Seth Stephens-Davidowitz articulates some ways of using social media that can contribute to envy and unhappiness. He writes: "We are all dimly aware that everybody else can't possibly be as successful, rich, attractive, relaxed, intellectual and joyous as they appear to be on Facebook. Yet we can't help comparing our inner lives with the curated lives of our friends."[14] Social media use can nurture the fear that you are not as happy, successful, liked, followed, or recognized as you should be, given how happy, successful, liked, followed, and recognized other people around you seem to be.

In their study of Facebook, Hui-Tzu Grace Chou and Nicholas Edge discovered that "those who have used Facebook longer agreed more that others were happier, and agreed less that life is fair, and those spending more time on Facebook each week agreed more that others were happier and had better lives."[15] People often express envy through what is called *social comparison*, an action that flattens the way they see themselves. Rather than see themselves in light of God's grace and unconditional love and apprehending their life's meaning as tied up in their identity as a beloved child of God, social media users determine how meaningful and fulfilling their lives are by social comparison.

Angie Zuo uses the term "social comparison" to describe social media's role in causing people to compare themselves to others. Zuo conducted two exploratory studies—a survey of 417 undergraduates and a study that assessed 127 participants before and after a Facebook profile evaluation task—and in so doing identified ties between Facebook use, social comparison, self-esteem, and mental health.[16] She found that emotional investment and the amount

12. Hui-Tzu Grace Chou and Nicholas Edge found that Facebook users who had more Facebook friends whom "they did not personally know as their Facebook friends . . . agreed more that others had better lives." See "'They Are Happier,'" 119.

13. Krasnova et al., "Envy on Facebook," 12.

14. Stephens-Davidowitz, "Don't Let Facebook."

15. Chou and Edge, "'They Are Happier,'" 117.

16. Zuo, "Measuring Up," 1. Another study of college students examined the correlation between using Facebook and body consciousness and concluded, "For both women and men, Facebook involvement predicted objectified body consciousness, which in turn predicted greater body shame and decreased sexual assertiveness." Manago et al., "Facebook Involvement," 1.

of time users spent on Facebook correlated with greater amounts of social comparison. And, not surprisingly, "high levels of social comparison predicted lower self-esteem and poor mental health."[17]

The fact that social media sites constantly display numbers (e.g., number of friends, likes, replies, shares, snaps) gives rise to the wounding action of social comparison. Numbers are a straightforward way to compare and contrast one person against another, but certain people and particular types of posts will inevitably get higher numbers. In a research study of 555 Facebook users, posts about achievements and children got the most likes and comments.[18] It is unclear whether this was because people genuinely liked these types of posts more than any other type or because people felt obligated to like these kinds of posts more.[19] Similarly, a study of mothers who used Facebook found that posts related to their children received much higher rates of feedback, likes, and comments than posts that were unrelated to their children.[20] Birth announcements usually receive the most attention.[21]

Social comparison is tricky because comparing oneself to others can be subconscious. When scanning posts on a newsfeed or viewing stories, we can evaluate what other users are saying, doing, and sharing without realizing it. One moment, we are merely scanning posts and noticing things, like who is having fun, who has lots of friends or followers or shares, and whose content is garnering attention; the next moment, we are comparing ourselves to them. Passively scrolling through our feed without engaging in critical reflection easily turns into social comparison.

It is tough to scan social media newsfeeds and stories and keep in mind what is not being posted. Stephens-Davidowitz explains that the mundane realities of people's lives are not captured on social media. He writes: "Americans spend about six times as much of their time cleaning dishes as they do golfing. But there are roughly twice as many tweets reporting golfing as there are tweets reporting doing the dishes."[22] Most people are uninterested in posting about themselves doing their dishes because it is an ordinary part of life. In the case of not posting ordinary activities, social media users are not necessarily disguising the truth; rather, most users do not post about routine activities for the simple reason that those activities are boring. Consequently, as we scan our social media newsfeeds, it is important to remember that

17. Zuo, "Measuring Up," 1.
18. Seidman, "What Can You Learn?"
19. Seidman, "What Can You Learn?"
20. Morris, "Social Networking Site Use," 1279.
21. Morris, "Social Networking Site Use," 1278.
22. Stephens-Davidowitz, "Don't Let Facebook."

other users post what they think will be interesting to their audience, not the whole of their lives.

Stephens-Davidowitz also compares Facebook posts with Google search data: "On social media, the top descriptors to complete the phrase 'My husband is . . .' are 'the best,' 'my best friend,' 'amazing,' 'the greatest' and 'so cute.' On Google, one of the top five ways to complete that phrase is also 'amazing.' . . . The other four: 'a jerk,' 'annoying,' 'gay,' and 'mean.'"[23] Most social media users choose not to post about the embarrassing, sad, or hurtful things that happen in their lives unless it can be viewed as humorous or socially acceptable; likewise, they tend to avoid publicizing the difficult questions, bad thoughts, and feelings they face for fear that they could be misunderstood, seen in a poor light, marginalized, or ignored. It is critical to help social media users in your community reflect on the ways that social media presents a limited view of what is going on in people's lives. In this respect, social media can be fruitfully compared to other short interactions one witnesses, for example, during coffee hours at church, when overhearing chats at the grocery store, or when observing couples sharing a meal at a restaurant. Like each of these short interactions, social media posts provide limited information about other people's lives. Unfortunately, in order to cope with envy, social media users feel the need to constantly share how happy they are and to promote themselves in their posts.

Impression Management

After her study of college students at thirteen campuses, Donna Freitas concluded that college students face enormous pressure to look perfect online— not just happy but blissful, ecstatic, and fabulously successful—something related to what she calls the "happiness effect."[24] Freitas found that young adults are desperate to avoid letting peers see any signs of weakness or failure.[25] The happiness effect is a vicious cycle: young people feel pressure to appear happy at all times; they constantly post happy things on social media, and they regularly see happy posts from friends, which gives rise to feelings of inadequacy because said youth compare how happy they feel to their friends' happy posts. Additionally, young people even feel inferior to their own happy posts because they do not actually feel happy all of the time.[26] In their study on envy, Hanna Krasnova and research team members discovered another social

23. Stephens-Davidowitz, "Don't Let Facebook."
24. Freitas, *Happiness Effect*, 14.
25. Freitas, *Happiness Effect*, 71.
26. Freitas, *Happiness Effect*, 14.

media phenomenon, which they termed the "self-promotion-envy spiral": when users feel envious of other users engaging in self-promotion, they cope with their envy by posting self-promotional content.[27] In other words, users can purposely present a flattened version of themselves, reducing their lives to happy moments and successes. People do this in person too, but it is easier to cover up feelings and failures online. When users are unreflective about their social media posts and get caught up in the happiness effect and self-promotion-envy spirals, users usually hurt both themselves and other people.

Mediated Hostility

Much of the animosity online is related to people believing that ends justify means. A good example is my reply to my Facebook friend's yoga pants post. I thought my attempts to make this person feel as small as possible and look as theologically ignorant as possible were justifiable because I was standing against misogyny. I still think his post was wrong—both logically and theologically—but I disrespected and mistreated him. My means compromised my ends. And as far as I know, nothing I hoped for happened. Angry new media users often negate or never reach their well-intentioned ends by the way they communicate on social media sites and through devices.

On social media, there are certain subjects that, when discussed, are especially likely to incite rage, contempt, disgust, and "flame wars" among users—the chief example being politics. A flame war is a "lengthy exchange of angry or abusive messages between users of an online forum or other discussion area."[28] Flame wars can happen online between friends, family members, and people you do not know. When researchers at the Pew Research Center studied the political atmosphere on social media, they discovered that "over half of polled social media users (59%) find discussing politics online to be frustrating and stressful" and that "nearly one-third of social media users (31%) say they have changed their settings in order to see fewer posts from someone in their feeds because of something related to politics, while 27% have blocked or unfriended someone for that reason."[29] The idea of people being divided over political ideals is not new. However, since it is easier through mediated forms of communication (e.g., Facebook) to minimize the humanness of yourself and other people and to interact with a person's ideas without having to actually interact with the person, hostility in a new media milieu manifests itself in ways that are particularly painful.

27. Krasnova et al., "Envy on Facebook," 12.
28. "Flame War."
29. Duggan and Smith, "Political Environment on Social Media."

Harassment

Harassment is viewed as normal online since so many people have experienced or at least witnessed it.[30] The Pew Research Center surveyed 4,248 US adults and discovered that "41% of Americans have been personally subjected to harassing behavior online, and an even larger share (66%) has witnessed these behaviors directed at others." Harassment was defined in this study as "offensive name-calling" (27% of participants said this had happened to them), "purposeful embarrassment" (22%), "physical threats" (10%), "stalking" (7%), "sustained harassment" (7%), and "sexual harassment" (6%).[31] These forms of harassment include sending unkind, vulgar, or threatening messages or replies and sending unwanted advancements. Harassment is especially harmful when it occurs through mediated communication because devices make it even easier for harassers to see their victims as objects instead of as humans with feelings, families, friends, stories, and perspectives.

While several forms of harassment are direct (e.g., stalking), others are indirect (e.g., forwarding messages between themselves and others or sharing private messages publicly); consequently, new media users are not always aware that such indirect actions can themselves constitute harassment. Posting untrue information about someone is a form of harassment that is not often acknowledged as such, yet 26% of participants in the Pew study noted that they have had untrue information about themselves posted online without their permission, most often about their character or reputation (17%). Another form of harassment is shaming—posting or editing photos to embarrass, humiliate, or hurt someone else; insulting someone's looks or sexual behavior or gender; or demeaning groups because of their religion, political affiliations, sexual orientation, education, abilities, race, or ethnicity.

Cyberbullying

Researchers Andrew Beale and Kimberly Hall found that online bullying between youth, also referred to as "electronic bullying" or "cyberbullying," happens through emailing, instant messaging, and using chat rooms or "voting booths" to deliberately torment others.[32] They describe the last of these as follows: "Voting or polling booths offer users the opportunity to create Web pages that allow students online to vote for [the] 'ugliest,' 'fattest,' 'dumbest,'

30. The forms of harassment discussed in this section were gathered from a list of questions in a survey on harassment conducted by the Pew Research Center. See A. Smith and Duggan, "Crossing the Line."

31. "Shareable Quotes."

32. Beale and Hall, "Cyberbullying," 8.

and so on, boy or girl at their school."[33] Concrete examples of cyberbully-ing include sending cruel text messages; spreading rumors by email; posting mean statements on social networking sites; and distributing embarrassing pictures, videos, websites, or fake profiles. Cyberbullying is particularly prob-lematic because it can be done anonymously, thereby making it difficult (and sometimes impossible) to trace their source. Furthermore, cyberbullying mes-sages and images can be distributed quickly to a wide audience, and deleting inappropriate or harassing messages, texts, and pictures after they have been shared is extremely challenging.[34]

In the most tragic cases, youth have committed suicide after being bullied online. In late 2017, Ashawnty Davis took her own life, at just ten years old, after a classmate posted a video of her being bullied.[35] Her parents have been willing to share their grief so that other parents can know the signs of cyberbullying. PureSight (http://www.puresight.com/) is a website dedicated to telling the stories of teens who took their own lives after being bullied online or through some other form of mediated communication, like texting.

Empathy Burnout

A considerable portion of the content on the internet features startling stories, grief, and violent imagery. Because social media users are confronted with more suffering than they can meaningfully respond to, new media further produces the problem of empathy burnout. When I talk to groups about new media, one common issue is users feeling so bombarded by tragedy, lament, and suffering that they begin to lose their sensitivity to what they are viewing. New media users can become numb to the pain of others and have a hard time empathizing with them. "Empathy burnout" or "compassion fatigue" are terms normally reserved for people who work in difficult fields, like social work, who encounter suffering daily.

The *amount* of suffering encountered online and the *velocity* with which we encounter it can be overwhelming. The internet has a way of flattening the way we see pain by normalizing pain and suffering. People consume sto-ries about the pain of others, share stories of pain, and even gossip about others' misdeeds or misfortunes without thinking much about it. Empathy burnout can also lead to new media users simply clicking an emoji, sharing an article, or replying to a post and feeling like they have done their part in responding to critical issues like sexual harassment or dismantling systemic

33. Beale and Hall, "Cyberbullying," 9.
34. "What Is Cyberbullying."
35. Lake, "'Just Devastating.'"

racism.[36] Another reaction is to do nothing since it can feel futile to do any-thing in response to the suffering one encounters online. The internet can cause users to believe their field of social responsibility has enlarged so much that everyone is a neighbor and everything is a responsibility. Since people obviously cannot help everyone and do everything, they often end up helping no one and doing nothing.

For some social media users, their instinct is to turn away from the inter-net's anxiety, suffering, and "bad news." Users want to turn off social media, not usually to spend time with God praying about what they encountered online or thinking about ways to respond concretely to the suffering, but rather, merely to avoid the issues. However, such withdrawal is a privilege reserved for a select few, because users cannot get off social media and get away from bad news if what is happening in the news directly affects their life—the way they are treated, their family, their work, their future, or where they live.

Always On

A considerable portion of American adults report that they go online "al-most constantly" (nearly 21%), and 42% say they are online multiple times per day.[37] Similarly, 45% of teenagers report that they are online "almost constantly."[38] Frequent use of mobile phones can disturb sleep and cause stress in youth and adults. For youth, sleep-related problems tend to be con-nected to staying on their phones too late at night to text and talk to their friends, watch movies and TV, and scroll through social media newsfeeds and websites.[39] Quality sleep is essential for well-being. Over time, lack of sleep causes vulnerability to mental health issues. For example, inadequate sleep has been linked to symptoms of depression in youth and adults. Perhaps unsurprisingly, the feeling (and sometimes the reality) that you need to be near your phone at all times ("availability demands") and being awakened by phone notifications while sleeping are factors that reduce the quality and length of your sleep.[40]

---

36. The comedians at Saturday Night Live performed a musical number, "Thank You, Scott," to critique precisely this sort of thin participation online. In it, a man sits on a couch and with a few clicks of his phone feels good about himself because he has done his part to raise aware-ness about issues like the refugee crisis. "Thank You, Scott—SNL."

37. Perrin, "One-Fifth of Americans."

38. M. Anderson and Jiang, "Teens, Social Media."

39. Lemola et al., "Adolescents' Electronic Media Use"; Hale and Guan, "Screen Time and Sleep"; Woods and Scott, "#Sleepyteens."

40. Thomée, Härenstam, and Hagberg, "Mobile Phone Use and Stress."

Mental Distress

Time online (along with emotional investment in social media) is linked to increased mental distress.[41] Participating online—posting, replying, producing content—has been shown to *reduce loneliness*, but a recent study of over 1,700 young people between ages nineteen and thirty-two discovered that social media use is also significantly associated with *increased depression*.[42] Social media use is also linked to anxiety. A study of emerging adults found that not only could time online result in greater symptoms of anxiety but also that increased daily social media usage was significantly associated with more severe levels of anxiety.[43]

It is unclear whether there is a causal link between the rise in suicide among teenagers in recent years and the rise in mobile phone purchases for teens, which have given teens the ability to be on social media constantly. However, there is sufficient evidence that social media use can contribute to some of the reasons suicidal ideation occurs: less in-person interaction and less sleep coupled with increased social comparison and negative feelings.[44] In addition, when self-expression online is shamed, disregarded, or rejected, new media users can experience destructive feelings, like despondency and meaninglessness. Stanford social psychologist Heejung Kim explains, "Depending on the dominant assumptions and expectations of cultural systems, self-expression has different psychological, physical, and social impacts"; that is, how other people perceive and respond to one's self-expression affects one's mental, emotional, and physical well-being as well as one's relationships.[45]

Suicidal ideation and suicide attempts are serious contemporary issues that need to be addressed by Christian communities, given that "suicide is the second leading cause of death in people aged 15 to 34 years and is a top 10 cause of death across all age groups in the United States."[46] Furthermore, in 2017, the most shared article on Facebook discussed the suicide of Chester Bennington, the lead singer of the popular band Linkin Park,[47] and a

41. Researchers Heather Cleland Woods and Holly Scott (University of Glasgow) used questionnaires to inquire about social media use among 467 teenagers. This study found that "overall and night-time specific social media use along with emotional investment in social media were related to poorer sleep quality, lower self-esteem as well as higher anxiety and depression levels." "Pressure to Be Available."

42. Lin et al., "Social Media Use and Depression"; Deters and Mehl, "Facebook Status Updates."

43. Vannucci, Flannery, and Ohannessian, "Social Media Use and Anxiety," 163.

44. Twenge, "Teen Mental Health."

45. Kim, "Culture and Self-Expression," under "Concluding Thoughts."

46. Vahabzadeh, Sahin, and Kalali, "Digital Suicide Prevention."

47. Rayson, "Most Shared Facebook Content 2017."

Grammy Song of the Year nomination that same year was a song titled "1-800-273-8255," the telephone number of the National Suicide Prevention Hotline. Christian communities need to address the ways passive, unreflective, negative, and excessive new media use are impacting people's lives, especially as new media use can nurture destructive feelings.

The Transparency Problem

Increasing capacity for recognizing when we are diminishing the humanness of ourselves or other people requires reflection on our social media use, and too often social media users cannot or do not take time to reflect on their online actions. This has been termed "the transparency problem."[48] Tackling passive, unreflective, negative, and excessive new media use requires addressing the transparency problem, a multifaceted issue that was brought to light through a research study of young people, although it is actually a multigenerational problem.[49] The transparency problem draws attention to several issues. Generally, people have trouble actively reflecting on their media experiences, naming the ways that media shape their views, and articulating what they learn from their online participation.[50]

Myriad possible reasons for the transparency problem can be given. One likely explanation is the pace of technological change. It has been difficult for institutions to keep up with changing needs regarding new media literacy, and therefore a limited number of adults have spent time in a Christian community critically reflecting on new media sites and devices and their own social media use.[51] Without adults who have been taught to critically examine new media, children and youth will also lack this education. Alongside this, some adults assume (wrongly) that media literacy skills are naturally acquired by young people because they are "digital natives." Media scholars, such as danah boyd,

48. Jenkins et al., *Confronting the Challenges*, 15.

49. Jenkins and his coresearchers focused on young people in their research for the book *Confronting the Challenges of Participatory Culture*.

50. Jenkins et al., *Confronting the Challenges*, 15.

51. Media literacy, also called "digital literacy," "social media literacy," "new media literacy," and so on, is a trending focus of research. See Hobbs, "Media Literacy"; K. Walsh, "5 Selected Frameworks." However, there is not agreement about exactly what media literacy is or how one knows if they have become media literate. This is because media literacy is complex. It is not merely a skill set, though media scholars have identified important competencies for navigating media. Jenkins et al. identified eleven necessary "new media literacies," describing them as "a set of core social skills and cultural competencies that young people should acquire if they are to be full, active, creative, and ethical participants in this emerging participatory culture" (*Confronting the Challenges*, 105–6). Media literacy is plural (contains several elements), contextual (relates to particular circumstances), and socially negotiated (discussed with others). See Pewhairangi, "6 Top Experts," under "Dr. Doug Belshaw."

who research teenagers have contested terms like "digital native" because some teens use technology frequently but not all do, and more importantly, all teens need guidance related to using social media and technology. Further, boyd argues that labeling youth as "digital natives" can mislead adults to believe that teens are more capable of navigating media than adults and thus do not need their help.[52]

The transparency problem also manifests itself as difficulty parsing messages, analyzing the quality of the information we receive, and separating fact from falsehood.[53] One example is the spreading of false rumors online. A research study discovered that false rumors take approximately fourteen hours to be debunked,[54] but significant damage can be done in fourteen hours with the power of the internet. The website Emergent (http://www .emergent.info) keeps track of the most shared false rumors. When I checked the site on December 12, 2017, one of the most shared was that Willie Nelson was dead; over 400,000 people had shared this false rumor on Twitter.[55] Fortunately, there are websites that track rumors so that social media users can determine whether the information they are receiving online is true or false.[56] Unfortunately, too many social media users spread information before verifying its truthfulness.

Practicing Discernment

Practicing discernment helps with detecting to what degree and in what ways people's use of new media is being governed by malformed visions of the good life versus being oriented by Christian visions of true life. Attending to the transparency problem and reducing wounding actions and destructive feelings caused by media use require processes of discernment that help your community to address new media design, make decisions about new media use, and discern God's invitations in new media experiences. These are imperative actions for confronting the profound brokenness of the new media landscape. Since discernment helps Christian communities to be continually receptive to God's grace and the Spirit's leading, each aspect of discernment for hybrid faithful living involves prayer.

52. Boyd, *It's Complicated*, 176.
53. Jenkins et al., *Confronting the Challenges*, 22–24.
54. Zubiaga et al., "How People Orient," 16.
55. "Most Shared."
56. According to the site's tagline, Emergent is "a real-time rumor tracker." PolitiFact (http:// www.politifact.com) "is a fact-checking website that rates the accuracy of claims by elected officials and others who speak up in American politics." See Adair, "Principles of PolitiFact."

Interested conversation is itself a discernment process. However, there are also other methods of discernment that your community can use to support interested conversation about new media. One such method is group spiritual direction, which involves meeting in groups to share, pray, sit in silence, listen to one another and to the Spirit, and discuss what the Spirit reveals to group members.[57] Mark Lau Branson's practical theology method is another. Branson's method involves cycles of action and reflection with steps such as naming and analyzing current praxis, studying Scripture for insights on current praxis, and shaping new praxis through imagining and experimenting.[58]

New Media Design

Early adopters of social media thought that media platforms would be democratic places where people would not be judged based on gender, education, or appearance and, therefore, would be able to build more authentic relationships. This optimism continues to some extent, especially in some Christian settings where people view the internet as simply a tool for evangelism. The fact is that social media sites are not neutral spaces and new media devices are not neutral tools. Therefore, flourishing in a new media landscape is not a matter of merely using technology well or being technologically innovative.

New media needs to be designed for flourishing because the way social media sites are designed *matters*. Christian communities need to discern ways to address new media design, though this is extremely difficult work. Openly articulating, in compelling ways, Christian visions of flourishing in a new media landscape is a powerful first step. Such visions are grounded in particularities of Christian faith, while genuinely confronting new media issues that affect all people's lives. By clearly articulating the values, desires, and practices worth pursuing in this new media landscape, Christian communities will be taking an issue that moves people (social media) and shining the light of the gospel on it.[59] Christian communities can share publicly both in person and in mediated forms (videos, blogs, websites, social media) what sort of new media is worth making. Doing so can inspire tech companies and, in particular, their user-experience designers to design social media sites and new media devices and apps with features that nurture human flourishing.[60]

---

57. Dougherty, *Group Spiritual Direction*.
58. Branson and Martínez, *Churches, Cultures, and Leadership*, 42–45.
59. "Conversation with Miroslav Volf."
60. I was inspired by the Institute of Buddhist Studies (http://www.shin-ibs.edu) to include this possibility. The institute requested proposals from scholars who want to help them

For example, I can imagine user-experience designers of new media being inspired by Christian visions of flourishing life to be dedicated to designing social media sites that nurture practices like compassion (a value grounded in the life and ministry of Jesus) rather than social comparison.

Members of Christian communities can also participate in advocacy work that hold technology companies accountable to designing new media that nurtures flourishing. Advocacy work can also involve encouraging user-experience designers at tech companies to focus on creating design features of new media that invite activities that nurture connection rather than contribute to diminished humanness and mental distress. Christian communities can also choose to give money to tech companies or advocacy groups that are committed to advancing new media that nurtures well-being. For instance, your community could support app creators who offer free education courses or your community could support designers of haptic technology (kinesthetic communication) who are helping stroke victims retrain their brains so paralyzed body parts can become active again.[61] While most Christian communities are limited in their capacity to nurture changes in new media design, they can nonetheless advocate for and support these changes to the extent that they are able.

Decisions

While Christians have limited control over new media design, they have more control over the *kinds* of media they personally use, *how* they use media, and *why*. Given that we live under the conditions of the false life, no tool or app or social media site will be exclusively designed, developed, and used in view of Christian visions of true life. Eventually swords will be turned into plowshares (Isa. 2:4), and one day every tool will be redeemed and nurture flourishing life, but in the meantime, some tools and social media sites nurture flourishing more than others. Christian communities can help their members be discerning about what tools and social media sites they use. They can teach their members to use some design features of social media platforms and not others. Members can be encouraged to think about what they are trying to accomplish (the ends they have in mind) and which devices or social media sites they will use to accomplish their goals.

It is also critical for Christian communities to be discerning about the types of technology the organization itself will use for its activities. This type of decision-making process could begin with trying to understand what kinds of new media

---

identify and cultivate new models of public theology for a project related to technology and presence.

61. Bhandari, "Mind-Controlled Device."

are already being used. Leaders of various ministries or departments in your organization could be interviewed to find out what types of new media they are using, why, and to what effect. Next, your community could seek to understand the forms of new media, especially social media sites, that community members are using in their personal lives, as well as what they use that media for and why. Leaders and other community members can also be asked about what new media they think the Christian community as a whole should consider using.

In order to make informed decisions about which new media the organization will use, your community will need to assess both new media that is being used and the mediums people desire to use. For example, Christian communities can think about the aim of the tech company that built a particular site, app, or tool, as well as the activities the new media encourages and its embedded values. Explicit values can be determined by viewing the website for the platform, tool, or app (read its "about" page and its values and mission statements); implicit values can be assessed based on critical reflection of how the site, app, or tool works and how the new media gets and keeps people's attention. For example, here is my assessment of Twitter:

Twitter

Explicit Aim: "We believe in free expression and think every voice has the power to impact the world."[62]

Activities:
- Type tweets of 280 characters or less with the ability to tag other users (individuals and organizations).
- Collect followers and follow others (Twitter quantifies both).
- Read tweets of users you follow.
- Read "moments" (five categories of curated events that happened today).
- Receive notifications of who has followed you, retweeted you, and so on.
- Send/receive messages between users.
- Receive curated tweets based on what's trending, your location, and who you follow.

Explicit Values: "now" (the present moment/what is happening right this second), civic engagement, direct dialogue: one-on-one or one-to-many

Implicit Values: brevity, speed, being followed and retweeted (forms of attention and recognition)

---

62. "Values," Twitter.

Once the community has determined a new media's aim, activities, and values, the community could discuss and pray about the following types of questions: Does the site or tool support activities, aims, and values of Christian visions of true life? Specifically, how does the tool or site nurture connection? Given its design, what ministry aims could this tool support? And does the new media (or any of its design features) encourage any activities that diminish humanness or may cause mental distress? Also, what does the new media in question encourage people to desire? Should we use all features of the new media or only some, or should we not use it at all?

Assessing tools and sites will help your community discern how to treat various new media. According to the Gospel narratives, Jesus did not treat all technology the same. For example, Jesus rejected the system of currency exchange that was set up at the temple in Jerusalem (Matt. 21:12–16; Luke 19:45–47; John 2:13–16). But Jesus used some technologies exactly as they were meant to be used (e.g., the scroll of Isaiah in Luke 4:17). Additionally, Jesus used tools for ministry purposes when such tools did not negate his aims. For instance, Jesus preached from a boat so a large crowd on the shore could hear him (Luke 5). As I described in chapter 4, sometimes Jesus transformed a technology (as he did with the cross, which he transformed from a technology of violence to a technology of love). Decision-making regarding what new media to use, and how and why to use it, will be contextual.

Finally, Christian communities need to think about how to discern with community members which online resources are beneficial and theologically sound. Since many of your members get resources for faith formation online, your community could encourage individuals to bring resources they find valuable into in-person gatherings. The community can read or view such materials and discuss who they were created by, what organizations endorse them, why they are theologically sound (or not), and how they nurture (or do not nurture) faith formation. Assessing online resources together is a way of modeling and practicing discernment about new media's resources.

Questioning as Quest

Another aspect of hybrid faithful living is encouraging community members to reflect on their new media and hybrid living experiences. Inviting such a process of discernment requires facilitators who ask powerful questions—questions that are curious, compelling, and capacious.[63] The questions I have in mind are ambiguous, personal, and evoke anxiety because they invite us

---

63. My creative and reflective husband, Paul Gorrell, helped me to describe the kinds of questions Jesus asked.

to think about things that matter to us.[64] Jesus himself often asked such powerful questions:

> "Who among you by worrying can add a single moment to your life?" (Matt. 6:27)
>
> "Why would people gain the whole world but lose their lives?" (Mark 8:36)
>
> "And what about you? Who do you say that I am?" (Luke 9:20)
>
> "What do you think? Which one of these three was a neighbor to the man who encountered thieves?" (Luke 10:36)

Jesus's questions were curious in the sense that he was genuinely interested in what other people believed and how they perceived the world. His questions were also compelling because they did not have simple answers. And his questions were capacious so that people could relate and respond to him, his parables, and his sermons in light of their context, no matter what that context was.[65]

In *Learning as a Way of Leading*, Stephen Preskill and Stephen Brookfield discuss the importance of inquiry, noting that "learning to ask questions is not an interrogatory project but a way of inviting people to wonder." When community members are invited to wonder, they are being invited into the learning process, into discovery. Preskill and Brookfield explain, "*Questioning* is derived from the word *quest*. When we pose questions we initiate a quest, a journey into the unknown or the poorly understood. Through questions we search out the unknown and unfamiliar, but we also reexamine the familiar. Sharp, incisive, focused questioning has a way of pushing people forward to uncover more. So questioning is part of the quest to live more fully and adventurously."[66]

I imagine there are Christian communities who are afraid to encourage facilitators to ask difficult questions or to create a learning space where conversation may go in any direction. However, this new landscape demands communities who welcome questions to which they don't have the answers.[67] The answers for how to live and what to do (especially regarding new media) are neither straightforward nor easily found.

64. Block, *Community*, 106.
65. For a meaningful way to lead your community in answering questions Jesus asked throughout the gospels see Croasmun, *Let Me Ask You a Question*.
66. Preskill and Brookfield, *Learning as a Way of Leading*, 127. Stephen Preskill is a former professor who studies leadership for social justice. Stephen Brookfield is a scholar of adult education and a professor at the University of St. Thomas in Minneapolis.
67. Preskill and Brookfield, *Learning as a Way of Leading*, 131.

The types of questions that are asked need to be open to the entire spectrum of experience with forms of new media. These sorts of questions aim to understand how people's use of new media is creating and preventing possibilities; producing and navigating challenges; connecting and distancing people; nurturing and inhibiting learning; extending and preventing spiritual disciplines; and supporting and thwarting love, joy, and peace.

Discussing Feelings

I was speaking to a room full of college students about social media. I shared stories and photos, and then I posed two social media scenarios for them to discuss with those sitting next to them. This lecture was similar to others that I had given, but I decided to ask this group a new question. I invited the students to take out their smartphones and answer one open-ended question through an online survey: "In general, what three emotions do you experience when using social media?" Below is a word cloud that represents the students' responses. The largest words are the ones that were reported most frequently.

disgust okay anger wonder upset amusement fomo

frustration happiness anxiety whistfulness satisfaction

nostalgia regret good thing surprise connection super self though apathy envy really state interest

jealousy excitement mostly wanderlust laughter sadness nothing validation

none curiosity mood connectedness humor something obsession boredom

new feel joy occasional indifference übermensch stress sometime

I showed the students the survey results on the screen behind me.[68] As I began reading the words out loud, there was occasional laughter, but mostly the students just nodded their heads in silence. After I finished reading, it seemed they were contemplating the seriousness of their responses. Many of the words in this word cloud represent challenges related to passive, uncritical, and negative use of new media: frustration, jealousy, sadness. Some of the

---

68. "Übermensch" (in the word cloud) is a word Friedrich Nietzsche uses in his writing and is German for "Superman," "Overman," or "Super-human." The college students had just read some of Nietzsche's work for their Life Worth Living course, which I teach with a team of colleagues at Yale University.

words, however, point to the possibilities of new media: interest, connection, excitement, joy. All of these words represent the experiences of real human beings—the real ways that new media impacts their lives. The act of naming and discussing feelings regarding new media is empowering and healing.

It is important for people to reflect on how their use of new media makes them feel—whether it nurtures positive or negative emotions and, in all cases, why: Why is new media making me feel insensitive, happy, depressed, or otherwise? When users can think about how new media makes them feel and why, they can be empowered to make necessary changes. For example, I teach college students to get offline when they notice they are feeling hopeless, depressed, or anxious and to try to find someone to do an activity with in person, like taking a walk outside or having a meal with a friend.

As your community listens to members' experiences related to new media, much will be uncovered—members' self-perceptions, beliefs and desires regarding relationships, sense of social responsibility, joys, hopes, laments, worries, and frustrations. Ultimately, asking powerful questions and discussing feelings leads to people sharing their stories.

Storytelling

There are several important reasons to make storytelling a regular practice in learning communities.[69] First, human beings are dialogical.[70] Language provides us with the ability to understand our experiences and integrate the meanings of those experiences.[71] Humans communicate in order to make meaningful sense of their lives.[72] In other words, human beings "know reality *storiedly*."[73] When humans are attentive to what has happened and verbalize experiences by way of stories, they can create meaningful associations between activities and thoughts and emotions, which is an important facet

---

69. It is important to have intentional facilitators who are interested in hearing from everyone in the learning community and who teach the group about the importance of being present, listening during storytelling, and respecting people's stories by not taking them out of the community without permission.

70. Taylor, *Ethics of Authenticity*, 33.

71. Berger and Luckmann, *Social Construction of Reality*, 64. Douglas Fisher, Nancy Frey, and Carol Rothenberg write, "Language, in other words, is how we think. It's how we process information and remember. It's our operating system." "Why Talk Is Important."

72. Fisher, Frey, and Rothenberg write, "*Telling* students what you want them to know is certainly a faster way of addressing standards. But *telling* does not necessarily equate to *learning*. . . . Oral language is the foundation of literacy, and as such, it requires focused attention in planning" ("Why Talk Is Important," emphasis original). For instructional strategies for integrating purposeful student (and congregant) talk, see Fisher, Frey, and Rothenberg, *Content-Area Conversations*.

73. J. Smith, *Desiring the Kingdom*, 14.

of memory consolidation.[74] Anderson and Foley write: "We use stories to construct meaning and communicate ourselves to one another."[75] Stories help people make sense of who they are, where they have been, and where they are headed.[76] This is why "stories are privileged and imaginative acts of self interpretation. . . . We retell incidents, relate occurrences, and spin tales in order to learn what occurred, especially *to me*."[77] Stories help people engage in transformative learning because stories invite people to encounter new information while feeling safe. Sharing stories and listening to one another's stories cause people to inquire, be curious, and "hunt" their assumptions, important aspects of the practice of discernment.[78]

Second, storytelling provides opportunities for another important practice: listening. Sharing stories regarding new media experiences is an incredible way for members of a Christian community to be invested in each other's lives. Storytelling can even help to heal the way community members see each other and themselves. Sharing stories exposes the critical matters in the community related to new media that need to be ministered to.[79] The nature of new media—namely, its participatory aspects—encourages people to have a voice and to participate. New media can give new shape to ministry activities like preaching, teaching, music, and liturgy. This sort of consideration could involve listening to more voices on a regular basis.

As the community listens to stories, the group can be attentive to ways new media use has contributed to friendship, learning, hope, prayer, collaboration, and missional engagement, as well as conflict, anxiety, loneliness, and distraction. The community should be listening for stories the community can rejoice over, as well as stories of concerns and needs the learning community can lament. The community might be asked by a facilitator to consider the

---

74. Berger and Luckmann, *Social Construction of Reality*, 64; they note that language provides human beings with the ability to understand their experiences and integrate the meanings of those experiences. (See also Kandel, *In Search of Memory*, 210). Incoming information has to be thoroughly processed in order to be remembered for a long time. This requires attentiveness and meaningful association.

75. H. Anderson and Foley, *Mighty Stories*, 4.

76. Carr, *Shallows*, 196–97.

77. H. Anderson and Foley, *Mighty Stories*, 5 (emphasis original).

78. Brookfield, *Teaching for Critical Thinking*, 7–11.

79. Storytelling about new media experiences can happen offline and online. Christian communities can create opportunities for people to share stories in person during worship services, in small groups or Bible studies, in focused Christian education settings, like youth group or Sunday school, or over a meal or coffee. Storytelling can happen in imaginative ways too. For example, groups can put newsprint paper on a wall and invite community members to write down phrases or draw pictures that represent their experiences. Online, community members can share stories by uploading videos, writing blog posts, or participating in a forum or a survey.

following questions, and others like them, as they listen to these stories: Are group members feeling seen, heard, understood, and loved online? Is social media use nurturing relationships? Is new media helping people to love and know God? How is media shaping people's perceptions? Is our new media use distorting our views of how we should lead our lives, how we should feel, and what we should pursue? As the community listens together, the community seeks the guidance of the Spirit to help answer questions and minister to one another.

A third reason for storytelling is that humans need to tell and listen to stories in order to discern God's movement within their lives and contexts.[80] It can be difficult to articulate God's activity in our lives and easy to miss God's presence and agency, especially in online contexts.[81] However, by pointing out the possibility that the Spirit is speaking and leading in this new media milieu and then telling stories about new media experiences, community members will not only be open to the possibility of God meeting them in their new media use but will also be more receptive to God's activity in these experiences.[82] Anderson and Foley explain, "When we are willing to admit the possibility of God's presence in ordinary human events, we will be more likely to fashion our human narratives—composed of so many such events—in light of that presence. Ordinary life is transformed when we recognize that our stories bear the presence of God. When we can acknowledge the possibility of God's presence in our daily living, it is possible for us to weave the divine narrative into the stories we fashion."[83] Storytelling gives Christian communities an opportunity to acknowledge what is going on in people's lives and to listen for the moments where God's reconciling love can speak into human situations.

Ultimately, we use new media under the conditions of the false life. We will be governed at times by malformed desires. In our neediness, fear, and sin, our seeing and relating will be flattened, and we will commodify relationships and participate in wounding actions. Regularly sharing new media stories and reflecting on experiences with a Christian community also helps members to discern when they fail. Naming failures provides opportunities for confession and repentance and a renewed commitment to hybrid faithful living.

80. Groome, *Sharing Faith*, 215, 250.

81. Of course, people can tell stories and wrongly associate human activities with God. However, this is a reason we need to be more practiced at sharing testimonies and storytelling in communities, not less.

82. To learn more about listening to the Holy Spirit and discerning God's activities through conversation, see Branson, *Memories, Hopes, and Conversations*; Roxburgh, *Joining God, Remaking Church*.

83. H. Anderson and Foley, *Mighty Stories*, 40.

Each of the wounding actions described in this chapter are reasons for you and your community *to be engaged* and *invested* in understanding and responding to the implications of a lack of seeing and relating to God's love in our new media milieu. In chapter 6 I explore how to nurture a hybrid, healing community by developing hybrid Christian practices and helping members of your community to design a rule for life in a new media landscape.

interested conversation in practice

Discussion Questions Related to Wounding Actions

1. What are passive scrolling and passive following, and why can both be problematic?
2. Do you find yourself comparing your life to other people's social media posts?
3. How has the happiness effect or the self-promotion/envy spiral affected you or people you know?
4. Have you witnessed online harassment or cyberbullying? How can our community address these issues?
5. Have you ever gotten really angry while using social media? Why? What happened?
6. Have you ever unfriended or blocked someone? Why? What happened?
7. Do you feel like you have to be "always on"? Why or why not?

Compelling, Curious, Capacious Questions

1. How do you make decisions about what to respond to online?
2. Have you ever been frustrated or sad about new forms of technology? What causes frustration or sadness for you?
3. When have you had a joyful experience online? Describe a time when you felt heard, affirmed, or understood online.
4. How does social media help you love God and others and/or prevent you from loving God and others?
5. When have you had a painful experience online? Describe a time when you felt unheard, bullied, left out, or misunderstood online.

6. What are the top three feelings you experience when using social media, and why do you think this is so?

7. Have you ever disagreed with someone or had someone disagree with you on a social media platform or through a technological device? What happened?

8. Have you ever cried or been overcome with sadness by something that you saw or read on social media? What happened?

Questions for Theological Reflection on Personal Stories

1. Why does the story that has just been heard matter to God?

2. How does faith in God help us understand the story (perhaps differently)?

3. What are the Christian-related issues embedded in the story we just heard?

4. Do the issues in the story remind you of any biblical stories or stories from the Christian tradition that might have something to offer the community?

5. What revelations or illuminations have you gained?

6. In light of the story, what might God's invitation be to this community?

six

glorious possibilities

Jesus announced, lived, and inaugurated a new social order, an alternative to violence, exclusion, and separation. Jesus went so far as to promise us this alternate reality. It is no fantastical utopia, but a very real and achievable peace—by the grace of God. He called it the *Reign* or *Kingdom of God*. It is the subject of his inaugural address (Luke 4:14–30), his Sermon on the Mount (Matthew 5–7), and most of his parables.

Richard Rohr, "Jesus's Alternative Reality"

Megan Phelps-Roper used to be a member of Westboro Baptist Church, the most controversial church in the United States. Westboro Baptist is infamous for protesting anyone and everyone—other churches, schools, various organizations, events (even funerals)—and carrying signs with cruel messages written on them, such as "God hates you." In 2009, Phelps-Roper started using Twitter. In an incredible TED talk delivered in 2017, she describes how Twitter users showed her the power of engaging with the Other and contributed to massive changes she made in her life. At first, the people she encountered through Twitter were "the digital version of the screaming hordes" she had seen at protests her whole life. But then constructive, meaningful conversations began to happen, and some of these conversations happened in person. For example, a Twitter follower she had been dialoging with for a few months showed up to an event she was picketing. He brought her a Middle Eastern dessert from Jerusalem, where he lived, and she brought him kosher chocolate; they talked while she was holding a "God hates Jews" sign. As she explains,

"The line between friend and foe was becoming blurred. We had started to see each other as human beings and it changed the way we spoke to one another. It took time, but eventually these conversations planted seeds of doubt in me."[1]

Ultimately, Phelps-Roper left Westboro Baptist Church. She explains, "My friends on Twitter took the time to understand Westboro's doctrines, and in doing so, they were able to find inconsistencies I had missed my entire life." She describes how the care shown to her by strangers on the internet was growing evidence that outsiders were not the demons she had been led to believe. Her perspective began to shift, and she realized she needed to leave; one of her sisters eventually left with her. Phelps-Roper and her sister found "light and a way forward" from some of the very communities she had protested. For example, they stayed with a Jewish family, slept on their couch, cooked with them, and talked with them about theology, Judaism, and life. She explains: "They treated us like family. They held nothing against us and again, I was astonished." Phelps-Roper nurtured hybrid relationships, and she and the friends she made faithfully practiced hybrid peacebuilding, generosity, forgiveness, and interreligious dialogue. Her story exemplifies new media's glorious possibilities.

Hybrid Healing Communities

As I described in the last chapter, interested conversation regarding new media requires *interest in hybrid faithful living*. Hybrid faithful living encompasses the true life of righteousness, peace, and joy—online and in person. Hybrid faithful living necessitates both practicing discernment and nurturing a hybrid healing community. Christian communities shaped by the dualistic approach have mission statements, staff job descriptions, activities, worship services, and programs that are imagined in narrow terms (e.g., relating to in-person interactions only) and performed in physical spaces (usually within the walls of a single building). In contrast, hybrid healing communities aim to join in Jesus's ministry of holistic healing and conduct ministry in both physical and digital spaces, during in-person and mediated communication, and through how they use both old forms of media and new media. Hybrid, healing communities are concerned with the pursuit and embodiment of Christian visions of true life no matter where they are or what they are doing in the new media landscape.

A Christian vision of true life desires peace (right circumstances), which in Jesus's ministry looked like wanting every human being to belong to a healing community marked by ever-increasing love, compassion, forgiveness, relief,

---

1. Phelps-Roper, "I Grew Up."

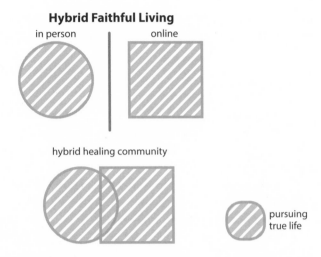

Hybrid Faithful Living

in person | online

hybrid healing community

pursuing true life

vision, and freedom. A Christian vision of flourishing also has right actions—righteousness. Desiring righteousness is desiring to participate in the truthful seeing and relating of Jesus by abiding in God's love and being receptive to the Spirit's promptings. Jesus's life and ministry personified righteousness: prayer and fasting, healing, providing relief, recognizing others, being compassionate and generous, forgiving, and breaking cycles of violence. However, members of Christian communities cannot merely desire to be like Jesus—for example, desire to be forgiving and then immediately become forgiving people. They need to develop forgiveness as a *practice* over time; members of Christian communities need to participate in a forceful combination of liturgies, sacraments, rituals, actions, disciplines, and habits that help them to become forgiving people.[2] Similarly, a "practitioner of medicine" is one who has participated in a series of behaviors or activities over time such that the person has become "practiced." Additionally, just as people choose to make commitments that help them remain faithful in marriage, members of Christian communities can also make commitments that will help them abide in God's love in a new media milieu. In short, nurturing a hybrid, healing community occurs through *dedication to developing hybrid Christian practices and designing a rule for life in a new media landscape.* Designing a rule for life is a way of cultivating kingdom-oriented desires, convictions, and habits through rituals and routines informed by Christian visions of flourishing life. Developing hybrid Christian practices and designing a rule that includes such

2. Branson, "Defining Practices and Disciplines," 1. Mark Branson and I also discussed definitions of practices when I was his instructor-in-training for Practices of Christian Community, a fall 2015 class at Fuller Theological Seminary.

practices helps with inhibiting new media's profound brokenness while also seizing new media's glorious possibilities.

Christian Education

Christian education in a new media milieu includes helping members of Christian communities attend to interrelations between their practices and their beliefs and desires. As L. Gregory Jones explains, "Ancient catechesis was predicated on the understanding that our convictions are embodied in material practices and desires, that our desires are always already being educated and formed in one way or another through our convictions and activities, and that our practices are the carriers of beliefs and desires."[3] Catechesis and other forms of Christian education in a new media milieu help community members reflect on living an integrated life in physical and digital spaces.

Such Christian education necessitates regularly including terms like "online," "social media," "new media use," "internet spaces," "physical and digital spaces," "devices," "smartphones," "digital practices," "iPads," and "hybrid living" into our vocabulary to make it clear that there is a relationship between new media and Christian faith. It should be common in Christian communities to talk about social media sites the way Christian communities talk about other spaces in people's lives.

Sharing in Christlikeness

A Christian vision of the good life has as its center the desire to surrender to and then share in God's love (because it's irresistible). To join in God's unconditional love is to also share in Christlikeness. For Christians, living into true life looks like imaging God, and "if we are to image God, we have to be formed according to God's own image—the second person of the Trinity—in something like the way Jesus was."[4] This formation into God's image comes from participating in God.[5] The participation of individuals and their communities "in Christ" is a collaborative process wherein God's agency *and* human agency actively work together.[6] Being converted into the image of Christ is a dynamic and life-shaping *act of grace* that is ongoing and

---

3. Jones, "Beliefs, Desires, Practices," 194.

4. Tanner, "Image of the Invisible," 120.

5. Tanner, "Image of the Invisible," 130. This participation will always be in an imperfect fashion during human life, as Tanner explains (129–30).

6. Dwight Zscheile writes, "A missional view of God offers rich resources for reenvisioning how disciples might be formed in the power of the Spirit for faithful participation in the

Sharing in Christlikeness

God's
agenda

Human
agenda

holistic; it encompasses the physical, moral, social, intellectual, emotional, and spiritual dimensions of the self and, for that reason, has purchase on all aspects of a person's life and a community's life together.[7]

Participating in God does not happen without human openness to and welcome of the Spirit's leading. In her poem "Annunciation," Denise Levertov writes that "the engendering Spirit did not enter her [Mary] without consent. God waited."[8] Reflecting on this poem in an Advent meditation, Cynthia Bourgeault noted that "God waited, the whole wheels of creation awaited a yes from a human being, that is formed not with gritted teeth and humble knuckled under obedience, but an active intelligence . . . an act of seeing which is at the same time an act of participation, a yes which is not passive but active."[9] God's agency is involved in our agency.[10] The ability to say yes and to participate in Christ is a mysterious act of grace. Since we are "in Christ" (1 Cor. 1:30) and Christ lives in us (Col. 1:27), we have received the grace of God (Acts 4:33; 15:11; Rom. 1:5; 1 Cor. 1:4) and the Holy Spirit was sent by Jesus (John 14:16) and forms human beings into Christlikeness.[11] By God's grace, like Jesus, we can be receptive to the Spirit's voice (Luke 4:18) and participate in Jesus's ongoing ministry.[12]

When Paul followed the voice of the Spirit in Acts, he followed Jesus.[13] Likewise, when we respond to the voice of the Spirit, we follow Jesus. Receptivity to the Spirit and engaging in the ministry of Jesus is an *art* and not

Triune God's communal, creative, and reconciling movement in the world." Zscheile, "Missional Theology," 1.

7. Steele, *On the Way*, 10. I am indebted to Theresa O'Keefe, associate professor of the practice of youth and young adult faith at Boston College, for this phrasing, which is based on a conversation we had at the Association of Youth Ministry Educators conference in the fall of 2015.

8. Levertov, "Annunciation."

9. Bourgeault, "Faculty Advent Messages."

10. Jennings, *Acts*, 2. Jennings writes: "God moves and we respond. We move and God responds." He adds, "Nevertheless this is God's drama."

11. Tanner, "Image of the Invisible," 120.

12. Ray S. Anderson uses the term "Christopraxis" to describe "the continuing ministry of Christ through the power and presence of the Holy Spirit." R. Anderson, *Shape of Practical Theology*, 29.

13. Jennings, *Acts*, 133.

a science. This artistic endeavor, like all forms of art in their creation, necessarily entails improvisation because sharing in Christlikeness is contextual and dynamic, just as Jesus's life was.[14] Improvisation requires imagination, creativity, and practice.

Improvisation also implies that Christian communities will get it wrong. Glen Stassen explains:

> To see churches [or other types of Christian communities] as on the side of Christ, and culture as over against Christ, is just the kind of hypocrisy and self-righteous judging that caused Christ to sound strong warnings again and again. *Churches* are part of the culture. Churches are made of clay and spirit—or clay and air. Their members and their leaders spend most of their days in the world and only a few hours or less in the church, and when they come inside, they bring the smells of the fields and the malls with them.[15]

It is essential to recognize that, like the kingdom of God, the church and the Christian life are *emerging realities*.[16] And to describe any of these realities requires paradoxical statements. For example, we say that the church "is the society of that new order of creation," but we also note that churches belong to "the old life that is passing away."[17] Like individuals and other cultural institutions, Christian communities are "just human entities on which God has taken mercy and which God is converting to God's self."[18] We are constantly being made new.

While it is not possible to perfectly image Jesus in this lifetime, in our attachment to and participation in God's love we can, like Jesus, embody Christian convictions and form our desires through Christian material practices. Christian practices cultivate Christian virtues, bear the fruit of the Spirit, and demonstrate faith.[19] Christians engage in Christian practices as participatory "enlightened witnesses"—that is, as people who have witnessed God's love and embody this love in the way they live.[20]

Unfortunately, the value of teaching Christian practices is often eclipsed by a value for information dissemination, as Jamie Smith points out in *Desiring the Kingdom*. "Christian education has absorbed a philosophical anthropology that sees human persons as primarily thinking things. The result has been an

---

14. Volf and Croasmun, *Life of the World*, 107–13.
15. Stassen, "New Vision," 224 (emphasis original).
16. Niebuhr, *"Responsibility of the Church,"* 59.
17. Niebuhr, *"Responsibility of the Church,"* 60.
18. Niebuhr, *"Responsibility of the Church,"* 61 (language altered to be gender neutral).
19. Tanner, "Image of the Invisible," 129–30; Bass, *Practicing Our Faith*, 5, 6–8.
20. Boyle, "Evening with Father Greg Boyle."

understanding of education largely in terms of *in*formation; more specifically, the end of Christian education has been seen to be the dissemination and communication of Christian ideas rather than the formation of a peculiar people."[21]

Christian education is less about disseminating knowledge (and less about telling people "do not sin") and more about focusing on what it means to abide in God's love by cultivating material Christian practices that shape us to love and desire God.[22] There are a number of Christian practices and spiritual disciplines that make up the Christian life and can be taught and practiced in hybrid ways by your community: listening, lamenting, honoring the body, confessing, praising, studying the Bible, showing gratitude, extending hospitality, keeping promises, reconciling, giving testimony, witnessing, showing mercy, practicing friendship, caring for the creation, celebrating, and participating in interreligious dialogue.[23] As foundational Christian practices are nurtured in a new media landscape, contrary practices, values, and beliefs are challenged.

Hybrid Christian Practices

Christian communities' work of joining with God in making the world into God's home—particularly through the preaching of good news and the acts of releasing, recovering, and liberating—takes shape in the form of hybrid Christian practices.[24] In the present social and technological landscape, it is

21. J. Smith, *Desiring the Kingdom*, 31.

22. J. Smith, *Desiring the Kingdom*, 68, 71. This is because "do not sin" is largely unhelpful. Instead, invite people to live into a vision of a new way of being that has concrete actions—ways they can perform their theology.

23. I codeveloped four courses at Fuller Theological Seminary that taught many of these Christian practices and spiritual disciplines. The majority of this list is the result of hybrid dialogue (in person and online) between numerous professors across multiple disciplines at Fuller. I am indebted to these professors for this list. For further reading on some of these practices, see Baab, *Power of Listening*; Barton, *Sacred Rhythms*; Billman and Migliore, *Rachel's Cry*; Bonhoeffer, *Life Together*; Boyle, *Tattoos on the Heart*; Brueggemann, *Praying the Psalms*; Conde-Frazier, "From Hospitality to Shalom"; Emmons, *Gratitude Works!*; King, *Stride toward Freedom*; Newell, *Listening for the Heartbeat*; Pohl, *Living into Community*; Rohr, *Things Hidden*; Tutu, *No Future without Forgiveness*; Willard, *Hearing God*; and Wirzba, *Food and Faith*.

24. In *Networked Theology*, Campbell and Garner describe the concept of "networked religion," identifying five characteristics of religious practice online (61–78). One characteristic of networked religion is "multisite reality," a concept that represents "the ways in which online practices are informed by wider beliefs as users integrate and seek to connect their online and offline patterns of life" (75). Another characteristic is "convergent practice," an aspect of digital religion where "people of faith transport and transform specific religious practices online" (70). Convergent practice is depicted as self-directed and individual (72–73). Nurturing a Christian community that cultivates hybrid Christian practices is a way of providing communal discernment for community members regarding hybrid faithful living and empowering members to critically and theologically reflect on individual renegotiations of beliefs, practices, and relationships online.

imperative that Christian communities frame the love of God and neighbor (which includes one's enemies) in terms of Christian practices that are integrated across physical and digital environments and practiced during in-person and mediated communication.

For example, if a youth group is teaching about hospitality, it is important to teach how embodying hospitality applies not only to in-person relating but also to social media interactions. If a worship service is teaching congregants about the Christian practice of reconciliation during in-person communication, this should include attention to the ways congregants can practice reconciliation online or through devices. Similarly, when teaching spiritual disciplines, Christian communities ought to explain the ways spiritual disciplines help Christians attend to God and God's invitations in both physical and digital spaces. For example, just as prayer can be practiced in a bedroom, prayerful habits can be cultivated while scrolling through a newsfeed. In *Making All Things New*, Henri Nouwen describes the activity of the Spirit as follows: "God speaks to us not only once in a while but always. Day and night, during work and play, in joy and in sorrow, God's Spirit is actively present in us. Our task is to allow that presence to become real for us in all we do, say or think."[25] Throughout the rest of this chapter, I will discuss specific hybrid Christian practices that I think are especially critical for leading our lives well in a new media milieu. I will provide examples of activities that nurture hybrid Christian practices and holistic healing and help break cycles of violence. My examples are merely meant to awaken your community's imagination. They are only starting points.

RHYTHMS OF REST

Your community can nurture habits related to regular rhythms of rest. It is helpful for a community to talk about the differences between leisure and rest and to talk about healthy ways to resolve boredom that do not entail using new media. Your community could also discuss why boredom is important by exploring its positive outcomes (e.g., creativity).[26] In your community, rest could take the form of Sabbath-keeping, taking one day a week off from using new media; habitually taking a day or a weekend to practice spiritual disciplines; going on a retreat without new media; or even dedicating one week a year to unplugging.[27] For members of Christian communities for

25. Nouwen, *Making All Things New*, 91.
26. Mann and Cadman, "Being Bored."
27. For further reading about the historic Christian practice of Sabbath-keeping and ways to cultivate this practice, see Heschel, *Sabbath*; Baab, *Sabbath Keeping*; and Muthiah, *Sabbath Experiment*.

whom long periods of silence and unplugging are unmanageable, rest could be something as simple as making a habit of taking a fifteen-minute walk or riding on transportation without looking at a device.

Additionally, community members can commit to helpful actions that limit access to and use of new media. People can place devices out of sight for a time period or have a basket that mobile phones go into during meals or during hours dedicated to other activities, like sleep. Technology hacks can help too—like setting one's email to update only every so often, disabling notifications from social media sites and smartphones, or restricting certain applications or social media sites for certain parts of the day. There are also apps and software that will help people monitor how much time they are spending online and remind them to take breaks. iPhone users can change their phone's display to black and white or "grayscale," which discourages passive use.[28]

Christian communities could also consider integrating periods of silence into community activities or designating particular days on the liturgical calendar for limiting the use of technology in the community's programming.[29] A thoughtful balance between engagement and unplugging in Christian communities' activities can minister to the feelings that I discussed in chapter 1: nostalgia, (unreflective) enthusiasm, anxiety, and apathy.

MERCY

If Jesus "has a brand," his brand is healing and inclusion. As Jesus cared for those who had few relationships, so also Christian communities can use some new media to care for and include the excluded. Practicing mercy helps people who are unseen feel seen. Truly seeing others (discussed in chap. 4) involves helping people see in themselves what God sees, recognizing practices of faith and love, and lifting up people who are being marginalized in person and online. Christian communities can talk together about the dehumanizing effects of new media and consider the actions through which Christians can use new media in loving ways that identify with and care for people of low social status. For example, in chapter 1 I discussed how taking photos of people in dire conditions and posting them online contributes to exploitation. A concrete way for Christian communities to practice hybrid mercy is to have ethical guidelines for taking and posting photographs, especially of people in low-wealth communities.[30]

28. Kirsch, "Change Your Screen."
29. "Pope Francis."
30. Gharib, "Volunteering Abroad?"

Christian communities can also explore ways that technology is being used to practice mercy and alleviate poverty and starvation. For instance, an app was developed by youth in Uganda that provides timely medical advice for pregnant women who live far away from doctors or do not have adequate health care.[31] Supporting technology like this is a meaningful way to practice mercy in a new media landscape.

Practicing mercy also includes considering the ways new media inspires formation of systems and institutional visions that marginalize people. For example, before designing an organizational system or vision for using new media, Christian communities can become aware of levels of access regarding new media within their group, the neighborhood, and other people the community feels called to minister to. Sometimes people are unable to participate online or in mediated communication because they do not have access to devices or the skills to use them.[32] Christian communities can be careful not to use new media in programming and communication that excludes people; or they can decide to share resources, including access to social media sites and to devices. It would also be appropriate for Christian communities to teach competencies necessary for participating online to those who have not had an opportunity to become media literate.

Advocacy

New media can be used by members to practice advocacy and to participate in transforming political structures so that they more closely align with Jesus's life and ministry. Advocacy entails engaging in justice work and entering into solidarity with people who are poor, disadvantaged, incarcerated, and oppressed. Practicing hybrid advocacy could look like inviting community members to use new media to research contemporary human rights issues or a specific issue like creation care. After researching online, members could come together in a physical or digital gathering to share what they have learned. Another habit that could develop the hybrid practice of advocacy is regularly inviting members to check out Facebook or Twitter feeds to see what is trending during an in-person gathering and use the content they find to pray together for the world.

31. "App to Uberize Care."
32. Jenkins and his research team describe this as the "participation gap" in *Confronting the Challenges*, xii, 15. Also, boyd has talked about how coding decisions on social network sites have negative implications for the less powerful and more vulnerable. See boyd, "Making Sense." See also Campbell and Garner's discussion of access and technology in *Networked Theology* where they provide important ways to practice justice regarding technology (128–33).

Members can also be encouraged to think about what they will do when they encounter an instance or story of suffering online and to have a plan they will carry out. For example, users can decide to meaningfully respond by replying, sharing, praying, and giving money. Advocacy might also take shape in the form of honoring important holidays, like National Women's Day, in person and online. Your community can create a space on the institution's website or Instagram account dedicated to creating conversation in light of significant holidays or special times in the year.

Christian communities who have access to new media can also use it to mobilize and recruit others toward common action and response.[33] Important and incredible things can happen when community members practice advocacy by sharing trending stories or using trending hashtags, as the examples of #metoo and #icebucketchallenge demonstrate. Tarana Burke founded the Me Too movement (https://metoomvmt.org) in 2006 "to help survivors of sexual violence, particularly young women of color from low-wealth communities, find pathways to healing." In 2017 the hashtag #metoo went viral, and crucial conversations about sexual violence gained national attention. In the summer of 2014, the hashtag #icebucketchallenge (http://www.alsa.org /fight-als/ice-bucket-challenge.html) was used to encourage donations for ALS (amyotrophic lateral sclerosis) research. Social media users filmed themselves pouring a bucket of ice water over their heads. The hashtag helped build awareness about the disease and spurred a huge increase in the ALS Association's research budget, raising $115 million in a few months.

Social media posts, blogs, and your organization's website can help share the stories of people who need support in order to raise awareness and rally provision for them. Similarly, new media can also be used to tell the stories of people who do vital advocacy work to support individuals and groups that are suffering. For example, Together Rising is an organization that "identifies what is breaking the hearts of our givers as they look around their world and their community, and then we connect our givers' generosity with the people and organizations who are effectively addressing that critical need."[34] One of their main activities is organizing Love Flash Mobs. Together Rising's website explains that "Love Flash Mobs are fundraisers in which thousands of strangers give [online] in order to meet a particular need in a matter of hours. Because we cap donations at $25 per giver during these campaigns, every giver is equally vital to meeting the specific need. Whether the donor is a child giving his accumulated allowance, or a single mother making room

33. See Rheingold, *Net Smart*, 221–23.
34. "What We're About."

in her strict budget, each giver is an essential part of the miracles we are able to make possible through our Love Flash Mobs."[35]

Informing your community of examples like Together Rising can encourage members to become excited about partnering with other Christian communities and organizations doing vital advocacy work. Sometimes Christian communities need to focus on supporting other groups that are engaged in advocacy and justice work rather than creating their own missional activities. Your Christian community can choose to be a part of Facebook groups run by activists in your city so you can know what is going on and attend events, vigils, protests, and meetings. Community members could also be encouraged to find the Facebook pages of social service groups in their neighborhoods and to "like" their pages and follow what those groups are doing with an eye toward providing assistance.

Compassion

For Paul, a significant mark of a Christian community is compassion (1 Cor. 12:26). In Romans 12, Paul is explicit about the kind of relating children of God should embody, presenting his readers with genuine ways of demonstrating love and relating well to other people. Verses 1–2 begin with a call for readers to offer their bodies as living sacrifices and to be transformed by the renewing of their minds. The sort of transformation Paul is after is explained in detail throughout the rest of the chapter. Paul invites readers to love others like they love their family members and to show others honor and meet their needs; he then goes on to explain what this kind of love, honor, and service looks like in concrete terms. In verse 15, he encourages readers to "rejoice with those who rejoice, weep with those who weep" (NRSV).[36] To truthfully see and relate to other people is to respond to what is happening in their lives.

It is easy to do the opposite, though, rejoicing when others weep and weep when others rejoice, especially when the "other" is someone we are competing with or comparing ourselves to or someone we have labeled as an enemy. This "other" could be a family member, a coworker, an old friend, or even a citizen of another country whom we have never met. When our perspective narrows and it appears that there is not enough—validation, success, social capital, recognition—for everyone, then it is only natural to rejoice when the "other" experiences pain. Likewise, it is only natural to weep when others

35. "Love Flash Mobs."
36. I am grateful to my friend and colleague Matt Croasmun for the insights he shared regarding this passage and social media engagement during a research seminar in the summer of 2017.

are rejoicing. If joy is construed as limited, then one will likely be inclined to view another's joy as coming at the expense of one's own access to joy.

Yet in Romans 12, readers are invited to enter into a community where people are bound together by their experiences of both joy and sorrow. The mark of a person who has a transformed mind will be that she sees another's joy or pain and embraces it, recognizing that their joy and their pain is also her joy and her pain; that is, the transformed person sees that, instead of needing to compete with another's joy and success, "we belong to each other."[37] She recognizes that joy is abundant rather than scarce.[38]

When the joy of other human beings is embraced as one's own joy and then returned back to them, joy is deepened that much more for the other and, mysteriously, for oneself. Similarly, when one sees pain, acknowledges it, gets close to it, takes it on, and shares in it, that pain is somehow transformed. While it is not necessarily weakened, the pain is seen for what it is: unjust, cruel, traumatizing. The transformation of another's pain that results when one truly sees and shares in it actually helps the suffering person by encouraging him or her to realize that he or she is not delusional. Sharing in someone else's pain says, "Your pain happened. And it matters *to me*." In fact, it matters so much that I am willing to use my resources—emotional and otherwise—to confront it with you. The acknowledgment that pain is real and awful is comforting because it says, "This should not have happened."

It seems that online Jesus would be keen to enter social media spaces looking for people he can mourn with and rejoice with. Christian communities can nurture habits that help people practice hybrid compassion. For example, Christian communities can make time during in-person gatherings to listen to people's joys and sorrows, and members of the community can be invited to thoughtfully and lovingly practice rejoicing with those who rejoice and weeping with those who weep. A leader can explain that actions like these are appropriate at all times—at work, in our homes, in our neighborhoods, and online. Christian communities could mindfully engage in this practice for a

37. Boyle, "Evening with Father Greg Boyle."

38. Mary Clark Moschella points out that pastors are often trained to be "pain specialists" because the majority of pastoral work is "focused on crises, such as illness, trauma, loss and grief, psychiatric illness, interpersonal violence, and disaster relief." Therefore, pastors are often "unaccustomed, untrained, and perhaps unable to care helpfully for people who are longing for the fullness of healing, hope, joy, strength, or well-being." Moschella asserts: "Just as pastoral counseling offers persons the opportunity to plumb the depths of their sorrows, it ought to be offering persons the opportunity to explore the heights and breadth of their experiences of grace, strength, goodness, beauty, and joy. Experiences of joy, when explored more fully, offer avenues for a deeper understanding of God's goodness and love." Moschella, "Calling and Compassion," 105–7.

specific period of time, in person and online, and then come back together to discuss what it felt like, how it went, why it was easy or difficult, and what fruits it bore.

TRUTH-TELLING

Truth-telling is a practice that nurtures vulnerability and the pursuit of truth, both of which are desperately needed in our new media milieu. Truth-telling is multilayered. First, it is personal. Seeing themselves the way God does, a truth-telling person feels no need to cover up their feelings and failings but, instead, feels free to share who they are with their community. Second, truth-telling is relational, so it concerns whether other people feel they can be truthful with you—that is, whether you are someone with whom people can be honest about who they are. I believe that behind the incessant posts on social media related to happiness and self-promotion is fear: fear of being unseen, fear of being unimportant, fear of not living a meaningful life. The practice of truth-telling allows people to release fear and openly share their feelings and failures. Christian communities can integrate activities for personal and relational truth-telling into their programming. For example, a community could create support groups (in person and online) and encourage these groups to be places where people can speak honestly about their lives. Also, members could be encouraged to act as "recognizers" online, where they give positive attention and recognition to others, a form of love in a world that seeks recognition.

Another layer of truth-telling is "affirming what is right and good."[39] Therefore, cultivating a practice of truth-telling entails not only creating space for honesty through naming failures but also making a dedicated effort to name and encourage the good that we see in others and in the world. Sometimes it is easier to tell the truth about what is wrong with the world than to tell the truth about what is good in the world. Yet, as Shane Claiborne says, "We can't just talk about what's wrong [protest]; we have to talk about what is right and protestify."[40]

Teaching community members to cultivate practices of truth-telling by encouraging them to affirm what is right and good could look like asking members to get on social media for a period of time and be intentional about looking for people to affirm and stories to share that talk about what is right and good in the world. After a designated period of time, community members could come back together in homes over a meal or during a worship service to

39. Pohl, *Living into Community*, 114.
40. Claiborne, "Abounding Joy."

talk about what happened. Members could respond to questions like: What did it feel like to look for what is right and good in the world? How did you affirm what is right and good? What did it feel like to affirm it? What are your criteria for goodness and rightness? How can theological reflection on the good help us be discerning about what makes something good?

In the youth group I led, every few months I would ask youth to text me two or three songs that they were playing on repeat. I would watch YouTube videos of the songs and find the lyrics. I would choose one song per week, and we would watch the video and look at the lyrics together. We discussed the lyrics and the following questions:

Why does this song resonate (or not) with you?

What is true about these lyrics?

Is there truth here that mirrors biblical truth?

Do these lyrics lie about the way the world really is or what God has revealed to us?

Activities like this teach community members to critically and theologically seek truth. In an age of "fake news" and "alternative facts," it is crucial to be truth-seekers.

There are institutional, systemic, and global levels of truth-telling (and lying) too. When injustice arises, truth-telling could look like turning on Facebook Live and recording events as they happen. Truth-telling could involve creating space in our Christian communities to lament horrific truths that have been uncovered or to confess when we have not lived or spoken truthfully. For example, your community could set up a physical or digital lament room where people can go to mourn and confess and receive prayer. All of the layers of truth-telling can be practiced both in person and online. We can share truthfully; be people who others feel they can be truthful with; regularly name and affirm the good we see in others; and seek, confess, and lament institutional, systemic, and global truths.

Peacebuilding

Howard Thurman describes the roots of hatred as "contact without fellowship, contact that is devoid of any of the primary overtures of warmth and fellow-feeling and genuineness."[41] Contact without fellowship is deficient relating. It is unsympathetic because it means I am unable to see myself in

41. Thurman, *Jesus and the Disinherited*, 75.

another's place, and an inability to sympathize can transform into ill will. Thurman describes ill will as a desire for the other to hurt or be harmed, which, in Thurman's words, is ultimately "hatred walking the earth."[42] Likewise, in her TED talk, Phelps-Roper explains that many of us want good things, like justice and freedom, but in our public discourse we exhibit many of the same destructive impulses that rule her former church. She says we have divided one another into camps: "No nuance, no complexity, no humanity."[43] In a new media milieu where wounding practices, like harassment, bullying, competition, and division are common, the life and ministry of Jesus teaches us to ask questions such as: "How do you stand against hate without becoming hate yourself?"[44] We are particularly susceptible to contact without fellowship during social media use.

Phelps-Roper provides concrete ways to overcome hatred and division and to engage in *contact with fellowship*, to use Thurman's words. She describes four things people did on Twitter that made real conversation possible. These steps of civil dialogue are excellent concrete activities for practicing peacebuilding: (1) don't assume bad intent, (2) ask questions, (3) stay calm, and (4) make the argument. I encourage your Christian community to practice these actions with one another. Near the end of her talk, Phelps-Roper says, "People often lament that digital communication makes us less civil, but this is one advantage that online conversations have over in-person ones. We have a buffer of time and space between us and the people whose ideas we find so frustrating. We can use that buffer. Instead of lashing out, we can pause, breathe, change the subject, or walk away, and then come back to it when we're ready."[45]

Another way to explore healthy ways of disagreeing online is to learn about and cultivate the historic Christian practice of peacebuilding, which is founded on a commitment to nonviolence. In the midst of conflict, peacebuilders aim to disrupt arguments and acts of rage and hatred with love rather than vengeance. Peacebuilding is courageous and active, not passive. As Martin Luther King Jr. explains, "The nonviolent resister's mind and emotions are always active. . . . The method is passive, physically, but strongly active spiritually."[46] Jesus did not advocate for a negative peace, the type of peace that comes from an unwillingness to participate in conflict, nor did he advocate for peace that is formed by violence. Practicing peacebuilding involves the willingness to

42. Thurman, *Jesus and the Disinherited*, 77–78.
43. Phelps-Roper, "I Grew Up."
44. Rohr, *Things Hidden*, 143.
45. Phelps-Roper, "I Grew Up."
46. King, *Stride toward Freedom*, 102.

engage in conflict with oppressive authority figures and structures, to cross social boundaries, to challenge the status quo, and even to suffer, all of which are forms of *active nonviolence*, as modeled by Jesus.

Dedication to nonviolence also requires a refusal to hate and instead a willingness to allow, by God's grace, "the love of God to act in the human heart."[47] Therefore, peacebuilders seek to win the friendship and understanding of enemies and nurture what King called the "beloved community" so that any "attack is directed against forces of evil rather than against persons who happen to be doing the evil." The objective of nonviolence is not just to defuse difficult situations but to renew or establish relationships.[48]

Christian communities can learn more about peacebuilding by being trained in the philosophy and practice of Kingian nonviolence, King's method of nonviolence that was inspired in part by the lives of Jesus and Gandhi.[49] My husband, Paul Gorrell, founded Peace Right Here, an organization that "works to reshape and recover imaginations to embrace, practice, and champion alternatives to violence." Peace Right Here trains individuals and groups in Kingian nonviolence and collaborates with artists to advance practices that nurture healthy relationships.[50] Peace Right Here also has a project called Wells of Peace, a multiplatform storytelling initiative that tells stories of peacebuilding.[51] The idea is to help people understand peace more fully and believe that peace really is possible. An additional way of practicing peacebuilding is to tell stories of Christians throughout history who have used nonviolence and love in the midst of violent situations to prevent further violence, create change, and even to make friends out of enemies. Christian communities can draw on Wells of Peace as a resource for inspiring community members to pursue peacebuilding.

Confession and repentance are other important aspects of peacebuilding. When I have said or done something hurtful, it is essential (when possible) to acknowledge, own, and repent of it both to God and to the person or group I have hurt. Community members can be encouraged to see some of the tools available through new media as helpful means of confessing and repenting because they allow people to choose their words carefully by allowing readers time and space before responding. If a community member has wounded someone, mediated communication may be the best way for them to confess and repent.

47. King, *Stride toward Freedom*, 104.
48. King, *Stride toward Freedom*, 102.
49. King, *Stride toward Freedom*, 93, 96–97, 101. There are several organizations that teach Kingian nonviolence across the country. See, for example, "Home," Nonviolent Schools Rhode Island.
50. "About," Peace Right Here.
51. "Wells of Peace."

Confession and repentance help begin the healing process and nurture another dimension of peacebuilding: forgiveness by the one wounded, a path demonstrated by the life of Jesus.[52] The practice of forgiveness is nurtured and practiced in the context of healing Christian community.[53] When members are wounded and tempted to choose retribution and hatred instead of forgiveness, the community provides listening, prayer, and sacraments, like baptism and the Eucharist, and points them toward forgiveness. Forgiveness involves forgoing vengeance; releasing debt, guilt, and shame; and committing to God the offense and the offender. Forgiveness comes in part by recognizing God's grace in our own lives and our new identity in Christ. We offer others to God, and God does the forgiving. Christ forgives through us.[54] It is not our work, but God's. Particular spiritual disciplines and actions help cultivate the hybrid practice of forgiveness in a Christian community; examples include reciting the Lord's prayer, using apps to practice centering prayer or various forms of meditation, journaling or blogging about experiences, or watching videos online that tell stories of forgiveness and then discussing them as a community.[55]

Design: New Media Rule for Life

A new media rule for life is a plan involving rituals and routines for living in a new media landscape. Members in the community design it for the sake of their individual lives, their families, the Christian community, and the world. A rule for life can be personal or communal; so an individual or family, housemates, or small group could create a rule together. Inviting members of your community to design a rule for life empowers members to be critically and theologically reflective about their use of new media. Empowering members will also help them make decisions when new forms of new media are created in the future. The term "rule" can give the impression that members are being asked to merely write up rules to live by. However, a rule for life is a rhythm *for life*, not a list of constraints. It is meant to nurture a life of flourishing. You could even call it a "rhythm for life" instead.

I want to be clear that I think people can use new media for enjoyment. I frequently use new media to watch television shows, movies, and music videos; listen to people's stories; and have fun with my friends and family by sharing videos and memes, texting during sports games, and so forth. Designing a rule

---

52. Rohr, *Things Hidden*, 149.
53. Rohr, *Things Hidden*, 213.
54. Volf, *Free of Charge*, 218.
55. See, for example, "Mother of Amish."

for life is *not* about deciding to never use new media for enjoyment; rather it is about inhibiting profound brokenness and living toward Christian visions of true life. I am inviting Christian communities to encourage members to be invested in thinking critically and theologically about how they will use new media, in being open to God's invitations in our new media landscape, and in regularly examining how God has been present to them in the midst of their hybrid lives.

A first question for designing a new media rule for life could be, What kind of people are we aiming to be when using new media? In order to answer this question, a rule for life should include specific hybrid spiritual disciplines and Christian practices for regularly attending to God and abiding in God's love in person and online. Given that new media is designed so that users are constantly on, Christian communities can discuss ways to direct some of the time and energy members spend connected to a device toward spiritual growth rather than impression management. For example, community members could download apps that will give them a prayer reminder at certain times of day, or apps for guided meditation or timed silence. Community members can also sign up for daily email and online devotions. Likewise, community members can be encouraged to be especially thoughtful about whom they friend or which groups they follow on Facebook, whom they follow on Instagram and Twitter, and which blogs they regularly visit.

Community members can have a vision for what kind of people they are aiming to be online by answering other questions like, What specific hybrid Christian practices do I want to cultivate? What will I do when I encounter suffering online?

A rule can also involve regular assessment of hybrid living through the prayer of Examen, a spiritual discipline that helps people review their day.[56] Richard Rohr points out that "the Bible illustrates both healthy and unhealthy religion, right in the text itself, and Jesus offers us a rather simple criterion by which to judge one from the other. It is not a head category at all, but a visual and practical one—'does it bear good fruit or bad fruit?' (Matt. 7:15–20; Luke 6:43–45). Jesus is almost embarrassingly practical."[57] Examen is a helpful spiritual discipline for discerning whether we are attending to God's invitations online and in person and whether our hybrid life is cultivating virtues like humility and integrity and helping us to bear the fruit of the Spirit (e.g., love, joy, peace, patience).

Another framing question for the new media rule for life could be, When will we use new media and when will we practice Sabbath-keeping or rest?

56. An example of a method of Examen is included at the end of this chapter.
57. Rohr, *Things Hidden*, 110.

Community members can discuss getting online for bounded sets of time and paying attention to how long they are online, perhaps by using an app that monitors the amount of time they spend online in order to be cautious about long periods of passive scrolling and following. Community members could also be encouraged to make a commitment in their rule for life related to paying attention to their feelings when using new media. Part of a rule for life is having a plan for what users will do when they feel particular emotions. For example, when they get angry while using new media, what happens next?

Another question that can guide the design of one's rule for life is, How will I decide what to post and reply to, what sorts of content to create, and what to buy or consume? Community members can write questions into their rules to ask themselves when engaging online or through devices. Here are some examples:

Is this information true?

Even though I find this funny, is it mean, hateful, racist, exploitative, and so forth?

Does this minimize the humanness of someone else?

Am I OK with my coworkers, peers, potential employers, family, and friends viewing this?

Additionally, community members could think about how they will respond when they see something false or hateful online or see that someone is being harassed, marginalized, or bullied. Members can be encouraged to think about their "tipping point"—that is, what it would take for them to do something about someone else's racist or otherwise cruel, exploitative, or hateful posts.

A rule for life can also include attending to buying practices. Community members can be encouraged to make a habit of putting things into online shopping carts and waiting a few hours or days and coming back to the cart to determine if they still want or need the items. A rule for life might include decisions like only buying in person or only buying certain items online or not clicking online advertisements.

Finally, community members may also want to consider who will keep them accountable to their rule for life. If it is a shared rule for life, what happens when someone in the house, small group, or youth group disregards the plan? A rule for life could include a time each year to reflect on the rule, when the individual or group can discern whether the rule needs to be edited, revised, or added to. Your community could come up with its own questions and make the design framework specific to your Christian community and context.

interested conversation in practice

New Media Rule for Life

Use the following questions to consider what kind of people we are aiming to be when we use new media:

1. How can we redirect some of the time and energy we spend connected to a device toward spiritual growth rather than impression management?
2. What specific hybrid Christian practices do we want to cultivate?
3. How can new media use help us to love God, love other people, share, give, create, pray, and tell stories?
4. What will we do when we encounter suffering online?
5. Who or what organizations will we give money to?
6. What issues will we stand up for online and how?
7. What will we do when we encounter political differences on social media?
8. What will we do when we get angry while using new media?
9. How will we disagree with someone else on social media or through texting or emailing?
10. At what point does internet use turn into voyeurism or exploitation?
11. What will we do when we encounter rejoicing online?
12. How will we assess our new media use (e.g., through Examen, story-telling, etc.)?

Use the following questions to consider how to make decisions when posting online, replying through devices, or producing content:

1. Is this information true?
2. Even though I find this funny, is it mean, hateful, racist, marginalizing, and so forth? Does it qualify as harassment, bullying, gossip, or lying?

3. Am I OK with my coworkers or peers, potential employers, family, and friends viewing this?
4. What is my tipping point when I see something bad happening online?
5. Am I affirming information or actions that are good and true?

Use the following questions to consider when to use new media and when to practice Sabbath-keeping or rest:

1. Where should we put devices at night?
2. When and how will I rest from using new media?
3. What are our online buying practices?
4. What sort of accountability should we have for this plan?
5. How often and when will we review this plan?

Examen

1. *Presence.* Spend time in God's presence to calm/quiet yourself. (2 min.)
2. *Invitation to the Holy Spirit.* Ask the Holy Spirit for discernment. (3 min.)
3. *Gratitude.* Review the previous twenty-four hours (online and in person) with gratitude. (5 min.)
4. *Review.* Review the previous twenty-four hours again, objectively, without judgment and without rationalizing or justifying, taking time to experience the whole range of emotions in the presence of God. Ask yourself questions that prompt you to consider times of both consolation and desolation online and in person. (5 min.)
   ➤ When was I most loving/most able to receive love?
   ➤ When was I hurtful/unloving?
   ➤ When did I not feel loved?
   ➤ When was I resistant to love?
5. *Examine.* Review the previous twenty-four hours again, examining your thoughts, reflections, and experiences (online and in person). Ask yourself questions that prompt you to consider how present you were to God and to others. (5 min.)
   ➤ How did I interact with others?
   ➤ Was I able to be present in conversations?

➤ When was God present to me?

➤ When was I present to God's activity?

6. *Response.* Allow God to invite you to respond in some way to what you have seen and experienced during your time of prayer; be open to receiving what God has for you. (5 min.)

epilogue

This book is an invitation to be *interested* in new media's glorious possibilities and profound brokenness. As members of Christian communities discover the breadth of new media's possibilities and the depth of its brokenness, it is difficult not to be compelled to talk with your Christian community about new media. Interested conversation is meaningful, imaginative, critically and theologically reflective, Spirit-guided, and fruitful conversation.

Interested conversation begins with assessing what type of conversation your community is already having about new media. Once you have done this, you can explore with your community the new media landscape: new media's connection to Christian faith; its meaning-filled activities; its distinctions, like hybridity; and its implications for Christian communities, such as the need to be hybrid Christian communities.

When your community realizes that new media's impact is connected not just to how people use it but also to how it is designed, your community can then critically reflect on cultural narratives that guide new media development and, consequently, people's use of new media. As your community makes sense of the malformed visions of the good life that shape new media and people's desires, beliefs, and practices, then your community can start to articulate visions of true life and live them well. Ultimately, the movements of interested conversation culminate with interest in hybrid faithful living, which requires committing to practicing discernment, developing hybrid Christian practices, and designing a rule for life for living in a new media landscape.

The challenges of new media—its malformed desires and wounding actions that result in destructive feelings—are troubling. There are many days that I feel overwhelmed being online and frustrated and exhausted using social media. I am tired of feeling tied to my smartphone and looking at it constantly.

It is equally maddening that everywhere I go other people are looking down at devices. Every once in a while, I would like to go back to 1990 and sit in our family's living room or on a bus or stand in line at the grocery store and remember what it was like to be with people before tablets and smartphones. However, I recognize that new media is not going away. The terrain is *new*. The world has changed, and so, as a Christian, I need to discern what God is doing in the midst of this new landscape.

This book intentionally includes many questions that your community can ask and answer together. Questions invite agency, signaling to listeners that they are being called to use their voices and participate—marks of a genuine community. And questions provide space for people to listen to the Spirit, join with God's activities, and discern what to do and how to live in the context God has called them to. In a digital age where people are overwhelmed with information, compelling, curious, capacious questions are foundational for teaching people how to think critically and theologically. I invite you to be intentional about when, where, and how you choose to pursue particular questions throughout this book with your community. Interested conversation is a dynamic, ongoing process that will most likely involve integrating its aspects into various parts of your institution's programs. For example, if you lead a church, movements of interested conversation can be engaged in through a sermon series, Bible studies, website development, small groups, youth and college groups, online discussions and activities, and Christian education hours.

When I am able to reflect on meaningful new media experiences, I think about new media keeping me connected to friends and family, as it does for so many others. I reflect on how much I have learned from people's posts, the articles they have shared, and the videos I have watched online. And my mind returns to youth group nights when we started conversations about God using the teenagers' own photos and videos.

Thankfully, because of God's grace, there are days that I am reminded of what is possible. Children like Karen Gilbo's daughter are connecting with peers without fear. Pastors like Jedidiah Haas are investing in people's lives through new media. Christian denominations are connecting their leaders and are lifting up female voices, as in the case of the Vineyard Movement. Christian leaders like Team World Vision's Lyndsey Deane Ratchford and Reverend Delonte Gholston are doing hybrid ministry, igniting people's passion for following Jesus, and inviting them to do so in concrete ways in physical and digital spaces. Christian communities are thinking critically and theologically about becoming hybrid, healing communities (although they have not used this phrase), and this encourages me too.

When I reflect on what is possible, activists and advocates for justice, love, and peace come to mind. I think of women like Tarana Burke and organizations like Together Rising and Peace Right Here using new media to invite people to speak up and speak out, give generously, and reshape imaginations to champion alternatives to violence. I am then reawakened to new media's power. I also think about Megan Phelps-Roper and am inspired. I am grateful for how she allowed social media to be a conduit for truly relating to people that she was told to hate. And the story of my high school friend, Aaron Jackson, continues to exemplify glorious possibilities—he impacted people's lives through social media, and people loved him through their replies, posts, photos, and messages, especially during his last days on earth. When I think about Aaron's story, my heart experiences unspeakable joy.

I am invested in creating awareness about how the design and use of new media contribute to profound brokenness. However, I am equally invested in advocating for Christian communities to discern, articulate, and live Christian visions of flourishing life. Christian visions of the good life encourage new media to be developed and used for the purpose of nurturing a hybrid, healing Christian community and living the true life of righteousness, peace, and joy in the Holy Spirit. While traversing the new media terrain, I try to keep in the forefront of my mind that God's love is unconditional and relentless, Jesus's ministry has not ended, and the Holy Spirit is leading us. God indeed is preparing God's home here—even online.

Thanks be to God, there are glorious possibilities.

bibliography

"About." Facebook. https://www.facebook.com/pg/facebook/about/?ref=page_in ternal.

"About." Peace Right Here. http://peacerighthere.org.

"About." RAWtools, Inc. https://rawtools.org/about-us/.

Adair, Bill. "Principles of PolitiFact." *PolitiFact*. June 3, 2013. http://www.politifact .com/georgia/article/2013/jun/03/principles-politifact/.

Adams, R. L. "10 Wildly-Successful Blogs That Earn Outlandish Incomes." *Forbes*. March 2, 2017. https://www.forbes.com/sites/robertadams/2017/03/02/top-in come-earning-blogs/#5c0eda472377.

Allen, Mike. "Sean Parker Unloads on Facebook: 'God Only Knows What It's Doing to Our Children's Brains.'" *Axios*. November 9, 2017. https://www.axios.com/sea n-parker-unloads-on-facebook-god-only-knows-what-its-doing-to-our-childrens -brains-1513306792-f855e7b4-4e99-4d60-8d51-2775559c2671.html.

Anderson, Herbert, and Edward Foley. *Mighty Stories, Dangerous Rituals: Weaving Together the Human and the Divine*. San Francisco: Jossey-Bass, 2001.

Anderson, Monica, and Jingjing Jiang. "Teens, Social Media and Technology 2018." Pew Research Center. May 29, 2018. http://www.pewinternet.org/2018/05/31/teens -social-media-technology-2018/pi_2018-05-31_teenstech_0-05.

Anderson, Ray S. *The Shape of Practical Theology: Empowering Ministry with Theo-logical Praxis*. Downers Grove, IL: InterVarsity Press, 2001.

Anić, Ines. "'A Hashtag a Day'—The Most Popular Hashtags and How to Use Them." *Wallery*. March 3, 2017. https://walleryapp.com/2017/03/03/popular-hashtags -how-to-use-them.

"App to Uberize Care for Expectant Mothers Developed by Ugandan Youth." United Nations Population Fund. UNFPA East and Southern Africa Press Release. June

15, 2017. http://esaro.unfpa.org/en/news/app-uberize-care-expectant-mothers
-developed-ugandan-youth.

"Augmented Reality." Apple. June 4, 2018. https://www.apple.com/ios/augmented
-reality.

Baab, Lynne M. *Fasting: Spiritual Freedom beyond Our Appetites*. Downers Grove,
IL: InterVarsity Press, 2006.

———. *Joy Together: Spiritual Practices for Your Congregation*. Louisville: Westminster John Knox, 2012.

———. *The Power of Listening: Building Skills for Mission and Ministry*. Lanham,
MD: Rowman & Littlefield, 2014.

———. *Reaching Out in a Networked World*. Herndon, VA: Alban Institute, 2008.

———. *Sabbath Keeping: Finding Freedom in the Rhythms of Rest*. Downers Grove,
IL: InterVarsity Press, 2005.

———. "Toward a Theology of the Internet." In *Digital Religion, Social Media and
Culture: Perspectives, Practices and Futures*, edited by Pauline Hope Cheong, Peter
Fischer-Nielsen, Stefan Gelfgren, and Charles Ess, 277–91. Digital Formations 78.
New York: Lang, 2012.

Barton, Ruth Haley. *Sacred Rhythms: Arranging Our Lives for Spiritual Transformation*. Downers Grove, IL: InterVarsity Press, 2006.

Bass, Dorothy C., ed. *Practicing Our Faith: A Way of Life for Searching People*. 2nd
ed. San Francisco: Jossey-Bass, 2010.

———. "What Is a Christian Practice?" Practicing Our Faith. March 2004. http://
practicingourfaith.org/what-christian-practice.

Bass, Dorothy C., and Craig Dykstra. "Times of Yearning, Practices of Faith." In
Bass, *Practicing Our Faith*, 1–12.

Bauman, Zygmunt. *Culture in a Liquid Modern World*. Cambridge: Polity, 2011.

Baym, Nancy K. *Personal Connections in the Digital Age*. Digital Media and Society.
Malden, MA: Polity, 2010.

Beale, Andrew V., and Kimberly Hall. "Cyberbullying: What School Administrators
(and Parents) Can Do." *The Clearing House* 81, no. 1 (2007): 8–12.

"#Being13: Inside the Secret World of Teens." CNN. https://www.cnn.com/specials
/us/being13.

Bellah, Robert. *Habits of the Heart: Individualism and Commitment in American
Life*. New York: HarperCollins, 1985.

Berger, Peter L., and Thomas Luckmann. *The Social Construction of Reality: A
Treatise in the Sociology of Knowledge*. Garden City, NY: Doubleday, 1966.

Bhandari, Tamara. "Mind-Controlled Device Helps Stroke Patients Retrain Brains
to Move Paralyzed Parts." Washington University School of Medicine, May 26,
2017, https://medicine.wustl.edu/news/bionic-hand-helps-stroke-patients-retrain
-brains-control-paralyzed-limbs.

Billman, Kathleen D., and Daniel Migliore. *Rachel's Cry: A Prayer of Lament and Rebirth of Hope.* Eugene, OR: Wipf & Stock, 2007.

Block, Peter. *Community: The Structure of Belonging.* San Francisco: Berrett-Koehler, 2009.

Boff, Leonardo. *When Theology Listens to the Poor.* Translated by Robert R. Barr. San Francisco: Harper & Row, 1988.

Bonhoeffer, Dietrich. *Life Together: The Classic Exploration of Christian Community.* New York: Harper SanFrancisco, 1954. Reprint, New York: HarperOne, 2009.

Borg, Marcus J. *Meeting Jesus Again for the First Time: The Historical Jesus and the Heart of Contemporary Faith.* San Francisco: HarperOne, 1994.

Bourgeault, Cynthia. "Faculty Advent Messages." Center for Action and Contemplation. https://cac.org/faculty-advent-messages/.

Bowler, Kate. *Blessed: A History of the American Prosperity Gospel.* Oxford: Oxford University Press, 2013.

Bowles, Nellie. "Early Facebook and Google Employees Form Coalition to Fight What They Built." *New York Times.* February 4, 2018. https://www.nytimes.com/2018/02/04/technology/early-facebook-google-employees-fight-tech.html.

boyd, danah. *It's Complicated: The Social Lives of Networked Teens.* New Haven: Yale University Press, 2014.

———. "Making Sense of Privacy and Publicity." Talk delivered at the SXSW Conference, Austin, Texas, March 13, 2010. http://www.danah.org/papers/talks/2010/SXSW2010.html.

Boyd, Jared Patrick. *Imaginative Prayer: A Yearlong Guide for Your Child's Spiritual Formation.* Downers Grove, IL: InterVarsity Press, 2017.

Boyle, Greg. "An Evening with Father Greg Boyle of Homeboy Industries." Lecture, Saint Thomas Moore Catholic Chapel, Yale University, New Haven, CT, September 19, 2017.

———. *Tattoos on the Heart: The Power of Boundless Compassion.* New York: Free Press, 2010.

Branson, Mark Lau. "Defining Practices and Disciplines." Unpublished manuscript. May 25, 2015.

———. *Memories, Hopes, and Conversations: Appreciative Inquiry, Missional Engagement, and Congregational Change.* 2nd ed. Lanham, MD: Rowman & Littlefield, 2016.

Branson, Mark Lau, and Juan Martínez. *Churches, Cultures, and Leadership: A Practical Theology of Congregations and Ethnicities.* Downers Grove, IL: IVP Academic, 2011.

Brookfield, Stephen D. *Teaching for Critical Thinking: Tools and Techniques to Help Students Question Their Assumptions.* New York: Jossey-Bass, 2011.

Brueggemann, Walter. *Praying the Psalms.* Winona, MN: Saint Mary's Press, 1986.

Campbell, Heidi, and Stephen Garner. *Networked Theology: Negotiating Faith in Digital Culture*. Grand Rapids: Baker Academic, 2016.

Carr, Nicholas. *The Shallows: What the Internet Is Doing to Our Brains*. New York: Norton, 2011.

Castells, Manuel. *Networks of Outrage and Hope: Social Movements in the Internet Age*. Malden, MA: Polity, 2012.

Cavanaugh, William T. *Being Consumed: Economics and Christian Desire*. Grand Rapids: Eerdmans, 2008.

Chen, Wu, Cui-Ying Fan, Qin-Xue Liu, Zong-Kui Zhou, and Xiao-Chun Xie. "Passive Social Network Site Use and Subjective Well-Being: A Moderated Mediation Model." *Computers in Human Behavior* 64 (2016): 507–14.

Chou, Hui-Tzu Grace, and Nicholas Edge. "'They Are Happier and Having Better Lives Than I Am': The Impact of Using Facebook on Perceptions of Others' Lives." *Cyberpsychology, Behavior, and Social Networking* 15, no. 2 (2012): 117–21.

Christian, Jayakumar. *God of the Empty-Handed: Poverty, Power, and the Kingdom of God*. Monrovia, CA: MARC, 1999.

Claiborne, Shane. "Abounding Joy: Grace and Its Consequences." Lecture, Yale Divinity School, April 4, 2018.

"Clean Water." World Vision. https://www.worldvision.org/our-work/clean-water.

Cohen, Jamie, and Paul Mihailidis. "Conducting Research Utilizing Social Media: Best Practices." In *Social Media: Pedagogy and Practice*, edited by Kehbuma Langmia, Tia C. M. Tyree, Pamela O'Brien, and Ingrid Sturgis, 85–102. Lanham, MD: University Press of America, 2014.

Conde-Frazier, Elizabeth. "From Hospitality to Shalom." In *A Many Colored Kingdom: Multicultural Dynamics for Spiritual Formation*, edited by Elizabeth Conde-Frazier, S. Steven Kang, and Gary A. Parrett, 167–210. Grand Rapids: Baker Academic, 2004.

Cone, James H. *The Cross and the Lynching Tree*. Maryknoll, NY: Orbis Books, 2011.

———. *God of the Oppressed*. New York: Seabury, 1975.

"A Conversation with Miroslav Volf and Tod Bolsinger." Fuller Theological Seminary, June 26, 2014. https://faith.yale.edu/news/conversation-miroslav-volf-and-tod-bolsinger.

Croasmun, Matthew. *Let Me Ask You a Question: Conversations with Jesus*. Nashville: Upper Room Books, 2018.

Crockett, M. J. "Moral Outrage in the Digital Age." *Nature Human Behaviour* 1 (2017): 769–71.

Cromwell, Derek. "26 Tips for Better Facebook Page Engagement." *Social Media Examiner*. October 3, 2016. https://www.socialmediaexaminer.com/26-tips-for-better-facebook-page-engagement.

Crouch, Andy. *The Tech-Wise Family: Everyday Steps for Putting Technology in Its Proper Place*. Grand Rapids: Baker Books, 2017.

Darvasi, Paul. "How Online Communities Lower Social Barriers for Kids across the Spectrum." *Connected Learning*. September 1, 2017. https://blog.connectedcamps .com/online-communities-lower-social-barriers-kids-across-spectrum.

Davidson, Cathy N. *Now You See It: How Technology and Brain Science Will Transform Schools and Business for the 21st Century*. New York: Penguin, 2012.

Dean, Kenda Creasy. *Almost Christian: What the Faith of Our Teenagers Is Telling the American Church*. Oxford: Oxford University Press, 2010.

DeLeire, Thomas, and Ariel Kalil. "Does Consumption Buy Happiness? Evidence from the United States." *International Review of Economics* 57, no. 2 (2010): 163–76.

de Souza e Silva, Adriana, and Daniel M. Sutko, eds. *Digital Cityscapes: Merging Digital and Urban Playspaces*. New York: Lang, 2009.

Deters, Fenne Grosse, and Matthias R. Mehl. "Does Posting Facebook Status Updates Increase or Decrease Loneliness? An Online Social Networking Experiment." *Social Psychological and Personality Science* 4, no. 5 (2013): 579–86.

Deutsche Welle. "Refugee Donations Surge after Aylan [*sic*] Kurdi Photo." May 9, 2015. http://p.dw.com/p/1GRSc.

"Digital Immigrant." Techopedia. https://www.techopedia.com/definition/28139 /digital-immigrant.

Dittmar, Helga. "Is Materialistic Value Orientation a Psychological Toxin?" Paper for a Yale Center for Faith and Culture consultation, March 3–4, 2017.

Donovan, Christa. "5 Things the Most Liked Instagram Photos Include." *Maximize Social Business*. https://maximizesocialbusiness.com/most-liked-instagram -photos-23966.

Dougherty, Rose Mary. *Group Spiritual Direction: Community for Discernment*. New York: Paulist Press, 1995.

Drescher, Elizabeth, and Keith Anderson. *Click 2 Save: The Digital Ministry Bible*. Harrisburg, PA: Morehouse, 2012.

Duggan, Maeve. "Online Harassment 2017." Pew Research Center. July 11, 2017. http://www.pewinternet.org/2017/07/11/online-harassment-2017.

Duggan, Maeve, and Aaron Smith. "The Political Environment on Social Media." Pew Research Center. October 25, 2016. http://www.pewinternet.org/2016/10/25 /the-political-environment-on-social-media.

Dunlop, Josh. "20 Websites Making the Most Money." *Income*. https://www.inco mediary.com/20-websites-making-the-most-money.

Edwards, Mark U., Jr. *Printing, Propaganda and Martin Luther*. Berkeley: University of California Press, 1994.

Eire, Carlos M. *Reformations: The Early Modern World, 1450–1650*. New Haven: Yale University Press, 2016.

El Issa, Erin. "2017 American Household Credit Card Debt Study." *NerdWallet*. https://www.nerdwallet.com/blog/average-credit-card-debt-household.

Ellison, Pat Taylor, and Patrick Keifert. *Dwelling in the Word*. St. Paul: Church Innovations Institute, 2011.

Emmons, Robert A. *Gratitude Works! A 21-Day Program for Creating Emotional Prosperity*. San Francisco: Jossey-Bass, 2013.

———. *Thanks! How Practicing Gratitude Can Make You Happier*. New York: Mariner, 2008.

"Ethics and Photography in Developing Countries." Unite for Sight. http://www.unite forsight.org/global-health-university/photography-ethics.

Ferré, John P. "The Media of Popular Piety." In *Mediating Religion: Conversations in Media, Religion, and Culture*, edited by Jolyon Mitchell and Sophia Marriage, 83–92. Edinburgh: T&T Clark, 2003.

Fisher, Douglas, Nancy Frey, and Carol Rothenberg. *Content-Area Conversations: How to Plan Discussion-Based Lessons for Diverse Language Learners*. Alexandria, VA: ASCD, 2008.

———. "Why Talk Is Important in Classrooms." October 2008. Association for Supervision and Curriculum Development. http://www.ascd.org/publications/bo oks/108035/chapters/Why-Talk-Is-Important-in-Classrooms.aspx.

"Flame War." *Oxford Dictionaries*. https://en.oxforddictionaries.com/definition /flame_war.

Fleming, David L. *What Is Ignatian Spirituality?* Chicago: Loyola Press, 2008.

"Forbes Profile: Mark Zuckerberg, Real Time Net Worth." *Forbes*. July 2, 2018. https://www.forbes.com/profile/mark-zuckerberg.

Foster, Richard J. *Celebration of Discipline: The Path to Spiritual Growth*. 3rd ed. San Francisco: Harper SanFrancisco, 2002.

Foucault, Michel. "Of Other Spaces, Heterotopias." *Architecture, Mouvement, Continuité* 5 (1984): 1–9.

Freitas, Donna. *The Happiness Effect: How Social Media Is Driving a Generation to Appear Perfect at Any Cost*. New York: Oxford University Press, 2017.

Gharib, Malaka. "Volunteering Abroad? Read This before You Post That Selfie." NPR. November 26, 2017. https://www.npr.org/sections/goatsandsoda/2017/11/26/5656 94874/volunteering-abroad-read-this-before-you-post-that-selfie.

Goodfellow, Mollie. "How Your Facebook 'Likes' Could Reveal More about Your Personality Than You Think." *Independent*. September 1, 2015. http://www.inde pendent.co.uk/news/your-facebook-likes-can-reveal-your-personality-traits-if -you-use-this-tool-10481372.html.

Gorrell, Angela. "Social Media, Churches, and Christian Formation." PhD diss., Fuller Theological Seminary, 2016.

Gould, Meredith. *The Social Media Gospel: Sharing the Good News in New Ways.* Collegeville, MN: Liturgical Press, 2013.

Green, Joel B. *The Gospel of Luke.* New International Commentary on the Old Testament. Grand Rapids: Eerdmans, 1997.

Groome, Thomas H. *Sharing Faith: A Comprehensive Approach to Religious Education and Pastoral Ministry: The Way of Shared Praxis.* Eugene, OR: Wipf & Stock, 1998.

Gutiérrez, Gustavo. *A Theology of Liberation: History, Politics, and Salvation.* Translated by Caridad Inda and John Eagleson. Maryknoll, NY: Orbis Books, 1988.

Hadad, Chuck. "Why Some 13-Year-Olds Check Social Media 100 Times a Day." *CNN.* October 13, 2015. https://www.cnn.com/2015/10/05/health/being-13-teens-social-media-study/index.html.

Haidt, Jonathan. *The Happiness Hypothesis: Finding Modern Truth in Ancient Wisdom.* New York: Basic Books, 2006.

Hale, Lauren, and Stanford Guan. "Screen Time and Sleep among School-Aged Children and Adolescents: A Systematic Literature Review." *Sleep Medicine Reviews* 21 (2015): 50–58.

Heifetz, Ronald A., and Martin Linsky. *Leadership on the Line: Staying Alive through the Dangers of Leading.* Boston: Harvard Business Review Press, 2002.

Hengel, Martin. *Crucifixion: In the Ancient World and the Folly of the Message of the Cross.* Philadelphia: Fortress, 1977.

Heschel, Abraham J. *The Sabbath: Its Meaning for Modern Man.* 1951. Reprint, New York: Bantam, 1999.

Hess, Mary. "Mirror Neurons, the Development of Empathy, and Digital Story Telling." *Religious Education* 107, no. 4 (2012): 401–14.

Hobbs, Renee. "Media Literacy." *Oxford Research Encyclopedia of Communication.* Forthcoming. https://doi.org/10.1093/acrefore/9780190228613.013.11.

"Home." Nonviolent Schools Rhode Island. https://nonviolentschoolsri.org.

"Home." World Vision International. https://www.wvi.org.

"Homepage." Vineyard Women. http://vineyardwomen.com.

hooks, bell. *Teaching to Transgress: Education as the Practice of Freedom.* Harvest in Translation. New York: Routledge, 1994.

Horsfield, Peter. *From Jesus to the Internet: A History of Christianity and Media.* Malden, MA: Wiley Blackwell, 2015.

"Human Trafficking." Polaris. https://polarisproject.org/human-trafficking.

Ignatius of Loyola. *The Spiritual Exercises of St. Ignatius: Based on Studies of the Language of the Autograph.* Translated by Louis J. Puhl. Chicago: Loyola University Press, 1951.

Jenkins, Henry. *Textual Poachers: Television Fans and Participatory Culture.* New York: Routledge, 1992.

Jenkins, Henry, Sam Ford, and Joshua Green. *Spreadable Media: Creating Value and Meaning in a Networked Culture*. New York: New York University Press, 2013.

Jenkins, Henry, Ravi Purushotma, Margaret Weigel, Katie Clinton, and Alice J. Robison. *Confronting the Challenges of Participatory Culture: Media Education for the 21st Century*. The John D. and Catherine T. MacArthur Foundation Reports on Digital Media and Learning. Cambridge, MA: MIT Press, 2009.

Jennings, Willie James. *Acts*. Belief. Louisville: Westminster John Knox, 2017.

———. "Theology of Joy: Willie James Jennings with Miroslav Volf." September 2014. Yale Center for Faith and Culture. https://www.youtube.com/watch?v=1f KD4Msh3rE&t=81s.

Jones, L. Gregory. "Beliefs, Desires, Practices, and the Ends of Theological Education." In *Practicing Theology: Beliefs and Practices in Christian Life*, edited by Dorothy Bass and Miroslav Volf, 185–205. Grand Rapids: Eerdmans, 2002.

Jurgenson, Nathan. "Defending and Clarifying the Term Augmented Reality." *The Society Pages*. April 29, 2011. https://thesocietypages.org/cyborgology/2011/04/29 /defending-and-clarifying-the-term-augmented-reality/.

———. "Digital Dualism and the Fallacy of Web Objectivity." *The Society Pages*. September 13, 2011. https://thesocietypages.org/cyborgology/2011/09/13/digital -dualism-and-the-fallacy-of-web-objectivity/.

———. "Digital Dualism versus Augmented Reality." *The Society Pages*. February 24, 2011. https://thesocietypages.org/cyborgology/2011/02/24/digital-dualism-ver sus-augmented-reality/.

Kallenberg, Brad. *God and Gadgets: Following Jesus in a Technological Age*. Eugene, OR: Wipf & Stock, 2011.

Kandel, Eric R. *In Search of Memory: The Emergence of a New Science of Mind*. New York: Norton, 2006.

Kant, Immanuel. *Groundwork of the Metaphysics of Morals*. Translated by Mary Gregor. 1998. Reprint, Cambridge: Cambridge University Press, 2012.

Kim, Heejung S. "Culture and Self-Expression." American Psychological Association. June 2010. http://www.apa.org/science/about/psa/2010/06/sci-brief.aspx.

King, Martin Luther, Jr. *Stride toward Freedom: The Montgomery Story*. The King Legacy. 1958. Reprint, Boston: Beacon, 2010.

Kirsch, Melissa. "Change Your Screen to Grayscale to Combat Phone Addiction." Lifehacker. June 5, 2017. https://lifehacker.com/change-your-screen-to-grayscale -to-combat-phone-addicti-1795821843.

Krasnova, Hanna, Helena Wenninger, Thomas Widjaja, and Peter Buxmann. "Envy on Facebook: A Hidden Threat to Users' Life Satisfaction." In *Proceedings of the 11th International Conference on Wirtschaftsinformatik*. Leipzig: Darmstadt Technical University, 2013.

Lake, Emma. "'Just Devastating' Ashawnty Davis Suicide—Girl, 10, Kills Herself after a Classmate Posted a Video Showing Her Being Bullied on Social Media." *The Sun.* December 1, 2017. https://www.thesun.co.uk/news/5042836/ashawnty -davis-10-suicide-after-bullying-social-media-video/.

Lanier, Jaron. *You Are Not a Gadget: A Manifesto.* New York: Vintage, 2011.

Lazarus, Natchi. *The Connected Church: A Social Media Communication Strategy Guide for Churches, Nonprofits and Individuals in Ministry.* CreateSpace Independent Publishing Platform, 2017.

Lemola, Sakari, Nadine Perkinson-Gloor, Serge Brand, Julia F. Dewald-Kaufmann, and Alexander Grob. "Adolescents' Electronic Media Use at Night, Sleep Disturbance, and Depressive Symptoms in the Smartphone Age." *Journal of Youth and Adolescence* 44, no. 2 (2015): 405–18.

Leung, Louis. "Net-Generation Attributes and Seductive Properties of the Internet as Predictors of Online Activities and Internet Addiction." *CyberPsychology and Behavior* 7, no. 3 (July 2004): 333–48.

Levertov, Denise. "Annunciation." In *A Door in the Hive*, 86–88. New York: New Directions, 1989.

Lin, Liu yi, Jaime E. Sidani, Ariel Shensa, Ana Radovic, Elizabeth Miller, Jason B. Colditz, Beth L. Hoffman, Leila M. Giles, and Brian A. Primack. "Association between Social Media Use and Depression among U. S. Young Adults." *Depression and Anxiety* 33, no. 4 (2016): 323–31.

Lindgren, Simon. "Towards a Heterotopology: Unlayering the Reality of Hybrid Media Culture." In *Hybrid Media Culture: Sensing Place in a World of Flows*, edited by Simon Lindgren, 139–48. Routledge Advances in Sociology 114. New York: Routledge, 2014.

Lindgren, Simon, Michael Dahlberg-Grundberg, and Anna Johansson. "Hybrid Media Culture: An Introduction." In *Hybrid Media Culture: Sensing Place in a World of Flows*, edited by Simon Lindgren, 1–15. Routledge Advances in Sociology 114. New York: Routledge, 2014.

Lohfink, Gerhard. *Jesus and Community: The Social Dimension of Christian Faith.* Minneapolis: Fortress, 1984.

"Love Flash Mobs." Together Rising. https://togetherrising.org/love-flash-mobs/.

Lua, Alfred. "Decoding the Facebook Algorithm: A Fully Up-to-Date List of the Algorithm Factors and Changes." October 18, 2017. https://blog.bufferapp.com/face book-news-feed-algorithm.

Manago, Adriana M., L. Monique Ward, Kristi M. Lemm, Lauren Reed, and Rita Seabrook. "Facebook Involvement, Objectified Body Consciousness, Body Shame, and Sexual Assertiveness in College Women and Men." *Sex Roles* 72, nos. 1–2 (2015): 1–14.

Mann, Sandi, and Rebekah Cadman. "Does Being Bored Make Us More Creative?" *Creativity Research Journal* 26, no. 2 (2014): 165–73.

McAnnally-Linz, Ryan. "An Unrecognizable Glory: Christian Humility in the Age of Authenticity." PhD diss., Yale University, 2016.

McLuhan, Marshall. *Understanding Media: The Extensions of Man*. New York: McGraw-Hill, 1964.

Michelfelder, Diane P. "Web 2.0: Community as Commodity?" In *The Good Life in a Technological Age*, edited by Philip Brey, Adam Briggle, and Edward Spence, 203–14. Routledge Studies in Science, Technology and Society. New York: Routledge, 2012.

Milgram, Paul, and Fumio Kishino. "Taxonomy of Mixed Reality Visual Displays." *IEICE Transactions on Information and Systems* E77-D, no. 12 (1994): 1321–29.

Miller, Vincent. *Consuming Religion: Christian Faith and Practice in a Consumer Culture*. New York: Continuum, 2003.

———. "Online, We Encounter Suffering from Afar: How Do We Respond?" *America: The Jesuit Review*. October 3, 2016. https://www.americamagazine.org/issue/geography-mercy.

"Mobile Fact Sheet." Pew Research Center. February 5, 2018. http://www.pewinternet.org/fact-sheet/mobile/.

Moltmann, Jürgen. *The Crucified God: The Cross of Christ as the Foundation and Criticism of Christian Theology*. London: SCM, 1974.

Morris, Meredith Ringel. "Social Networking Site Use by Mothers of Young Children." In *Proceedings of the 17th ACM Conference on Computer Supported Cooperative Work and Social Computing*, 1272–82. Baltimore: ACM Press, 2014.

Moschella, Mary Clark. "Calling and Compassion: Elements of Joy in Lived Practices of Care." In *Joy and Human Flourishing: Essays on Theology, Culture, and the Good Life*, edited by Miroslav Volf and Justin E. Crisp, 97–126. Minneapolis: Fortress, 2015.

"Most Shared." Emergent. http://www.emergent.info.

"Mother of Amish School Shooter Shares Amazing Story of Forgiveness." *CBS*. https://www.cbsnews.com/news/mother-of-amish-school-shooter-shares-amazing-story-of-forgiveness/.

Muñiz-Velázquez, Jose A., Diego Gomez-Baya, and Manuel Lopez-Casquete. "Implicit and Explicit Assessment of Materialism: Associations with Happiness and Depression." *Personality and Individual Differences* 116 (2017): 123–32.

Muthiah, Rob. *The Sabbath Experiment: Spiritual Formation for Living in a Non-Stop World*. Eugene, OR: Cascade, 2015.

Myers, Bryant L. *Walking with the Poor: Principles and Practices of Transformational Development*. Maryknoll, NY: Orbis Books, 2011.

Newell, J. Philip. *Listening for the Heartbeat of God: A Celtic Spirituality*. Mahwah, NJ: Paulist Press, 1997.

———. *Sounds of the Eternal: A Celtic Psalter*. Grand Rapids: Eerdmans, 2002.

Niebuhr, H. Richard. *"The Responsibility of the Church for Society" and Other Essays by H. Richard Niebuhr.* Edited by Kristine A. Culp. Louisville: Westminster John Knox, 2008.

Nietzsche, Friedrich. *Beyond Good and Evil: Prelude to a Philosophy of the Future.* Edited by Rolf-Peter Horstmann and Judith Norman. Translated by Judith Norman. Cambridge Texts in the History of Philosophy. Cambridge: Cambridge University Press, 2002.

Nouwen, Henri J. M. *Making All Things New: An Invitation to Spiritual Life.* San Francisco: Harper & Row, 1981.

———. *The Return of the Prodigal Son: A Story of Homecoming.* New York: Continuum, 1995.

O'Brien, Kevin. *The Ignatian Adventure: Experiencing the Spiritual Exercises of St. Ignatius in Daily Life.* Chicago: Loyola Press, 2011.

Osmer, Richard Robert. *The Teaching Ministry of Congregations.* Louisville: Westminster John Knox, 2005.

Painter, Christine Valters. *Lectio Divina—The Sacred Art: Transforming Words and Images into Heart-Centered Prayer.* The Art of Spiritual Living. Woodstock, VT: Skylight Paths, 2011.

Palmer, Parker J. *To Know as We Are Known: Education as a Spiritual Journey.* 1983. Reprint, New York: HarperCollins, 1993.

Pandey, Erica. "Sean Parker: Facebook Was Designed to Exploit Human 'Vulnerability.'" *Axios.* November 9, 2017. https://www.axios.com/sean-parker-facebook -was-designed-to-exploit-human-vulnerability-1513306782-6d18fa32-5438-4e60 -af71-13d126b58e41.html.

Perrin, Andrew. "One-Fifth of Americans Report Going Online 'Almost Constantly.'" Pew Research Center. December 8, 2015. http://www.pewresearch.org/fact-tank /2015/12/08/one-fifth-of-americans-report-going-online-almost-constantly/.

Peterson, Eugene H. *Eat This Book: A Conversation in the Art of Spiritual Reading.* Grand Rapids: Eerdmans, 2006.

Pewhairangi, Sally. "6 Top Experts Expose Digital Literacy Mistakes and How to Overcome Them." Finding Heroes. June 22, 2017. https://findingheroes.co.nz/2017/06 /22/6-top-experts-expose-digital-literacy-mistakes-and-how-to-overcome-them/.

Phelps-Roper, Megan. "I Grew Up in the Westboro Baptist Church. Here's Why I Left." TED talk presented at TEDNYC, New York, February 2017. https://www.ted .com/talks/megan_phelps_roper_i_grew_up_in_the_westboro_baptist_church _here_s_why_i_left.

Pohl, Christine. *Living into Community: Cultivating Practices That Sustain Us.* Grand Rapids: Eerdmans, 2011.

Polak, Emily L., and Michael E. McCullough. "Is Gratitude an Alternative to Materialism?" *Journal of Happiness Studies* 7, no. 3 (2006): 343–60.

"Pope Francis: Mass Is for Prayers Not Mobile Phones." *BBC*. November 8, 2017. http://www.bbc.co.uk/news/world-europe-41918906.

Pope, Stephen. "Expressive Individualism and True Self-Love: A Thomistic Perspective." *Journal of Religion* 71, no. 3 (1991): 384–99.

Potkay, Adam. *The Story of Joy: From the Bible to Late Romanticism*. New York: Cambridge University Press, 2007.

Preskill, Stephen, and Stephen D. Brookfield. *Learning as a Way of Leading: Lessons from the Struggle for Social Justice*. San Francisco: Jossey-Bass, 2009.

"Pressure to Be Available 24/7 on Social Media Causes Teen Anxiety and Depression." University of Glasgow. September 11, 2015. http://www.gla.ac.uk/news/headline_419871_en.html.

Rainie, Lee, and Barry Wellman. *Networked: The New Social Operating System*. Cambridge, MA: MIT Press, 2012.

Rayson, Steve. "The Most Shared Facebook Content 2017: The Top Viral Posts, Videos, and Articles." *Buzzsumo*. December 12, 2017. http://buzzsumo.com/blog/the-most-shared-facebook-content-posts-videos/.

"Refugee Crisis." World Relief. https://www.worldrelief.org/refugee-crisis/.

Reid, Barbara E. "'Do You See This Woman?' A Liberative Look at Luke 7.36–50 and Strategies for Reading Other Lukan Stories against the Grain." In *A Feminist Companion to Luke*, edited by Amy-Jill Levine and Marianne Blickenstaff, 106–20. FCNTECW 3. Cleveland: Pilgrim, 2001.

Rheingold, Howard. *Net Smart: How to Thrive Online*. Cambridge, MA: MIT Press, 2012.

Robinson, Martin, and Alan Roxburgh. "Changing the Conversation." *Journal of Missional Practice*, Autumn 2015. http://journalofmissionalpractice.com/changing-the-conversation/.

Rohr, Richard. "Church Was Supposed to Be an Alternative Society." Center for Action and Contemplation. Daily Email Meditation, May 9, 2018.

———. "Returning to Union." Center for Action and Contemplation. Daily Email Meditation, December 19, 2017.

———. *Things Hidden: Scripture as Spirituality*. Cincinnati: St. Anthony Messenger Press, 2008.

Root, Andrew. *Faith Formation in a Secular Age: Responding to the Church's Obsession with Youthfulness*. Ministry in a Secular Age 1. Grand Rapids: Baker Academic, 2017.

Rosa, Hartmut. *Social Acceleration: A New Theory of Modernity*. Translated by Jonathan Trejo-Mathys. New Directions in Critical Theory. New York: Columbia University Press, 2013.

Roxburgh, Alan J. *Joining God, Remaking Church, and Changing the World: The New Shape of the Church in Our Time*. New York: Morehouse, 2015.

Rudder, Christian. *Dataclysm: Who We Are (When We Think No One's Looking)*. London: Crown, 2014.

Schawbel, Dan. *Me 2.0: Build a Powerful Brand to Achieve Career Success*. New York: Kaplan, 2009.

Schnekloth, Clint. *Mediating Faith: Faith Formation in the Trans-Media Era*. Minneapolis: Fortress, 2014.

Scribner, R. W. "Oral Culture and the Transmission of Reformation Ideas." In *The Transmission of Ideas in the Lutheran Reformation*, edited by Helga Robinson-Hammerstein, 83–104. Worcester, Ireland: Irish Academic Press, 1989.

Seidman, Gwendolyn. "What Can You Learn about People from Facebook?" *Psychology Today*. July 2, 2015. https://www.psychologytoday.com/blog/close-encount ers/201507/what-can-you-learn-about-people-facebook.

Shamsian, Jacob. "Teens Are Obsessed with This One Snapchat Score That Can Make or Break Friendships." *Insider*. December 14, 2016. http://www.thisisinsider.com /teens-are-obsessed-with-snap-streaks-on-snapchat-2016-12.

"Shareable Quotes from Americans on Online Harassment." Pew Research Center. July 11, 2017. http://www.pewinternet.org/2017/07/11/shareable-quotes-from-ameri cans-on-online-harassment/.

Sharma, Rakesh. "How Does Facebook Make Money?" *Investopedia*. December 11, 2017. https://www.investopedia.com/ask/answers/120114/how-does-facebook -fb-make-money.asp.

Shirky, Clay. *Cognitive Surplus: How Technology Makes Consumers into Collaborators*. New York: Penguin, 2010.

Simonson, Peter. *Refiguring Mass Communication: A History*. Chicago: University of Illinois Press, 2010.

Smith, Aaron, and Maeve Duggan. "Crossing the Line: What Counts as Online Harassment?" Pew Research Center. January 4, 2018. http://www.pewinternet.org/20 18/01/04/crossing-the-line-what-counts-as-online-harassment/.

Smith, Christian, and Melinda Lundquist Denton. *Soul Searching: The Religious and Spiritual Lives of American Teenagers*. Oxford: Oxford University Press, 2005.

Smith, James K. A. *Desiring the Kingdom: Worship, Worldview, and Cultural Formation*. Grand Rapids: Baker Academic, 2009.

"Sophia." Hanson Robotics. http://www.hansonrobotics.com/robot/sophia/.

Southerland, Joel. *Digital Witness: A Social Media Primer for Churches*. Dallas: St. Paul Press, 2014.

Stassen, Glen H. "A New Vision." In *Authentic Transformation: A New Vision of Christ and Culture*, edited by Glen H. Stassen, D. M. Yeager, and John Howard Yoder, 191–270. Nashville: Abingdon, 1996.

Stassen, Glen H., and David P. Gushee. *Kingdom Ethics: Following Jesus in Contemporary Context*. Downers Grove, IL: IVP Academic, 2003.

Steele, Les L. *On the Way: A Practical Theology of Christian Formation*. Grand Rapids: Baker, 1990.

Stephens-Davidowitz, Seth. "Don't Let Facebook Make You Miserable." *New York Times*. May 6, 2017. https://www.nytimes.com/2017/05/06/opinion/sunday/dont -let-facebook-make-you-miserable.html?mcubz=3.

"St. Ignatius Loyola." Ignatian Spirituality. https://www.ignatianspirituality.com /ignatian-voices/st-ignatius-loyola.

"The Story of Stuff." December 2007, video. Dir. Louis Fox. Presented by Funders Workgroup for Sustainable Production and Consumption and Free Range Studios. http:// storyofstuff.org/movies/story-of-stuff.

Tanner, Kathryn. "In the Image of the Invisible." In *Apophatic Bodies: Negative Theology, Incarnation, and Relationality*, edited by Chris Boesel and Catherine Keller, 117–35. Transdisciplinary Theological Colloquia. New York: Fordham University Press, 2010.

Taylor, Charles. *The Ethics of Authenticity*. Cambridge: Harvard University Press, 1991.

———. *A Secular Age*. Cambridge, MA: Belknap, 2007.

"Thank You, Scott—SNL." YouTube video, 03:04, April 8, 2017. https://www.you tube.com/watch?v=QDydKwmrHFo.

Thiessen, Gerd. *The New Testament: A Literary History*. Minneapolis: Fortress, 2011.

Thomée, Sara, Annika Härenstam, and Mats Hagberg. "Mobile Phone Use and Stress, Sleep Disturbances, and Symptoms of Depression among Young Adults—A Prospective Cohort Study." *BMC Public Health* 11, no. 66 (2011). https://doi.org/10 .1186/1471-2458-11-66.

Thurman, Howard. *Jesus and the Disinherited*. 1949. Reprint, Boston: Beacon, 1976.

Turkle, Sherry. *Alone Together: Why We Expect More from Technology and Less from Each Other*. New York: Basic Books, 2011.

———. *Reclaiming Conversation: The Power of Talk in a Digital Age*. New York: Penguin, 2015.

Tutu, Desmond. *No Future without Forgiveness*. New York: Doubleday, 1999.

Twenge, Jean. "With Teen Mental Health Deteriorating over Five Years, There's a Likely Culprit." *The Conversation*. November 14, 2017. https://theconversation .com/with-teen-mental-health-deteriorating-over-five-years-theres-a-likely -culprit-86996.

"The Typology of Modern Slavery." Polaris. https://polarisproject.org/typology.

Underwood, Marion K., and Robert Faris. "#Being Thirteen: Social Media and the Hidden World of Young Adolescents' Peer Culture." https://www.documentcloud .org/documents/2448422-being-13-report.html.

Vahabzadeh, Arshya, Ned Sahin, and Amir Kalali. "Digital Suicide Prevention: Can Technology Become a Game-Changer?" *Innovations in Clinical Neuroscience* 13, nos. 5–6 (May–June 2016): 16–20.

"Values." Twitter. https://about.twitter.com/content/about-twitter/en_us/values.html.

van Dijck, José. *The Culture of Connectivity: A Critical History of Social Media.* New York: Oxford University Press, 2013.

Van Gelder, Craig. *The Ministry of the Missional Church: A Community Led by the Spirit.* Grand Rapids: Baker Books, 2007.

Vannucci, Anna, Kaitlin M. Flannery, and Christine McCauley Ohannessian. "Social Media Use and Anxiety in Emerging Adults." *Journal of Affective Disorders* 207 (2017): 163–66.

Vilhauer, Jennice. "This Is Why Ghosting Hurts So Much." *Psychology Today.* November 27, 2015. https://www.psychologytoday.com/blog/living-forward/201511/is-why-ghosting-hurts-so-much.

Volf, Miroslav. *Exclusion and Embrace: A Theological Exploration of Identity, Otherness, and Reconciliation.* Nashville: Abingdon, 1996.

———. *Free of Charge: Giving and Forgiving in a World Stripped of Grace.* Grand Rapids: Zondervan, 2005.

———. "Theology for a Way of Life." In *Practicing Theology: Beliefs and Practices in Christian Life,* edited by Dorothy Bass and Miroslav Volf, 245–63. Grand Rapids: Eerdmans, 2002.

Volf, Miroslav, and Matt Croasmun. *For the Life of the World: Theology That Makes a Difference.* Grand Rapids: Brazos, 2019.

Volf, Miroslav, and Ryan McAnnally-Linz. *Public Faith in Action: How to Think Carefully, Engage Wisely, and Vote with Integrity.* Grand Rapids: Brazos, 2016.

Walsh, Bryan. "Alan Kurdi's Story: Behind the Most Heartbreaking Photo of 2015." *Time.* December 29, 2015. http://time.com/4162306/alan-kurdi-syria-drowned-boy-refugee-crisis/.

Walsh, Kelly. "5 Selected Frameworks for Promoting Digital Literacy." *EmergingEdTech.* September 12, 2017. http://www.emergingedtech.com/2017/09/selected-frameworks-for-teaching-digital-literacy/.

Wang, Rong, Hongyun Liu, Jiang Jiang, and Yue Song. "Will Materialism Lead to Happiness? A Longitudinal Analysis of the Mediating Role of Psychological Needs Satisfaction." *Personality and Individual Differences* 105 (2017): 312–17.

Ward, Graham. *Cities of God.* London: Routledge, 2000.

———. *Cultural Transformation and Religious Practice.* Cambridge: Cambridge University Press, 2005.

"Web 2.0." Techopedia. https://www.techopedia.com/definition/4922/web-20.

"Wells of Peace." Peace Right Here. https://www.peacerighthere.org/wells-of-peace/.

"What Is Cyberbullying." stopbullying.gov. https://www.stopbullying.gov/cyberbul lying/what-is-it/index.html.

"What We're About." Together Rising. https://togetherrising.org/about/.

Willard, Dallas. *Hearing God: Developing a Conversational Relationship with God.* Downers Grove, IL: InterVarsity Press, 1999.

Wirzba, Norman. *Food and Faith: A Theology of Eating.* New York: Cambridge University Press, 2011.

Wise, Justin. *The Social Church: A Theology of Digital Communication.* Chicago: Moody, 2014.

Witvliet, John D. *Worship Seeking Understanding: Windows into Christian Practice.* Grand Rapids: Baker Academic, 2003.

Wolterstorff, Nicholas. *Justice in Love.* Grand Rapids: Eerdmans, 2011.

Woods, Heather Cleland, and Holly Scott. "#Sleepyteens: Social Media Use in Ado- lescence Is Associated with Poor Sleep Quality, Anxiety, Depression and Low Self- Esteem." *Journal of Adolescence* 51 (2016): 41–49.

"Word of the Year 2016 Is . . ." *Oxford Dictionaries.* November 16, 2017. https://www .oxforddictionaries.com/press/news/2016/12/11/WOTY-16.

"You." Apply Magic Sauce. https://applymagicsauce.com.

"YouTube: Our Brand Mission," YouTube video, 01:48, June 22, 2017, https://www .youtube.com/watch?v=kwmFPKQAX4g.

Zirschky, Andrew. *Beyond the Screen: Youth Ministry for the Connected but Alone Generation.* Nashville: Abingdon, 2015.

———. "Technology, Education, Adolescents, and Ministry." Plenary address at the annual meeting of the Association of Youth Ministry Educators, October 2015.

Zscheile, Dwight J. "A Missional Theology of Spiritual Formation." In *Cultivating Sent Communities: Missional Spiritual Formation,* edited by Dwight J. Zscheile, 1–28. Grand Rapids: Eerdmans, 2012.

Zsupan-Jerome, Daniella. *Connected toward Communion: The Church and Social Communication in the Digital Age.* Collegeville, MN: Liturgical Press, 2014.

Zubiaga, Arkaitz, Maria Liakata, Rob Procter, Geraldine Wong Sak Hoi, and Peter Tolmie. "Analysing How People Orient to and Spread Rumours in Social Media by Looking at Conversational Threads." *PLoS ONE* 11, no. 3 (2016), https://journals .plos.org/plosone/article?id=10.1371/journal.pone.0150989.

Zuo, Angie. "Measuring Up: Social Comparisons on Facebook and Contributions to Self-Esteem and Mental Health." Master's thesis, University of Michigan, 2014.

index